The Generation of 2000

Ontario Review Press Poetry Series

THE GENERATION OF 2000

Contemporary American Poets

edited by
William Heyen

ONTARIO REVIEW PRESS
Princeton, New Jersey

Library of Congress Cataloging in Publication Data

The Generation of 2000.

   1. American poetry—20th century.   I. Heyen,
William, 1940-
PS615.G38   1984   811'.5'08   84-14745
ISBN 0-86538-042-2
ISBN O-86538-043-0 (pbk.)

Distributed by Persea Books, Inc.
225 Lafayette St.
New York, NY 10012

AI: "Why Can't I Leave You?," "I Have Got to Stop Loving You," "One Man Down," and "The Hitchhiker" are from *Cruelty* by Ai. Copyright © 1970 by Ai. Reprinted by permission of Houghton Mifflin Co. "The Mortician's Twelve-Year-Old Son," "The Kid," "The Expectant Father," and "Pentecost" are from *Killing Floor* by Ai. Copyright © 1979 by Ai. Reprinted by permission of Houghton Mifflin Co.

Wendell Berry: "A Homage to Dr. Williams" is copyright © 1970 by Wendell Berry. Reprinted from his volume *A Continuous Harmony* by permission of Harcourt Brace Jovanovich, Inc. "My Great-Grandfather's Slaves" and "The Snake" are copyright © 1965 by Wendell Berry and reprinted from his volume *Openings* by permission of Harcourt Brace Jovanovich, Inc. "The Peace of Wild Things" is copyright © 1968 by Wendell Berry and reprinted from *Openings* by permission of Harcourt Brace Jovanovich, Inc. "Poem for J." is copyright © 1972 by Wendell Berry and reprinted from his volume *The Country of Marriage* by permission of Harcourt Brace Jovanovich, Inc. "The Lilies" and "Grief" are copyright © 1980 by Wendell Berry and reprinted from *A Part* by permission of North Point Press, Berkeley, California. "The Gift of Gravity," "The Wheel," and "In Rain" are copyright © 1982 by Wendell Berry and reprinted from *The Wheel* by permission of North Point Press.

Raymond Carver: "Bobber," "Prosser," "Your Dog Dies," "Forever," "Looking for Work," "Wes Hardin: From a Photograph," and "Marriage" are copyright © 1983 by Raymond Carver and reprinted from *Fires* by permission of Capra Press.

Lucille Clifton: "forgiving my father," "i once knew a man," "holy night," "the light that came . . . " "testament," "incandescence," "mother, I am," "perhaps," "explanations," "friends come," "to joan," "confession," and "in populated" are copyright © 1980 by the University of Massachusetts Press and reprinted from *Two-Headed Woman* by Lucille Clifton by permission of the author and The University of Massachusetts Press.

Norman Dubie: Excerpts from "Dark Spiralling Figures: An Interview," which first appeared in the *American Poetry Review* (1978), are copyright © by Julie Faye and

David Wojahn and reprinted with their permission. "The Hours," "Sacrifice of a Virgin in the Mayan Ball Court," and "Norway" are from *The City of the Olesha Fruit,* copyright © 1979 by Norman Dubie; "There Is a Dream Dreaming Us" and "The Everlastings" are from *The Everlastings,* copyright © 1980 by Norman Dubie. All are reprinted with the author's permission.

Tess Gallagher: "Black Money" and "Complicity" are copyright © 1976 by Tess Gallagher and reprinted from *Instructions to the Double* by permission of Graywolf Press. "The Ritual of Memories," "Under Stars," and "The Meeting" are copyright © 1978 by Tess Gallagher and reprinted from *Under Stars* by permission of Graywolf Press. "Tableau Vivant," copyright © by Tess Gallagher, first appeared in *The New Yorker,* and is published here with the author's permission.

Louise Glück: "The Racer's Widow" and "Cottonmouth Country" are copyright © 1968 by Louise Glück. From *Firstborn,* published by The Ecco Press in 1983. Reprinted by permission. "For My Mother," "For Jane Myers," and "Jeanne d'Arc" are copyright © 1975 by Louise Glück. From *The House on Marshland,* published by The Ecco Press in 1975. Reprinted by permission. "Descending Figure," "The Mirror," and "Dedication to Hunger" copyright © 1980 by Louise Glück. From *Descending Figure,* published by The Ecco Press in 1980. Reprinted by permission.

Albert Goldbarth: "Distances," "All-Nite Donuts," "Pleasures," "And Now Farley Is Going to Sing," "The Accountings," and "The Form and Function of the Novel" are copyright © 1973, 1974, 1976, 1980, 1981, 1983 by Albert Goldbarth and reprinted from *Original Light: New & Selected Poems 1973-1983* by permission of Ontario Review Press.

Michael S. Harper: "Don't they speak jazz?" first appeared in *TriQuarterly,* copyright © 1982 by Michael S. Harper, and is reprinted with his permission. "We Assume: On the Death of Our Son, Reuben Masai Harper," "Reuben, Reuben," "Dear John, Dear Coltrane," "Love Medley: Patrice Cuchulain," "Last Affair: Bessie's Blues Song," "Debridement: Operation Harvest Moon: *On Repose,*" "Grandfather," "Nightmare Begins Responsibility" are copyright © 1970, 1971, 1972, 1973, 1974, 1975, 1976, 1977 by Michael S. Harper and reprinted from *Images of Kin: New and Selected Poems* with the permission of University of Illinois Press.

Robert Hass: "San Pedro Road," "After the Gentle Poet Kobayashi Issa," "Measure," and "In Weather" are copyright © 1973 by Robert Hass and reprinted from *Field Guide* by permission of Yale University Press. "The Feast" is copyright © 1979 by Robert Hass and reprinted from *Praise,* published by The Ecco Press in 1979. Reprinted by permission. "Late Spring" is copyright © 1981 by Robert Hass and reprinted with his permission. "A Story About the Body" (from *The New Republic*) is copyright © by Robert Hass and reprinted with his permission.

William Heyen: "Birds and Roses Are Birds and Roses" and "Existential" are copyright © 1970 by William Heyen and reprinted from *Depth of Field* (Louisiana State University Press) by permission of the author. "Ram Time" and "Mother and Son" (both from *Poetry*) and "The Berries" (from *Poetry* and *Along This Water* [Tamarack Editions]) are copyright © 1981, 1982, 1983 by William Heyen and reprinted by permission of the author. "Poem Touching the Gestapo" (first published in *The Trains,* Metacom Press) and "The Children" (first published in *American Poetry Review* and then in *My Holocaust Songs,* William B. Ewert, Publisher) are copyright © 1980, 1981 by William Heyen and reprinted from *Erika: Poems of the Holocaust* by permission of the author and Vanguard Press, Inc.

Faye Kicknosway: "Gracie" and "Mr. Muscle-On" are copyright © 1974 by Faye

Kicknosway. From *A Man Is a Hook. Trouble.* Reprinted by permission of Capra Press. "In Mysterious Ways" is copyright © 1981 by Faye Kicknosway. From *Asparagus, Asparagus, Ah Sweet Asparagus.* Reprinted by permission of The Toothpaste Press. "The Horse," copyright © by Faye Kicknosway, first appeared in *Nimrod,* and is reprinted by permission of the author. "There Is No" is copyright © 1978 by Faye Kicknosway. From *Nothing Wakes Her.* Reprinted by permission of Oyster Press.

Paul Mariani: "Golden Oldie" is copyright © 1979 by Paul Mariani. From *Timing Devices* by Paul Mariani. Reprinted by permission of David R. Godine, Publisher, Boston. "The Girl Who Learned to Sing in Crow" is copyright © 1982 by Paul Mariani. From *Crossing Cocytus.* Reprinted by permission of Grove Press, Inc. "The Ring" (from *Tendril*), "News That Stays News" (from *The Hudson Review*), and "Then Sings My Soul" (from *il Cobald* [Genoa]) are copyright © by Paul Mariani and reprinted by permission of the author.

William Matthews: "The Search Party," copyright © 1970 by William Matthews, is reprinted from *Ruining the New Road;* and "Bring the War Home," copyright © 1975 by William Matthews, is reprinted from *Sticks and Stones;* both by permission of the author. "Taking the Train Home," which first appeared in *The Ohio Review,* copyright © 1974 by William Matthews; "In Memory of the Utah Stars," which first appeared in *The Iowa Review,* copyright © 1978 by William Matthews; and "Living Among the Dead," which first appeared in *The Ohio Review,* copyright © 1975 by William Matthews, are reprinted from *Rising and Falling;* and "Unrelenting Flood," which first appeared in the *American Poetry Review,* copyright © 1982 by William Matthews, is reprinted from *Flood;* all by permission of Little, Brown and Company in association with the Atlantic Monthly Press.

Heather McHugh: "Squeal," "Gig at Big Al's," and "Having Read Books" are copyright © 1977 by Heather McHugh. Reprinted from *Dangers* by Heather McHugh by permission of Houghton Mifflin Co. "Message at Sunset for Bishop Berkeley," "Brightness," "Meantime," "The Fence," "Form," and "Breath" are copyright © 1981 by Heather McHugh. Reprinted from *A World of Difference* by Heather McHugh by permission of Houghton Mifflin Co. "I Knew I'd Sing," which first appeared in *Kayak,* is copyright © by Heather McHugh, and reprinted by permission of the author.

Sandra McPherson: "Poppies" and "His Body" are copyright © 1970 by Sandra McPherson and reprinted from *Elegies for the Hot Season,* published by The Ecco Press in 1982. "Letter with a Black Border" is copyright © 1973 by Sandra McPherson and reprinted from *Radiation,* published by The Ecco Press in 1973. "Centerfold Reflected in a Jet Window" and "Open Casket" are copyright © 1978 by Sandra McPherson and reprinted from *The Year of Our Birth,* published by The Ecco Press in 1978. "For Elizabeth Bishop" and "Wings and Seeds" are copyright © 1982 by Sandra McPherson and reprinted from *Patron Happiness,* published by The Ecco Press in 1983. All poems reprinted by permission of The Ecco Press.

Judith Minty: "The End of Summer," "Wounds," "Prowling the Ridge," and "Burning Against the Wind" are copyright © 1981 by Judith Minty and reprinted from *In the Presence of Mothers* by Judith Minty by permission of the University of Pittsburgh Press. "Making Music" and "The Legacy" are copyright © 1973 by Judith Minty and reprinted from *Lake Songs and Other Fears* by permission of the author. "Orchids," which first appeared in *Hawaii Review,* is copyright © by Judith Minty and reprinted by her permission.

Robert Morgan: "Cedar" is reprinted from *Red Owl, Poems* by Robert Morgan, by permission of the author and W. W. Norton & Co., Inc. Copyright © 1972 by Robert Morgan. "Face" and "Pumpkin" are reprinted by permission of Louisiana State University Press from *Land Diving,* copyright © 1976 by Robert Morgan. "Mountain Bride" is reprinted from *Groundwork* by Robert Morgan, copyright © 1979 by Robert Morgan, by permission of Gnomon Press. "Passenger Pigeons" (from *Tendril*), "Buffalo Trace" (from *Carolina Quarterly*), "Uncle Robert" (from *Bluefish*), "Cow Pissing" and "Lightning Bug" are copyright © by Robert Morgan and published here with the author's permission.

Joyce Carol Oates: "Acceleration Near the Point of Impact" is from *Angel Fire,* copyright © 1973 by Joyce Carol Oates, and reprinted by permission of the author. "The Stone Orchard," "The Wasp," "Baby," "First Dark," "The Child Bride," and "Dreaming America" are copyright © 1982 by Joyce Carol Oates and reprinted from *Invisible Woman: New and Selected Poems 1970-1982* by permission of the Ontario Review Press. "Night" (from *Poetry*) and "New Jersey White-Tailed Deer" (from *Michigan Quarterly Review*) are copyright © by Joyce Carol Oates and reprinted here with the author's permission.

Gregory Orr: "Silence," "The Room," and "Love Poem" are copyright © 1973 by Gregory Orr and reprinted from *Burning the Empty Nests,* published by Harper & Row, by permission of the author. "The Project" and "Gathering the Bones Together" are copyright © 1975 by Gregory Orr and reprinted from *Gathering the Bones Together,* published by Harper & Row, by permission of the author. "After a Death," "Driving Home After a Funeral," "Spring Floods," "The Lost Children," "On the Lawn at Ira's," and "A Last Address to My Ghosts" are copyright © 1980 by Gregory Orr and reprinted from *The Red House,* published by Harper & Row, with the author's permission.

Robert Phillips: "Vital Message" copyright © 1973 by Quixote Press; "The Married Man" copyright © 1972 by *Choice* Magazine Inc.; "Decks" copyright © 1978 by *The Hudson Review* are from *The Pregnant Man* by Robert Phillips and reprinted by permission of Doubleday & Co., Inc. "The Persistence of Memory, the Failure of Poetry" and "Miss Crustacean" are from *Running on Empty,* copyright © 1981 by Robert Phillips, and reprinted by permission of Doubleday & Co., Inc. "Inside and Out," copyright © by Robert Phillips, first appeared in *The New Yorker* and is reprinted by permission of the author.

Marge Piercy: The prose excerpt from "Midgame: Making It Better, Truer, Clearer, More Gorgeous" is copyright © 1982 by Marge Piercy and reprinted from *Parti-Colored Blocks for a Quilt* with the permission of the author and The University of Michigan Press. "Burying blues for Janice" and "To be of use," copyright © 1973 by Marge Piercy, and "The market economy," copyright © 1978 by Marge Piercy, are reprinted from *Circles on the Water* by Marge Piercy, by permission of Alfred A. Knopf, Inc. "Let us gather at the river," "Hummingbird," "The watch," and "The common living dirt" are copyright © 1983 by Marge Piercy and reprinted from *Stone, Paper, Knife,* by Marge Piercy, by permission of Alfred A. Knopf, Inc.

Stanley Plumly: "Poetry and Intimacy," revised from its first appearance in *The Ohio Review,* is copyright © by Stanley Plumly and published here with his permission. "The Iron Lung," "Out-of-the-Body Travel," and "Now That My Father Lies Down Beside Me" are copyright © 1976 by Stanley Plumly and reprinted from *Out-of-the-Body Travel* by permission of The Ecco Press. "Posthumous Keats," "My Mother's Feet," "Blossom," "American Ash," and "Waders and Swimmers"

Crazyhorse), "The Mystery of the Caves" (from *Poetry*), and "Singles" (from *The Ohio Review*) are copyright © by Michael Waters and reprinted by permission of the author.

C. K. Williams: "Downwards" and "A Day for Anne Frank" are copyright © 1969 by C. K. Williams and reprinted from *Lies* by permission of the author. "The Rampage" is copyright © 1971 by C. K. Williams and reprinted from *I Am The Bitter Name* by permission of the author. "Blades" is copyright © 1977 by C. K. Williams and reprinted from *With Ignorance* by permission of the author. "Floor" and "Tar" are copyright © 1983 by C. K. Williams and reprinted from *Tar: Poems by C. K. Williams* by permission of Random House, Inc.

Charles Wright: "The New Poem," copyright © 1971 by Charles Wright, first appeared in *The Venice Notebook* published by Barn Dream Press, Boston, and is reprinted from *Hard Freight* by permission of Wesleyan University Press. "Blackwater Mountain," copyright © 1972 by Charles Wright, first appeared in *Poetry* and is reprinted from *Hard Freight* by permission of Wesleyan University Press. "Cloud River" (from *Three Rivers Poetry Journal*), "Spider Crystal Ascension," and "Clear Night" (from *The New Yorker*) are copyright © 1977 by Charles Wright, and reprinted from *China Trace* by permission of Wesleyan University Press. "Holy Thursday," "Laguna Blues," and "Portrait of the Artist with Hart Crane" are copyright © 1977, 1978, 1979, 1980, 1981 by Charles Wright and reprinted by permission of Random House, Inc., from *The Southern Cross* by Charles Wright.

Contents

NORMAN DUBIE

TESS GALLAGHER

LOUISE GLÜCK

WILLIAM PITT ROOT

ROBERT SIEGEL

CHARLES SIMIC

DAVE SMITH

Preface

*Henry James . . . had come since to regard Whitman as the
greatest American poet. . . . Edith Wharton, hearing James read
"Lilacs," . . . found "a new proof of the way in which, above a
certain level, the most divergent intelligences walk together like
gods."*

from *Walt Whitman: A Life*
by Justin Kaplan

For several years now I've attempted to define for myself that gen-
eration of American poets to which I might belong. I've not been
successful in any clear way, have again and again caught myself con-
tradicting myself or being contradicted by a particular poet's life or
work. But I've kept making these attempts, I've realized, because I've
needed to feel part of something, not necessarily a "movement" or
"group" or "school" with cloned characteristics, but of a community of
those poets of my approximate age who began writing and publishing
when I did, who will lose the earth approximately when I will and
who, for this reason among others, are now deepening into their lives
and poetry in many of the ways I am.

In one of his notebooks Theodore Roethke refers to "the exhaust-
ing fight against the inner fatigue, the soul sickness." I connect
Roethke's struggle, one felt by most poets, with the fact that poetry is
a lonely activity in this America in which the life of the spirit itself
seems increasingly to be in danger of obliteration, and when I've read
and/or heard and/or met the contributors to this book, I've felt the
kinship I've needed to feel. The generation is in the poems them-
selves, of course, or it is nowhere. Underneath the various voices, un-
derneath the various subject matters that serve in the best poems to
reach into what all true poetry has always been about, I believe that
what I've called "The Generation of 2000" reveals itself here. I know
it as I feel it. I feel it as I enter the poems.

There is a very limited audience for quality poetry in America. The
best work seldom reaches the shelves of the dominant fast-book
chains now fixtures in shopping malls built on what were once farms
across the country. Television sells books now, but (perhaps fortu-
nately) the poet is still felt to be too trivial or uninteresting or unbal-
anced or esoteric to appear on talk shows. Poetry does not make it into
the "Books in the Media" displays at the mall stores, and if there is a

poetry section, it consists of leatherette gilt-edged gift books or the latest insipid collection by some sweet singer, maybe a relative that a publisher decided to make famous. But genuine poetry will always guard its own integrity fiercely, and will always be necessary. It will not dilute itself to sell itself. In the most important sense, it is not for sale, and won't be. Nor will it condescend to us. We will have to reach up to it to discover its very real abilities to sustain us. In his essay included here, Wendell Berry quotes William Carlos Williams: "It is difficult / to get the news from poems / yet men die miserably every day / for lack / of what is to be found there."

I won't belabor the obvious difficulties there were in making a selection. I wish I could have included more poets (and perhaps a future edition of this anthology will). I've leaned toward a larger number of selections by fewer poets rather than vice versa. Each contributor has published at least two substantial collections of poetry, most several more. Each, in my opinion, is dedicated to the art, has made poetry a central part of his or her life, and is more than likely to keep the faith, to keep writing. I read as widely as I could, discovered poets and poems that came to be important to me. Once I decided to include a poet, I aimed to make a selection, as limited as it would have to be, that would be representative of the poet's best work. Often, the poet helped choose poems, helped make me see and hear poems that I hadn't been up to before. Usually the selections include both early and later work, and suggest the different sides of the nature of each poet. This anthology, of course, hopes to be just a beginning, hopes to incline the reader toward the poets' books.

After I edited *American Poets in 1976*, one of the poets included wrote to me to say that another poet in the book was "the enemy," and that if he'd known "the enemy" was going to be in my anthology, he himself would have refused inclusion. I don't understand this kind of thinking. I have my own preferences, have a feeling myself for the poetry I most care for—some of the poets here write the kinds of poems I would most like to write, and some do not—but an anthology is a gathering, to my mind, of various aesthetics. Each poem here, I believe, whatever musics I prefer among them, is a work of language-integrity, and this is an eclectic book. Its aim is to reach that level where "the most divergent intelligences," both of readers and contributing poets, may come together.

What I feel poetry to be will, of course, be embodied in my poems and in the poems by others that I've chosen, and not in what I may come to say about them. But I'll hazard one observation now. If there is an editorial slant that helped form this wide-ranging collection, it is one against the kind of quasi-surrealist poem that Wallace Stevens made fun of when he said that "To make a clam play an accordion is to invent, not to discover." It is understandable but tragic that there is so much distracting silliness and indulgence in poetry during this critical point in human history, a time when all life on earth is threatened. Earlier, to suggest what I feel to be the rooted concerns of the poets of this generation I most believe in, I used the phrase "lose the earth" rather than the simple word "die." The poets *2000* brings together are not dadaists or faddists or stand-up comics, and they are not aestheticians tripletalking ethereal voices, but are poets of long-staring at the things of this world. Poetry's language is not overtly didactic, of course, does not beat us over our heads with blunt sticks. It discovers what it knows and feels as it comes to be itself, as it unfolds itself during its own present language again and again. But, as Stevens says, "Poetry has to be something more than a conception of the mind. It has to be a revelation of nature. . . ." It will be this in myriad ways, certainly, but not by the sort of false wit whereby bivalves play "Lady of Spain." At the same time, this is not a book of what Louis Simpson calls "deadly solemnity." The contributors here (and I as editor) take chances, I believe, endorse that necessary "wildness" that Emerson called for in the American poet.

My oldest contributors (Wendell Berry and Mark Strand) were born in 1934, my youngest in 1948 and 1949 (Heather McHugh and Michael Waters). Although in essential ways dates do not matter—a contemporary poet may of course feel closer to Li Po or Walt Whitman than to T. S. Eliot or Allen Ginsberg—literary generations in twentieth-century America seem to be about fifteen years wide, as is this one. Not one of the poets in this book is included in the best anthology of the previous generation of poets (most of whom were born in the Twenties), A. Poulin, Jr.'s *Contemporary American Poetry* whose youngest contributor, Imamu Amiri Baraka, was born in 1934. As time goes by, some of the poets in *2000* may of course resist the particular boundaries of this book and move backward or forward into other constellations.

I want to thank my contributors for various kindnesses, particularly for their willingness to provide the prose pieces (most of which were written especially for this book) that now accompany their poems in intriguing ways. I've provided brief biographical and bibliographical notes on each poet, but have kept critical commentary to a minimum. The opinionated critical introductions often favored by other anthologists usually seem to me to curdle quickly as they set up preconditions for the reading of the poems in ways that the poets' own essays, suggestive and complementary, do not. . . . A note of special gratitude, also, to Raymond Smith of Ontario Review Press for his faith in this project, his help with permissions and other details, his guidance along the way.

It may be that by the year 2000, because of accelerating economic and technological pressures that are forcing students overwhelmingly into business/computer/scientific fields, we will have a nation of imbalance, one in which the leavening qualities of the humanities to help us know ourselves and our earth, to help us laugh and curse and sing and pray, to help us order our priorities in life-giving ways will be seriously compromised. In its own small way, this anthology hopes to be a counterweight to that tendency. There are poems here that can help us realize, as Whitman says in "To Think of Time," "that the purpose and essence of the known life, the transient, / Is to form and decide identity for the unknown life, the permanent." During a time when we have been numbed by hourly exposure to news of unimaginable tragedies around the globe, there are poems here to help us imagine again, and feel, and become human again, soul-restoring poems. This anthology hopes to be an edge that cuts away at cant and complacency all the way to 2000 and beyond. This most recent generation of American poets will bear out the faith we place in it now. This anthology is dedicated to the faithful reader.

W.H.
January, 1984

The Generation of 2000

AI

AI *was born in 1947 in Arizona, and holds degrees from the University of Arizona (1969) and the University of California at Irvine (1971). Her first book,* Cruelty, *was published in 1973.* Killing Floor, *her second, was the Lamont Poetry Selection for 1978. Other of her many prizes and awards include a Guggenheim Fellowship and an Ingram-Merrill Award. A new manuscript of poems is tentatively titled* Sin.
(Photo by Brad Franckum)

Memories

1

One day, in summer, in Tucson, Arizona there were two goats: one black, one white. The black goat was mine. I was ten, my sister six. The goats thrived, began to jump on the roof of my grandfather's Ford pickup. That's when he said, *I'm gonna kill those sonsofbitches.* And so he did, on one hot, dry Sunday in July, while assorted great-aunts, great-uncles, cousins, my great-grandmother and great-grandfather, and Papa (who was to barbecue) looked on. While the goats' cries drifted in through the open kitchen windows, my sister and I sat at the table with our heads bowed.

A few weeks later, my grandfather decided to kill Piggy, the pet pig. When Piggy was very young, I had dropped a watermelon on his back and now he limped. He would follow us about the yard like a dog and would even have gone into the house if we had let him. But now, he'd die too. My grandmother, mother, sister and I were upset, but my grandfather didn't care. Sometimes when I am down on men, I can't help remembering that and thinking that's how men are—like my grandfather. Beasts. That women, children and animals only exist to be ruled, to be slaughtered by men who cry over the loss of a football game, but who can go out one day and kill millions. But people are not so simple as that and I did have some revenge when Piggy died: his meat made everyone who ate it sick.

My black goat had the most incredible yellow eyes which later became "rain, like black cats' eyes" in the poem "I Have Got To Stop Loving You." The kidney in the poem was really Piggy's, which as he hung lifeless from the wooden stake, my grandmother quickly cut from him and took to the house where she put it in boiling water with slices of lemon. She said the steam would cure colds, and she had my sister and me bend over the pot and breathe. This is the closest I have ever come to autobiography in my poems. If someone asked me how I got the poem from these episodes in my childhood, I wouldn't be able to tell. I only know that these two memories lived inside me for over ten years, then suddenly, as I tried to get over a crush on a man, flowed out of me onto paper. The man wasn't worth it; he has faded from my memory, but Piggy and my black goat are alive.

2

When I was fourteen, I babysat for a nurse who worked in a rest home. She had two daughters, aged three and six. Sometimes, a young man would come over on a motorcycle. He was thin, wore a black leather jacket, levis, and carried a long comb in his back pocket. He would wrestle and play with the little girls. I disapproved. Eventually, I wasn't needed anymore and I forgot the job and the man, until a few years later, when a man, the man on the motorcycle, was picked up by the police and charged with murdering two teenage girls, the daughters of a doctor. He had buried them in the desert, and took the police and showed them. The newspaper was full of the details. He and his friends had spent most of their time cruising Speedway, Tucson's main drag, while listening to their favorite song, "Who Do You Love" by the blues singer Bo Diddley. When *Life* picked up the story, it called Speedway the "ugliest street in America." The man went to prison. I went to college. But we both became poets. The man was murdered in prison. I carry on. My notebooks, my paper and pens, my typewriter and books, my struggle to stay afloat in a field that gives few tangible rewards. It's got to be love that keeps me writing year after year, as I cripple along with too little money, occasionally fantasizing some other career. But writing in a sense isn't a career; it's an eternal apprenticeship. As long as I can hold a pen, as long as I can dictate, or speak into a microphone, I'm a student, I'm under the guidance of a master not unlike God, the patriarchal God of the Jews, who in His kabbalistic aspect *Din*, is judgement, power (*geburah*) and fear (*pahad*). I wonder if the murderer ever felt this? Did he feel God looking over his shoulder when he wrote, or yes, the faces of those two murdered girls like two infinitely patient, infinitely understanding angels?

When I wrote the poem "The Hitchhiker," I was trying to understand the murderer. But I didn't really. I saw a man like Abraham, an Abraham of Satan's, not God's, a man who would sacrifice others, who felt good when it was over, but I didn't know the whole story, don't about anybody, including myself. I only know the master is here, one hand on my shoulder, the other one guiding my hand. *Write*, he says, and I do.

Why Can't I Leave You?

You stand behind the old black mare,
dressed as always in that red shirt,
stained from sweat, the crying of the armpits,
that will not stop for anything,

stroking her rump, while the barley goes unplanted.
I pick up my suitcase and set it down,
as I try to leave you again.
I smooth the hair back from your forehead.
I think with your laziness and the drought too,
you'll be needing my help more than ever.
You take my hands, I nod
and go to the house to unpack,
having found another reason to stay.

I undress, then put on my white lace slip
for you to take off, because you like that
and when you come in, you pull down the straps
and I unbutton your shirt.
I know we can't give each other any more
or any less than what we have.
There is safety in that, so much
that I can never get past the packing,
the begging you to please, if I can't make you happy,
come close between my thighs
and let me laugh for you from my second mouth.

I Have Got to Stop Loving You

So I have killed my black goat.
His kidney floats in a bowl,
a beige, flat fish, around whom parasites, slices of lemon,
break through the surface of hot broth, then sink below,
as I bend, face down in the steam, breathing in.
I hear this will cure anything.

When I am finished, I walk up to him.
He hangs from a short wooden post,
tongue stuck out of his mouth,
tasting the hay-flavored air.
A bib of flies gathers at his throat
and further down, where he is open
and bare of all his organs,
I put my hand in, stroke him once,
then taking it out, look at the sky.
The stormclouds there break open

and raindrops, yellow as black cats' eyes, come down
each a tiny river, hateful and alone.

Wishing I could get out of this alive, I hug myself.
It is hard to remember if he suffered much.

One Man Down

Your brother brings you home from hunting,
slung over your horse, dead,
with the wild boar tied down beside you.
I ask no questions.

He throws the boar at my feet,
hands me the red licorice he promised.
I drop my shawl
and his hands cover my breasts.
He whispers of a dress in town,
while I unbutton my skirt.

I sit on the ground, waiting,
while he loosens his belt.
He smiles, swings it across my face,
then pushes me back. I keep my eyes open.
The hound's paws bloody the tiles
lining the flower bed.
The bitch walks behind him, licking his tracks.
I scratch the flesh above me.
The odor of fresh meat
digs a finger in my nostrils.
The horse rears,
your body slides from the black saddle
like a bedroll of fine velvet.
I laugh, close my eyes, and relax.

The Hitchhiker

The Arizona wind dries out my nostrils
and the heat of the sidewalk burns my shoes,
as a woman drives up slowly.

I get in, grinning at a face I do not like,
but I slide my arm across the top of the seat
and rest it lightly against her shoulder.
We turn off into the desert,
then I reach inside my pocket and touch the switchblade.

We stop, and as she moves closer to me, my hands ache,
but somehow, I get the blade into her chest.
I think a song: "Everybody needs somebody,
everybody needs somebody to love,"
as the black numerals 35 roll out of her right eye
inside one small tear.
Laughing, I snap my fingers. Rape, murder, I got you
in the sight of my gun.

I move off toward the street.
My feet press down in it,
familiar with the hot, soft asphalt
that caresses them.
The sun slips down into its cradle behind the mountains
and it is hot, hotter than ever
and I like it.

The Mortician's Twelve-Year-Old Son

Lady, when you were alive
I'd see you on the streets,
the long green dress with the velvet flower
sewn dead center between your breasts
so tightly I could never get a look inside.

Now the gas lamps half-light the table,
washing the sheet that covers you with shadows.
A few strands of your dyed red hair
hang nearly to the floor,
as if all your blood had run there to hide.

I lift the sheet, rub the mole on your cheek
and it comes off black and oily on my hand.
I bend over your breasts and sing,
love, sister, is just a kiss away.

I cover each nipple with my mouth.
Tonight, just a kiss away.

The Kid

My sister rubs the doll's face in mud,
then climbs through the truck window.
She ignores me as I walk around it,
hitting the flat tires with an iron rod.
The old man yells for me to help hitch the team,
but I keep walking around the truck, hitting harder,
until my mother calls.
I pick up a rock and throw it at the kitchen window,
but it falls short.
The old man's voice bounces off the air like a ball
I can't lift my leg over.

I stand beside him, waiting, but he doesn't look up
and I squeeze the rod, raise it, his skull splits open.
Mother runs toward us. I stand still,
get her across the spine as she bends over him.
I drop the rod and take the rifle from the house.
Roses are red, violets are blue,
one bullet for the black horse, two for the brown.
They're down quick. I spit, my tongue's bloody;
I've bitten it. I laugh, remember the one out back.
I catch her climbing from the truck, shoot.
The doll lands on the ground with her.
I pick it up, rock it in my arms.
Yeah. I'm Jack, Hogarth's son.
I'm nimble, I'm quick.

In the house, I put on the old man's best suit
and his patent leather shoes.
I pack my mother's satin nightgown
and my sister's doll in the suitcase.
Then I go outside and cross the fields to the highway.
I'm fourteen. I'm a wind from nowhere.
I can break your heart.

The Expectant Father

The skin of my mouth, chewed raw, tastes good.
I get up, cursing, and find the bottle of Scotch.
My mouth burns as darkness, lifting her skirt,
reveals daylight, a sleek left ankle.
The woman calls. I don't answer.
I imagine myself coming up to my own door,
holding a small reed basket in my arms.
Inside it, there is a child,
with clay tablets instead of hands,
and my name is written on each one.
The woman calls me again and I go to her.
She reaches for me, but I move away.
I frown, pulling back the covers to look at her.
So much going on outside;
the walls could cave in on us any time, any time.
I bring my face down
where the child's head should be and press hard.
I feel pain, she's pulling my hair.
I rise up, finally, and back away from the bed,
while she turns on her side
and drags her legs up to her chest.
I wait for her to cry,
then go into the kitchen.
I fix a Scotch and sit down at the table.
In six months, it is coming, in six months,
and I have no weapon against it.

Pentecost

for Myself

Rosebud Morales, my friend,
before you deserted,
you'd say anyone can kill an Indian
and forget it the same instant,
that it will happen to me, Emiliano Zapata.
But my men want more corn for tortillas,
more pigs, more chickens, more chilis

and land.
If I haven't got a gun or a knife,
I'll fight with a pitchfork or a hoe,
to take them from the bosses,
those high-flying birds,
with the pomade glistening on their hair,
as they promenade into their coffins.
And if I'm killed, if we're all killed right now,
we'll go on, the true Annunciation.

Rosebud, how beautiful this day is.
I'm riding to meet Guajardo.
He'll fight with me now,
against Carranza.
When I get to the hacienda, it's quiet.
Not many soldiers,
a sorrel horse, its reins held
by a woman in a thin, white American dress
and Guajardo standing on a balcony.

I get off my horse and start up the steps.
My legs burn, my chest,
my jaw, my head.
There's a hill in front of me;
it's slippery, I have to use my hands to climb it.
At the top, it's raining fire and blood
on rows and rows of black corn.
Machetes are scattered everywhere.
I grab one and start cutting the stalks.
When they hit the ground,
they turn into men.
I yell at them.
You're damned in the cradle,
in the grave, even in Heaven.
Dying doesn't end anything.
Get up. Swing those machetes.
You can't steal a man's glory
without a goddamned fight.
Boys, take the land, take it; it's yours.
If you suffer in the grave,
you can kill from it.

WENDELL BERRY

WENDELL BERRY *was born in 1934 in Henry County, Kentucky, where he now lives and farms.* "Such history as my family has," *he writes,* "is the history of its life here. All that any of us may know of ourselves is to be known in relation to this place." *He holds two degrees from the University of Kentucky, Lexington, and is a past fellow of both the Guggenheim and Rockefeller foundations. He is the author of more than a dozen books including* A Place on Earth *and* The Memory of Old Jack *(novels),* Recollected Essays 1965-1980 *and* The Gift of Good Land *(prose), and* Clearing, A Part, *and* The Wheel *(poetry).*
(Photo by Tanya Berry)

A Homage to Dr. Williams

I have always been attracted to the work of William Carlos Williams because of his use of the art of writing as an instrument by which a man may arrive in his place and maintain himself there. I am still involved in comprehending the implications of such a labor, but this has been the fascination and the solace I have found in him from the first. He has always about him the excitement of the awareness that poetry, as much as the axe or the plow, is a necessity of discovery and settlement, and of the husbanding and neighboring that must follow.

His poems and stories and essays record the lifelong practice of citizenship, the unceasing labor of keeping responsibly conscious of where he was. He knew, as few white Americans have ever known, that a man has not meaningfully arrived in his place in body until he has arrived in spirit as well, and that the consummation of arrival is identification:

> Say it! No ideas but in things. Mr.
> Paterson has gone away
> to rest and write. Inside the bus one sees
> his thoughts sitting and standing. His
> thoughts alight and scatter. . . .
> *(Paterson,* Book One)

What he accomplished was a sustained and intricate act of patriotism in the largest sense of that word—a thousand times more precise and loving and preserving than any patriotism ever contemplated by officials of the government or leaders of parties.

At times the usefulness of his work has been made so vivid to me that what I know of him has become part of what I know of myself. One such time was an overcast day late in the summer of 1962. I was riding a bus out of New York City across the marshes and the industrial suburbs of New Jersey. That fall I was to take a job in New York, and I was hunting a place to live. I was between places, uprooted, alien in that place, deeply depressed. And then I suddenly thought of Williams—all those lovely poems that had grown out of and so heartily savored the life of such places as I saw—and I felt wonderfully comforted and relieved. Life was possible there after all! I had known it for years! And though I never found a place to live in New Jersey, Williams' poems have helped to satisfy me of the possibility of life wherever I have lived. It occurs to me now that no more could be asked of a poet. No more could be asked of a man.

The necessity, the *usefulness*, of poetry! Williams was certain of it. Man cannot live by bread alone, and Williams' work is full of the assurance that he is providing us the staff of life. In the great love poem of his last years, "Asphodel, that Greeny Flower," as in other poems, he speaks directly of it:

> Look at
> > what passes for the new.
> You will not find it there but in
> > despised poems.
> > > It is difficult
> to get the news from poems
> > yet men die miserably every day
> > > for lack
> of what is to be found there.

A poem was never, for him, merely an object of art; it was not a specialist's product. He spoke of poetry as the life force, not a "creative act" but one of the acts of the creation, a part of the sum of

> All that which makes the pear ripen
> > or the poet's line
> > > come true!
> > > > ("Deep Religious Faith")

It is the power by which a man gifted and trained in verse might find speech and so, in his way, clarify himself and his neighborhood.

In his poems he did not speak as a poet but as a man. Having come up under the influence of the more superficial techniques of "explication," which encouraged us to read everything as if it were an exercise, I was slow to recognize this. Having learned to think of him as a poet in the specialist sense, I was slow to see him; in "The Host" for instance, a man speaking in worship:

> There is nothing to eat,
> > seek it where you will,
> > > but of the body of the Lord.
> The blessed plants
> > and the sea, yield it
> > > to the imagination
> intact.

While the experts haggle whether God is dead, as if that could be settled by somebody's argument, here is something of the life of God where none of them have yet suspected it: in the world, in a poet's book.

In the same way I was slow to see anything political in Williams. And yet he is full of concern for politics, for matters important to the community of us. But he does not speak as a politician. He could not quit being a poet in order to become political any more than he could quit being a man in order to become a poet. One thinks of the effort he made toward the end of his life to speak of the bomb, to contain it in an order of comprehension, as though in answer to a feeling of community obligation. Or there is the brilliant anger of the poem "To Elsie" in *Spring and All,* in which his concern for women and their fate offers a profound political measure:

> young slatterns, bathed
> in filth
> from Monday to Saturday
>
> to be tricked out that night
> with gauds
> from imaginations which have no
>
> peasant traditions to give them
> character

And he goes on to speak of a servant girl, Elsie, whose voluptuous ungainly body was

> addressed to cheap
> jewelry
> and rich young men with fine eyes
>
> as if the earth under our feet
> were
> an excrement of some sky
>
> and we degraded prisoners
> destined
> to hunger until we eat filth

Is that political poetry? As I care to use the adjective, it is. It would be perfectly useless and bewildering, perhaps, to the average politician, a political specialist. But how serviceable and clarifying it is, once we have set aside the current abstractions and categories of politics. The poem is telling us precisely what is wrong with us. And yet, because of the exacting energy of its love for the girl and its grief over her, it simply *cannot* produce a high-toned political abstraction or slogan. By its nature it is a world apart from the dumbfounding earth-polluting blither (The Great Society, The Great Leap Forward) characteristic of government talk from here to China. It fulfills itself in its facts, and does not rant or pontificate. It is preceded by a poem about "Banjo jazz" and is followed by one about lilacs. And far indeed from any political fashion that I know is his assertion—that I believe to be entirely correct—of the importance of peasant traditions.

The speech of politicians, political rhetoric, grows out of the pretense that the politician is not a man, but is somehow infallible. This sort of speech, no matter whose it is, is preparing the world to fight— to the last man—the final war. The poetry that is most useful to us, that has most devotedly sought the humble exactitude of the personal, never makes the deathly pretense of being more than human, and if we will read it, it will help to keep us from making such a pretense. What Williams exemplifies is that a man is most a poet— and, hard as it may be for us to believe it, most a citizen—when he is most humanely and exactingly a man. The measure that so obsessed him, the form and energy of the poetic line, what is it but the obligation and the distinction of a responsible manliness?

Looking back recently through some of his poems, I have been impressed again by the way certain passages I never particularly noticed before suddenly stand out, epigraphs for some new awareness I have come to, some new whereabouts of my concern. His work seems to keep ahead of me, like a man's shadow when he walks eastward in the afternoon, and I have the comfort of believing that I will not exhaust the delight I take in it.

My Great-Grandfather's Slaves

Deep in the back ways of my mind I see them
    going in the long days
    over the same fields that I have gone
    long days over.

I see the sun passing and burning high
　　over that land from their day
　　until mine, their shadows
　　having risen and consumed them.

I see them obeying and watching
　　the bearded tall man whose voice
　　and blood are mine, whose countenance
　　in stone at his grave my own resembles,
　　whose blindness is my brand.

I see them kneel and pray to the white God
　　who buys their souls with Heaven.

I see them approach, quiet
　　in the merchandise of their flesh,
　　to put down their burdens
　　of firewood and hemp and tobacco
　　into the minds of my kinsmen.

I see them moving in the rooms of my history,
　　the day of my birth entering
　　the horizon emptied of their days,
　　their purchased lives taken back
　　into the dust of birthright.

I see them borne, shadow within shadow,
　　shroud within shroud, through all nights
　　from their lives to mine, long beyond
　　reparation or given liberty
　　or any straightness.

I see them go in the bonds of my blood
　　through all the time of their bodies.

I have seen that freedom cannot be taken
　　from one man and given to another,
　　and cannot be taken and kept.

I know that freedom can only be given,
　　and is the gift to the giver
　　from the one who receives.

I am owned by the blood of all of them
who ever were owned by my blood.
We cannot be free of each other.

The Snake

At the end of October
I found on the floor of the woods
a small snake whose back
was patterned with the dark
of the dead leaves he lay on.
His body was thickened with a mouse
or small bird. He was cold,
so stuporous with his full belly
and the fall air that he hardly
troubled to flicker his tongue.
I held him a long time, thinking
of the perfection of the dark
marking on his back, the death
that swelled him, his living cold.
Now the cold of him stays
in my hand, and I think of him
lying below the frost,
big with a death to nourish him
during a long sleep.

The Peace of Wild Things

When despair for the world grows in me
and I wake in the night at the least sound
in fear of what my life and my children's lives may be,
I go and lie down where the wood drake
rests in his beauty on the water, and the great heron feeds.
I come into the peace of wild things
who do not tax their lives with forethought
of grief. I come into the presence of still water.
And I feel above me the day-blind stars
waiting with their light. For a time
I rest in the grace of the world, and am free.

Poem for J.

What she made in her body is broken.
Now she has begun to bear it again.
In the house of her son's death
his life is shining in the windows,
for she has elected to bear him again.
She did not bear him for death,
and she does not. She has taken back
into her body the seed, bitter
and joyous, of the life of a man.

In the house of the dead the windows shine
with life. She mourns, for his life was good.
She is not afraid. She is like a field
where the corn is planted, and like the rain
that waters the field, and like the young corn.
In her sorrow she renews life, in her grief
she prepares the return of joy.

She did not bear him for death, and she does not.
There was a life that went out of her to live
on its own, divided, and now she has taken it back.
She is alight with the sudden new life of death.
Perhaps it is the brightness of the dead one
being born again. Perhaps she is planting him,
like corn, in the living and in the earth.
She has taken back into her flesh,
and made light, the dark seed of her pain.

The Lilies

Hunting them, a man must sweat, bear
the whine of a mosquito in his ear,
grow thirsty, tired, despair perhaps
of ever finding them, walk a long way.
He must give himself over to chance,
for they live beyond prediction.
He must give himself over to patience,
for they live beyond will. He must be led

along the hill as by a prayer.
If he finds them anywhere, he will find
a few, paired on their stalks,
at ease in the air as souls in bliss.
I found them here at first without hunting,
by grace, as all beauties are first found.
I have hunted and not found them here.
Found, unfound, they breathe their light
into the mind, year after year.

Grief

The morning comes. The old woman, a spot
of soot where she has touched her cheek, tears
on her face, builds a fire, sets water to boil,
puts the skillet on. The man in his middle years,
bent by the work he has done toward the work
he will do, weeps as he eats, bread in his mouth,
tears on his face. They shape the day for its passing
as if absent from it—for what needs care, caring,
feeding what must be fed. To keep them, there are only
the household's remembered ways, etched thin
and brittle by their tears. It is a sharp light
that lights the day now. It seems to shine,
beyond eyesight, also in another day
where the dead have risen and are walking
away, their backs forever turned. What
look is in their eyes? What do they say
as they walk into the fall and flow of light?
It seems that they must know where they are going.
And the living must go with them, not knowing,
a little way. And the dead go on, not turning,
knowing, but not saying. And the living
turn back to their day, their grieving and staying.

The Gift of Gravity

All that passes descends,
and ascends again unseen
into the light: the river

coming down from sky
to hills, from hills to sea,
and carving as it moves,
to rise invisible,
gathered to light, to return
again. "The river's injury
is its shape." I've learned no more.
We are what we are given
and what is taken away;
blessed be the name
of the giver and taker.
For everything that comes
is a gift, the meaning always
carried out of sight
to renew our whereabouts,
always a starting place.
And every gift is perfect
in its beginning, for it
is "from above, and cometh down
from the Father of lights."
Gravity is grace.
All that has come to us
has come as the river comes,
given in passing away.
And if our wickedness
destroys the watershed,
dissolves the beautiful field,
then I must grieve and learn
that I possess by loss
the earth I live upon
and stand in and am. The dark
and then the light will have it.
I am newborn of pain
to love the new-shaped shore
where young cottonwoods
take hold and thrive in the wound,
kingfishers already nesting
in a hole in the sheared bank.
"What is left is what is"—
have learned no more. The shore
turns green under the songs
of the fires of the world's end,
and what is there to do?
Imagine what exists

so that it may shine
in thought light and day light,
lifted up in the mind.
The dark returns to light
in the kingfisher's blue and white
richly laid together.
He falls into flight
from the broken ground,
with strident outcry gathers
air under his wings.
In work of love, the body
forgets its weight. And once
again with love and singing
in mind, I come to what
must come to me, carried
as a dancer by a song.
This grace is gravity.

The Wheel

for Robert Penn Warren

At the first strokes of the fiddle bow
the dancers rise from their seats.
The dance begins to shape itself
in the crowd, as couples join,
and couples join couples, their movement
together lightening their feet.
They move in the ancient circle
of the dance. The dance and the song
call each other into being. Soon
they are one—rapt in a single
rapture, so that even the night
has its clarity, and time
is the wheel that brings it round.

In this rapture the dead return.
Sorrow is gone from them.
They are light. They step
into the steps of the living
and turn with them in the dance

in the sweet enclosure
of the song, and timeless
is the wheel that brings it round.

In Rain

1.
I go in under foliage
light with rain-light
in the hill's cleft,
and climb, my steps
silent as flight
on the wet leaves.
Where I go, stones
are wearing away
under the sky's flow.

2.
The path I follow
I can hardly see
it is so faintly trod
and overgrown.
At times, looking,
I fail to find it
among dark trunks, leaves
living and dead. And then
I am alone, the woods
shapeless around me.
I look away, my gaze
at rest among leaves,
and then I see the path
again, a dark way going on
through the light.

3.
In a mist of light
falling with the rain
I walk this ground
of which dead men
and women I have loved
are part, as they

are part of me. In earth,
in blood, in mind,
the dead and living
into each other pass,
as the living pass
in and out of loves
as stepping to a song.
The way I go is
marriage to this place,
grace beyond chance,
love's braided dance
covering the world.

4.
Marriages to marriages
are joined, husband and wife
are plighted to all
husbands and wives,
any life has all lives
for its delight.
Let the rain come,
the sun, and then the dark,
for I will rest
in an easy bed tonight.

RAYMOND CARVER

RAYMOND CARVER *was born in Clatskanie, Oregon, in 1939. His early years, when he was straining to become a writer, were precarious. "But I learned some things along the way," he has written. "One of the things I learned is that I had to bend or else break. And I also learned that it is possible to bend and break at the same time." He has taught at the Universities of Iowa, Texas, and California, and in 1983 he resigned his chair at Syracuse University in order to accept a Mildred and Harold Strauss Living Award. His books of fiction include* Will You Please Be Quiet, Please? *(1976),* What We Talk About When We Talk About Love *(1981), and* Cathedral *(1983). He has published three collections of poetry:* Near Klamath *(1968),* Winter Insomnia *(1970), and* At Night the Salmon Move *(1976).* Fires *(1983) is a collection of essays, poems, and stories.*

(Photo by Tess Gallagher)

Occasions

Every poem I've written has been, for me, an occasion of the first order. So much so, I believe, that I can remember the emotional circumstances that were at work when I wrote the poem, my physical surroundings, even what the weather was like. If pressed, I think I could come close to recalling the day of the week. At least, in most instances, I can remember whether the poems were written during the week or on a weekend. Most certainly I can remember the particular time of day I wrote them—morning, midday, afternoon or, once in a great while, late at night. This kind of recall is not true of the short fiction I write, especially the stories I wrote early in my career. When I look back at my first book of stories, for example, I have to glance over the copyright dates to even get a fix on the year the stories were published, and from that I can guess—give or take a year or two—when they must have been written. It's only in a few isolated instances that I can recall anything in particular, or out of the ordinary, about when I wrote them, let alone what I was feeling at the time I did so.

I don't know why it is that I recall so clearly the time and circumstances surrounding each poem, yet don't recall much about the composition of these stories. I think partly it has to do with the fact that, in truth, I feel the poems are closer to me, more special, more of a gift received than my other work, even though I know, for sure, that the stories are no less a gift. It could be that I put a more intimate value finally on the poems than I do the stories.

My poems are of course not literally true—the events didn't actually happen, or at least the stuff in the poems didn't happen in the way I say it does. But, like most of my fiction, there is an autobiographical element to the poems. Something resembling what happens in them did happen to me at some time or another, and the memory stayed with me until it found expression. Or often what is being described in the poem was to some degree a reflection of my state of mind at the time of writing it. I suppose in a large way then the poems *are* more personal than my stories and hence more "revealing."

In poetry, my own or someone else's, I like narrative. A poem doesn't have to tell a story with a beginning, middle and end, but for me it has to keep moving, it has to step lively, it has to spark. It may move in any direction at all—back in time, far into the future, or it may veer off onto some overgrown trail. It may even cease to be earthbound and go out seeking habitation with the stars. It might speak in a voice from beyond the grave or travel with salmon, wild geese, or locusts. But it isn't static. It *moves*. It moves and though it may have mysterious elements at work in it, its development is intrinsic, one thing suggesting something else. It shines—or at any rate I hope it shines.

Each of my poems that the editor has seen fit to include in this anthology touches upon a real-life concern or situation that pressed upon my life with some degree of urgency when that particular poem was written. To that degree I suppose the poems could be called narrative or story poems for they are always *about* something. They have a "subject." One of the things each one is "about" is what I thought and felt at the time I wrote it. Each poem preserves a specific moment in time; and when I look at one I can see the frame of mind I was in at the time I wrote it. Reading my poems now, I am in a very real sense looking back over a rough, but true map of my past. So in a way they are helping hold together my life, and I like that idea.

"Bobber," the oldest poem in the group, was written one fine June morning in a motel room in Cheyenne, Wyoming, on my way from Berkeley to Rock Island, Illinois. A year and a half later, in the fall of 1969, I was living in Ben Lomond, California, a few miles north of Santa Cruz, and it was there I wrote "Prosser." I woke up one morning thinking about my father. He'd been dead for two years, but had appeared that night in the margins of a dream I'd had. I tried to pin something down from the dream, but couldn't. But that morning I began to think about him and began to recall some hunting trips we'd made together. Then I clearly remembered the wheat fields we'd hunted over together, and I recalled the town of Prosser, a little place where we often stopped for something to eat in the evening once we'd finished hunting. It was the first town we came to after we left the wheatfield country, and I suddenly remembered how the lights would appear to us at night, just as they do in the poem. I wrote it quickly and, seemingly, effortlessly. (This may be one of the reasons I'm especially fond of this poem. But if I were ever asked which is the favorite of any poem I've written, this one would be it.) A few days later that same week I wrote the poem "Your Dog Dies." That one, too, came quickly and didn't seem to require much revision.

"Forever" was different. I wrote the poem in 1970, just before Christmas, in a workroom in a garage in Palo Alto; and it was a poem that I must have written fifty or sixty times before I felt I had it right. I remember that when I wrote the first draft it was raining hard outside. I had this worktable set up in the garage, and every now and then I would look out of the little garage window toward the house. It was late at night. Everyone inside the house was asleep. The rain seemed a part of that "Forever" I was approaching in my mind.

"Looking for Work" was written the following August, in the afternoon, in an apartment house in Sacramento during a confusing and difficult summer. My children and my wife had gone to the park. The temperature was nearly a hundred degrees, and I was barefoot and in swimming trunks. When I walked across the tile floors of the apartment, my feet left tracks.

"Wes Hardin" was also written in Sacramento. But it came a few months later, in October, and in a different residence, a house on a deadend road called, if you can believe it, Lunar Lane. It was early in the morning, eight o'clock or so, and my wife had just left the house to drop the children off at school and go on to her job. I had the day in front of me, a rare day in which to write, but instead of trying to write anything I picked up a book that had come in the mail and began to read about outlaws of the old West. I came to a photograph of John Wesley Hardin and stopped there. In a little while, I roughed out the poem.

"Marriage" is the most recent poem in this particular group of poems and was written in a two-room apartment in Iowa City in April 1978. My wife and I had been separated for months. But we had gotten back together on a trial basis for what, as it turned out, would prove to be a very short time. But we were trying once more to see if we could put our marriage back together. Our children, both of them grown now, were someplace in California, pretty much on their own. Still, I was worried about them. I was also worried about myself and my wife and our marriage of twenty-some years that we were making one final effort to preserve. I was alive with apprehensions of all sorts. I wrote the poem in the evening, my wife in one room and I in the other. The fears I was experiencing found a place to go.

The reconciliation didn't work out, but that's another story.

Bobber

On the Columbia River near Vantage,
Washington, we fished for whitefish
in the winter months; my dad, Swede—
Mr. Lindgren—and me. They used belly-reels,
pencil-length sinkers, red, yellow, or brown

flies baited with maggots.
They wanted distance and went clear out there
to the edge of the riffle.
I fished near shore with a quill bobber and a cane pole.

My dad kept his maggots alive and warm
under his lower lip. Mr. Lindgren didn't drink.
I liked him better than my dad for a time.
He let me steer his car, teased me
about my name "Junior," and said
one day I'd grow into a fine man, remember
all this, and fish with my own son.
But my dad was right. I mean
he kept silent and looked into the river,
worked his tongue, like a thought, behind the bait.

Prosser

In winter two kinds of fields on the hills
outside Prosser: fields of new green wheat, the slips
rising overnight out of the plowed ground,
and waiting,
and then rising again, and budding.
Geese love this green wheat.
I ate some of it once too, to see.

And wheat stubble-fields that reach to the river.
These are the fields that have lost everything.
At night they try to recall their youth,
but their breathing is slow and irregular as
their life sinks into dark furrows.
Geese love this shattered wheat also.
They will die for it.

But everything is forgotten, nearly everything,
and sooner rather than later, please God—
fathers, friends, they pass
into your life and out again, a few women stay
a while, then go, and the fields
turn their backs, disappear in rain.
Everything goes, but Prosser.

Those nights driving back through miles of wheat fields—
headlamps raking the fields on the curves—
Prosser, that town, shining as we break over hills,
heater rattling, tired through to bone,
the smell of gunpowder on our fingers still:
I can barely see him, my father, squinting
through the windshield of that cab, saying, Prosser.

Your Dog Dies

it gets run over by a van.
you find it at the side of the road
and bury it.
you feel bad about it.
you feel bad personally,
but you feel bad for your daughter
because it was her pet,
and she loved it so.
she used to croon to it
and let it sleep in her bed.
you write a poem about it.
you call it a poem for your daughter,
about the dog getting run over by a van
and how you looked after it,
took it out into the woods
and buried it deep, deep,
and that poem turns out so good
you're almost glad the little dog
was run over, or else you'd never
have written that good poem.
then you sit down to write
a poem about writing a poem
about the death of that dog,
but while you're writing you
hear a woman scream
your name, your first name,
both syllables,
and your heart stops.
after a minute, you continue writing.
she screams again.
you wonder how long this can go on.

Forever

Drifting outside in a pall of smoke,
I follow a snail's streaked path down
the garden to the garden's stone wall.
Alone at last I squat on my heels, see

what needs to be done, and suddenly
affix myself to the damp stone.
I begin to look around me slowly
and listen, employing

my entire body as the snail
employs its body, relaxed, but alert.
Amazing! Tonight is a milestone
in my life. After tonight

how can I ever go back to that
other life? I keep my eyes
on the stars, wave to them
with my feelers. I hold on

for hours, just resting.
Still later, grief begins to settle
around my heart in tiny drops.
I remember my father is dead,

and I am going away from this
town soon. Forever.
Goodbye, son, my father says.
Toward morning, I climb down

and wander back into the house.
They are still waiting,
fright splashed on their faces,
as they meet my new eyes for the first time.

Looking for Work

I've always wanted brook trout
for breakfast.

Suddenly, I find a new path
to the waterfall.

I begin to hurry.
Wake up,

my wife says,
you're dreaming.

But when I try to rise,
the house tilts.

Who's dreaming?
It's noon, she says.

My new shoes wait by the door.
They are gleaming.

Wes Hardin: From a Photograph

Turning through a collection
    of old photographs
I come to a picture of the outlaw,
    Wes Hardin, dead.
He is a big, moustached man
    in a black suitcoat
on his back over a boardfloor
    in Amarillo, Texas.
His head is turned at the camera
    and his face
seems bruised, the hair
    jarred loose.
A bullet has entered his skull
    from behind

coming out a little hole
    over his right eye.

Nothing so funny about that
    but three shabby men
in overalls stand grinning
    a few feet away.
They are all holding rifles
    and that one
at the end has on what must be
    the outlaw's hat.
Several other bullets are dotted
    here and there
under the fancy white shirt
    the deceased is wearing
—in a manner of speaking—
    but what makes me stare
is this large dark bullethole
    through the slender, delicate-looking right hand.

Marriage

In our cabin we eat breaded oysters and fries
with lemon cookies for dessert, as the marriage
of Kitty and Levin unfolds on Public TV.
The man in the trailer up the hill, our neighbor,
has just gotten out of jail again.
This morning he drove into the yard with his wife
in a big yellow car, radio blaring.
His wife turned off the radio while he parked,
and together they walked slowly
to their trailer without saying anything.
It was early morning, birds were out.
Later, he propped open the door
with a chair to let in spring air and light.

It's Easter Sunday night,
and Kitty and Levin are married at last.
It's enough to bring tears to the eyes, that marriage
and all the lives it touched. We go on
eating oysters, watching television,

remarking on the fine clothes and amazing grace
of the people caught up in this story, some of them
straining under the pressures of adultery,
separation from loved ones, and the destruction
they must know lies in store just after
the next cruel turn of circumstance, and then the next.

A dog barks. I get up to check the door.
Behind the curtains are trailers and a muddy
parking area with cars. The moon sails west
as I watch, armed to the teeth, hunting
for my children. My neighbor,
liquored up now, starts his big car, races
the engine, and heads out again, filled
with confidence. The radio wails,
beats something out. When he has gone
there are only the little ponds of silver water
that shiver and can't understand their being here.

LUCILLE CLIFTON

LUCILLE CLIFTON *was born in 1936 in Depew, New York, and attended Howard University and Fredonia State Teachers College. In 1969 she received both the YM-YWHA Poetry Center Discovery Award and a grant from the National Endowment for the Arts. The author of many acclaimed books for children and* Generations: A Memoir *(1976), she won the 1980 Juniper Prize, an annual poetry award sponsored by the University of Massachusetts, for* Two-Headed Woman. *Her volumes of poetry are* Good Times *(1969),* Good News About the Earth *(1972), and* An Ordinary Woman *(1974). She and her husband have six children and live in Baltimore.*
(Photo by Layle Silbert)

So Far

My daughters lead me into the supermarket. When I am alone I hold my head down, watching for the arrows directing shoppers toward the doors. The doors are marked OUT and IN but if I am outside going in I invariably head for the door marked OUT. That, I have explained to my daughters, is because I am OUT and so the OUT door must be for me. They explain it to me each time but when faced with the moment I tend to make the same mistake. It is in trying to understand what the words mean. I think that much of my writing is in that attempt: to try to understand what the words mean. I know what I mean by them, and I know what they usually and generally mean, but what do they mean This time? Each This time is a new attempt at trying to understand, a new poem.

Growing up poor, and Black, and female and, yes, American, I also discovered early on that the world was full of things that were not what they seemed. I learned to try to look behind the form to find the substance. I learned that I was not even what I might have seemed. I learned that it was interesting to me to try to get at the face behind the face. I still do try.

I was blessed with toughness and humor and a loving heart. I was blessed with the ability to See as well as see, to Hear as well as hear, and with the ability to learn. I am grateful for that. Mostly though, I was born with the gift of being able to hear the music in the language and see the nobility in the people, that is, all the language and all the people. And for some reason, things poem up in me. Not always, but so far often enough. So far.

forgiving my father

it is friday. we have come
to the paying of the bills.
all week you have stood in my dreams
like a ghost, asking for more time
but today is payday, payday old man;
my mother's hand opens in her early grave
and i hold it out like a good daughter.

there is no more time for you. there will
never be time enough daddy daddy old lecher
old liar. i wish you were rich so i could take it all
and give the lady what she was due
but you were the son of a needy father,
the father of a needy son;
you gave her all you had
which was nothing. you have already given her
all you had.

you are the pocket that was going to open
and come up empty any friday.
you were each other's bad bargain, not mine.
daddy old pauper   old prisoner,   old dead man
what am i doing here collecting?
you lie side by side in debtors' boxes
and no accounting will open them up.

i once knew a man

i once knew a man who had wild horses killed.
when he told about it
the words came galloping out of his mouth
and shook themselves and headed off in
every damn direction. his tongue
was wild and wide and spinning when he talked
and the people he looked at closed their eyes
and tore the skins off their backs as they walked away
and stopped eating meat.
there was no holding him once he got started;
he had had wild horses killed one time and
they rode him to his grave.

holy night

joseph, i afraid of stars,
their brilliant seeing.
so many eyes. such light.
joseph, i cannot still these limbs,

i hands keep moving toward i breasts,
so many stars. so bright.
joseph, is wind burning from east
joseph, i shine, oh joseph,   oh
illuminated night.

[the light that came]

the light that came to lucille clifton
came in a shift of knowing
when even her fondest sureties
faded away. it was the summer
she understood that she had not understood
and was not mistress even
of her own off eye. then
the man escaped throwing away his tie and
the children grew legs and started walking and
she could see the peril of an
unexamined life.
she closed her eyes, afraid to look for her
authenticity
but the light insists on itself in the world;
a voice from the nondead past started talking,
she closed her ears and it spelled out in her hand
"you might as well answer the door, my child,
the truth is furiously knocking."

testament

in the beginning
was the Word.

the year of Our Lord,
amen. i
lucille clifton
hereby testify
that in that room
there was a light

and in that light
there was a voice
and in that voice
there was a sigh
and in that sigh
there was a world.
a world a sigh a voice a light and
i
alone
in a room.

[incandescence]

incandescence
formless form
and the soft
shuffle of sound

who are these strangers
peopling this light?

lucille
we are
the Light

[mother, i am]

mother, i am mad.
we should have guessed
a twelve-fingered flower
might break. my knowing
flutters to the ground.

mother i have managed to unlearn
my lessons. i am left
in otherness. mother

someone calling itself Light
has opened my inside.

i am flooded with brilliance
mother,

someone of it is answering to
your name.

perhaps

i am going blind.
my eyes exploding,
seeing more than is there
until they burst into nothing

or going deaf, these sounds
the feathered hum of silence

or going away from my self, the cool
fingers of lace on my skin
the fingers of madness

or perhaps
in the palace of time
our lives are a circular stair
and i am turning

explanations

anonymous water can slide under the ground.

the wind can shiver with desire.

this room can settle.

this body can settle.

but can such a sound
cool as a circle
surround and
pray
or promise
or prophesy?

friends come

explaining to me that my mind
is the obvious assassin

the terrorist of voices
who has waited
to tell me miraculous lies
all my life. no

i say
friends
the ones who talk to me
their words thin as wire
their chorus fine as crystal
their truth direct as stone,
they are present as air.

they are there.

to joan

joan
did you never hear
in the soft rushes of france
merely the whisper of french grass
rubbing against leathern
sounding now like a windsong
now like a man?
did you never wonder
oh fantastical joan,
did you never cry in the sun's face
unreal   unreal? did you never run
villageward
hands pushed out toward your apron?
and just as you knew that your mystery
was broken for all time
did they not fall then
soft as always
into your ear
calling themselves Michael

among beloved others?
and you
sister   sister
did you not then sigh
my voices   my voices   of course?

confession

father
i am not equal to the faith required.
i doubt.
i have a woman's certainties;
bodies pulled from me,
pushed into me.
bone flesh is what i know.

father
the angels say they have no wings.
i woke one morning
feeling how to see them.
i could discern their shadows
in the shadow. i am not
equal to the faith required.

father
i see your mother standing now
shoulderless and shoeless by your side.
i hear her whisper truths i cannot know.
father i doubt.

father
what are the actual certainties?
your mother speaks of love.
the angels say they have no wings.
i am not equal to the faith required.
i try to run from such surprising presence;
the angels stream before me
like a torch.

[in populated]

in populated air
our ancestors continue.
i have seen them.
i have heard
their shimmering voices
singing.

NORMAN DUBIE

NORMAN DUBIE *was born in Barre, Vermont, in 1945. His degrees are from Goddard College and the University of Iowa, where he taught for four years. Currently a member of the English Department at Arizona State University in Tempe, he has won the Bess Hokin Award from* Poetry, *and a Guggenheim Fellowship. In addition to several limited editions, he has published* Selected and New Poems *(1983), which includes work from four previous full-length collections,* In the Dead of Night *(1975),* The Illustrations *(1977),* The City of Olesha Fruit *(1979), and* The Everlastings *(1980).*

(Photo by Jeannine Dubie)

from Dark Spiralling Figures: An Interview

(Julie Fay and David Wojahn conducted an interview with Norman Dubie on Nov. 4 and 5, 1977, in Tempe, Arizona.)

WOJAHN: What do you feel the purpose of poetry is?

DUBIE: It's like the point in geometry. Eugenio Montale thought, strangely, that poetry is born to understanding when it is actually presented, but that it has not yet come to life unless it has sufficient power to continue to act on its own purpose. This purpose is beyond the poet's instructions, dissolving, perhaps then returning itself to the exact situation of life which had made it possible. And only in that instant is the figure of understanding complete, and the poem bonds with life as Shelley dreamed it would.

WOJAHN: You were raised in New England and were the son of a minister. How has this background affected your writing?

DUBIE: Well, both things count: the fact that my father was a minister and that I was raised in the north country in New England. I remember vividly that while we lived on this peninsula off Bath, Maine, we were in another culture and in another time. There were still kerosene lanterns in the houses of the fishermen. Many houses were without electricity, and their ways were dated too. Also, leaving that peninsula was hard. There I was, a twelve-year-old, realizing I had a longing for this place that shouldn't have existed at all. I would never again find the nineteenth century. Anyway, I was really being raised in the manner of the nineteenth century, where it was a popular convention to bother children with great literature. The exposure to Dickens, Conrad, Thomas Mann, Dostoevski, Turgenev, and Chekov must have affected me tremendously and must continue to, I believe. I love to tell stories in my poems. I write a narrative poem often, and I'm confident that I employ many of the strategies of a Chekov, a Turgenev, or Thomas Mann; those three were perhaps most important to me. To answer the other part of it—my father being a minister: my father was an insurance executive and he came home from work one day and stepped out into the orchard, and, feeling some sort of spark, suffered a conversion and decided to go into the ministry. He somehow never forgot his original lowly membership in the church. Consequently, his ministry was radical and provocative and tended toward the left. It was always exciting for us. My father was often in trouble with the lions, and the Christians. . . .

WOJAHN: Where do your poems come from? . . . Do you keep mental or written notes on a figure you'd like to treat in a poem?

DUBIE: What you're really asking about is my writing habits. All my poems come out of a daily writing habit. It doesn't even all get committed to paper. For as long as I've been writing, I've been training myself to make renderings which are sometimes very impressionistic. I know that they range through the day, as the light changes. I might come home with nothing in my head but two alternate descriptions of a tree in noon shade. I do write every day, and I've learned how to let go; I believe that's where the best poems come from, from the letting-go of the unconscious. If you aggravate images within yourself, something will materialize on paper. If you're willing to commit yourself to paper you'll discover what it is that the poem's discovered. Writing isn't painful for me; it's just a pleasure. . . .

WOJAHN: You mentioned syntax before, and I wonder if we might return to that. The music in your poems often seems to come from distorted syntax. Can you talk about that?

DUBIE: Such matters are entangled with your nerve fiber, and I'm not sure that I can talk about it. I know what it feels like, and I know when I've achieved a discordant passage in a poem. I simply accept it as a vehicle. It can be counterpointed. I know it often has to do with eluding unrhymed iambic pentameter, because there are integral phrases within my work that really define themselves and become measured. . . .

FAY: When did you write your first poem?

DUBIE: I was actually eleven when I wrote my first poem. My mother has my earliest poems tucked away, hidden away somewhere in a breakfront or bureau or an old sofa in the attic; I don't know. I've explored all of these places and I haven't been able to find them, so I can't destroy them. Actually I wouldn't any longer, but there was a time when it was very important for me to start again and to destroy everything that I'd done. I've been writing for twenty-one years, and for the first twelve years I repeatedly purged myself in that way, starting again. . . .

FAY: Your most recent work strikes me as being more personal and lyrical than before. Many of your new poems are autobiographical;

that is, Norman Dubie seems to emerge as a character. Do you feel that you're moving away from the need for a persona?

DUBIE: Yes, absolutely, and of course, because I do write a great deal and I do write obsessively, I'm able to disabuse myself of mannerisms and obsessive themes and obsessive strategies, just because I see them repeated so often that I become bored with them myself. So, consequently, I've been made weary of the repeated effect of the monologue. I've also felt that I'm at a point where I ought to be able to talk about characters near and dear to me and I ought to be able to talk about myself. I've created this third-person narrator, this interloper, who is a fictive personality who has nevertheless emerged in my poetry. . . . I think that I've done so many poems in voices, that they've all formed naturally, inevitably into a single voice, which is a detached voice that can now risk contact with my life, the terms of my life, the details of my life. . . .

FAY: You were a male nurse at one point in your life. How do you feel that that experience has affected your poetry?

DUBIE: The work in the hospitals had a large effect on my poetry. I was going to school at Goddard. As freshmen, we were told to go away for half the year to work and to "get our hands dirty." I haven't begun to tap my memories of the hospitals; they're so various; there is so much individual suffering from all of that. I don't know when I'll possibly begin to exhaust it all. But at least it has me rooted in a very real world that we like to look away from. I felt, going in there as a writer, that I was learning how to observe things that were difficult to observe. I also felt that I ought to be at ease, even though I was up to my ears in shit, piss, and blood. I wanted to overcome a lot of embarrassments that we feel for our bodies. And so, I came to that point on one incredibly muggy, hot afternoon in this Catholic hospital in Manchester, New Hampshire, where a bus driver was "going out"—he was going bad, dying. He had had a double colostomy, two resectionings of the intestine, and neither would take. He had the worst odor. You couldn't possibly imagine! He was on a charity ward, and we weren't able to keep other patients in there with him; he was, in effect, there alone. We were going to draw straws to see who would sit with him to change his gauze and vaseline bandages and do his vital signs every fifteen minutes. . . . I spent the afternoon and evening with him, listening to something that I haven't listened to since, which was a little concert out in the gazebo on the Common. There was a band playing familiar songs, and there was a very exuberant tuba player, who I watched much of the time. As I watched the tuba player and the tuba

with its very suggestive form, I watched all the great footage of intes-
tine that had been interrupted and was sort of glistening in this funny
half-light that I had in the ward. The bus driver and I had the most
vaporous conversation all throughout that concert. I touched his
death; I was taking his pulse at the moment when he died. At that
moment, out in the gazebo, they were concluding this dark, spiralling
figure from a Mahler song. And so, he went out of the body, which
had become such a cruel joke for him, in escort with that lovely, as-
cending musical figure, and art began to take on a new meaning for
me. I began from that evening to believe that our earthly existence, as
it is sensitive to duplicities of creation, is just a spiritual exercise that
perpares us for the leaving of the body. . . . Nothing was repulsive
anymore. Suddenly, without inhibitions, I saw, I think with great de-
spair, how it is that we all suffer more or less constantly, and I want to
be able to engage that suffering so as to transcend it.

The Hours

for Ingrid Erhardt (1951-71)

The meadows are empty. There are two villages:
One to the north and another to the south.
It's first light, and the two villages are striking
Their two bells. This is a green valley
That has an echo. Now, the bell to the south
Follows immediately the bell in the north.
So when the bell to the north is struck
Its echo is not heard by anyone for it is lost
In the sound from the south. A pilgrim
Has just climbed down into the valley.
Does he believe that he hears
One, two or four bells working in the morning?

This much is clear: when the bells stopped
The pilgrim thought, at first, that he had
Heard last that bell to the north, followed
By the bell to the south, followed by the echo
Of the bell, to the south. So he would tell us

That there are three bells being struck
In the morning. But
You know how after hearing bells
You seem to carry them around
For some time inside your skull? And, also,
The echo of the bell to the north that is lost
So often each morning, where does it go?

Perhaps, it goes where the pilgrim is going. And
Neither north, nor south. We will all be lost,
Even down to the very last memories that others have
Of us, and then these others who survived us, they
Too will be lost. There were many more bells
Than we thought, they will

Never stop for us, as waking to them we realize that
Throughout our lives, in the light and in the dark,

We were always counting our losses.

Sacrifice of a Virgin in the Mayan Ball Court

There are the many red birds holding a document
That is written in red,
Red lettering flocking on the page
And off from it at each corner; each corner is appointed
A single colorless bird, perhaps, drained
Like the virgin beneath it.
This, then, is the ceiling! At the center of the room

There is a priest at a stone table. On the table
There is the girl: a breast hangs smoking on its
Hinge of skin, there's an opening in her chest
And her heart has been carried off on a cold plate.
This little vacancy in the girl's chest is
Like a small pond turning red at sunset, is,
For this society of men dressed in bright feathers,
Their *only* antecedent for true feeling! There is

This red emergency of birds above a priest, and a
Painted confusion of stars at his feet.

Last night, outside Phoenix in the desert, among
The creosote and the flowering agave-plants, the body

Of yet another nude girl was discovered by children.
She had been stabbed repeatedly. The sheriff
Insists that he is looking in West Phoenix
For a middle-aged man, *a psychopath who will seem
Perfectly ordinary to his family and friends.*

Imagine them this past weekend outside Flagstaff
Beside a pond that is turning red at evening,
And, *there,* at the center of the pond standing
In a small boat is the man:

He is hated, he is *wanted*—and
Soon, perhaps, he'll be hunted
In the mountains north of the desert.
In the Mayan Ball Court he was the antecedent
Of all time and space! And isn't he, after all, sick

At heart and in his stomach, while shocked he again walks
Out of the desert staring at his red hands
That are like two red fluttering birds?

He is returning to our world: to
Its religions and its ball courts. Returning, and

To kill. *Again!*

Norway

for Elizabeth Paūs

The raw slopes of meat are stabbed with pikes
And the flesh of the whale is torn away
With the use of hands and feet. Here and there
A gull cries. This fish turned to oil, the oil turning
To a carbon band around the chimney of a crystal lamp,

And, at midnight, a man closes his book. He sighs,
Closes his eyes,

And, then, it is there in the purple haze of his mind
That the whale leaps
For a last time; dancing a little, just an element
Of white oval light in a lamp.
It has spread past the seated man,
Past the table at his right hand to a sleeping dog,
But it failed at touching the far corner
Of the room—its tiny vase of blue and black pansies stands

With the smudged faces of exhausted whalers,
Their red arms stirring the big iron pots while
Above them on the deck a cabin boy leans on a broom,
Stopped at his work, his mouth open: he just gazes
At a brain of a whale
That is steaming like a newborn calf outside
In the early spring rain that has turned to hail.

There Is a Dream Dreaming Us

We are seven virgins. Seven lamps.
Each with a different animal skin on our shoulders.
We had crowns made of black mulberry with the pyracantha,
Its white flowers in corymbs spotted with yellow fruit.
On my forehead, in charcoal, is the striking digit
Of an asp, and with all of this we were nearly nude.

The procession to the pyramid began at the pavilion
At the very edge of the thirteen acres that were sacred.
We walked ahead of everyone with our priest,
But we are the last to leave this world for the portico
And the first gallery which is dark and cold.

We stood on the terraced face of the pyramid witnessing
The long entrance of the king's family.
The queen carried a lamb made of papyrus: its eyes
Were rubies. The Queen's brother was dressed

In little rattles made of clay.
Even the King's nursery followed him with two slaves

To the chamber where we would all stay.
The sun no longer touched us on the plateau. It was lost

Making the sand dunes beyond the cataract rise and fall
Like water rushing toward us.
The glass doll was smashed above the portico,
And the doors began to close! We were inside the galleries
Of sun and flour and our seven lamps guided us
To the underground chamber. We could no longer hear
The drums leaving the inner acre.
I am the initial lamp and so I broke the last bottle

And from the bottle sand poured:
This last gate had two flanking chambers full with sand
And on it was the weight of marble columns,
Columns that joined the limestone slab that was
The last seal lowering now as the sand spills
Into two fern boxes on the floor.

The children had all been smothered and washed in oils,
All of the family is poisoned.
They sprawl around the sarcophagus which is open.
The priest has stabbed my six companions—it is
A noise like a farmer testing river soil.
I'm to drain the cup of wine that the King's mother
Handed me before dying. I was the *first lamp,* but
This is my story. I spilled the wine down my leg
And pretended to faint away. The priest thinking everyone
Had crossed from his world stopped his prayer. He walked
To the girl with the third lamp.
He kissed my dead sister on the lips. He ripped the silk
From her breasts. And then he fell on her.
Her arms were limp, I imagine even as they would be
If she were alive doing this with him.

The heat must have been leaving her body. He, finishing,
Turned to me: what I saw was the longest
Of the three members of an ankh, all red, and from it
Came a kind of clotted stream.

But his strength was leaving him visibly; he put his
Dagger in his neck and bled down his sleeve.
I don't understand. But now

I am alone as I had planned.
I'm a girl who was favored in the market by the King.
I've eaten the grapes that the slaves carried in for him:
If someone breaks into this tomb in a future time how
Will they explain the dead having spit grape seeds
Onto a carpet that was scented with jasmine?
The arrogance of the living never had a better monument
Than in me. I am going to sleep
In a bed that was hammered out of gold for a boy
Who was Pharaoh and King of Egypt. My father died free.
My mother died a slave, here, at this site after being
Whipped twice in a morning. In the name of Abraham

I have displaced a King. I picked him up
And put him in the corner, facing in and kneeling.
He would seem to be a punished child.
What he did? I will tell you; you will be told many times again:

He killed four thousand of my people
While they suffered the mystery of this mountain appearing
Where there was nothing but moving sands and wind!

The Everlastings

In the village it must be a clear night with the light of a red
Star twisting down the water
Filling the distant mouth of our narrow fjord . . .

Snow blankets the sleeping mustard, thistle and gorse!

Two longships have been brought up on forms:
Their bellies are checkered with tar and goatskins.
The wind is up in the bones. The dogs
Are peaceful. I have died
On a beach in France. A monk
And I did battle. I wish I could burn the little icon
Of the nut-fairy; its red berries in the triangular seed-box
And the roof of furze and maple. It was a gift
From the King, my father. Tonight here in the water I feel
Closer to my mother . . .

In the frescoes
Of the lives of the saints, there's hibiscus, rhubarb
And roses sketched on wet plaster, each flower
Outlined by a fine bone pencil, and when the lime

Touches the air the watercolors
Become thin, speckled—

A daubing of light
in the cobwebs suspended between a stag's antlers.
Saint Odoacer, our fourth pope, brought to the lepers
The fanaticism of the rose
With its old, unfolding characteristics of fire.

He embalmed the Viking's daughter,
Scooping out her breads and heart: in their place
He laid sticks of balsam with salt.
He put spices inside her skull.
He sat her in a jar with the knees snapped, brought back
Under her jaws.

The jar filled with wild, languorous honey!

My stomach is opened. My sword fell at the Viking's collar,
Leaving the body above the silver braided waist—
Arm and shoulder dropping into the surf.

The moon sits on my shield, lighting the circle
Of oxskulls
Which the goldsmith staggered, every third one, with
Delicately hammered suns . . .

My daughter's womb was put in an ark of osier and sedge;
Taken out over the waters in a votive ship . . .
On my shield, at the center of the oxskulls, there is
A silver wreath, all of this worked into its carapace
That is the brine-soaked shell of a sea-tortoise. I cracked the Pope's
Skull with it. I have scattered his monks!
I no longer dream of long oars breaking up
In the drifting lakes of kelp. The loadstone,
In its sock of pig intestine, spins to the south? Not Odin
Calling? The fingers of the fog are white like every ninth wave
Across our bow.

My daughter was born in a pine forest in mid-summer.

To die at dawn is to wash down with hot ale the raw red livers
Of sea-turtles. *Is to smile at my father!* What I feel
Is not fear, it's more the sudden circumspection
Of deer just before they follow the white roebuck who leaps
Over horizons.

    HAIL NORTHMAN! HOW IS IT? No, he'll think that
    I'm taunting him. He could be free in the tides? There was
        blood
    All over him and sea foam like the saliva of wild dogs.
    His beard stood in the sun like laden papers
    Of honeycomb. In the lives of the saints there are red stars,
    And one is painted over another, crossing out the eyes
    Of the unicorn and lion. The Norsemen thought the frescoes
    Were secret maps to the Underworld, and they'll voyage
        anywhere:

They have pulled oars while caught in maelstroms. They filled
Sails while being dragged down into the blood-sworls
Of their thumbs. I love their pandemonium. Listen—

It is the thunder at dawn!

TESS GALLAGHER

TESS GALLAGHER *was raised where she was born in 1943, between the Strait of Juan de Fuca and the Olympic Mountains in northwestern Washington. Her parents worked in logging (silver in "Black Money" is turned black by sulphur, a pulp-mill by-product); later, her father became a longshoreman and bought a farm to teach his five children things "not learned in books." Tess, the oldest, began working as a journalist at sixteen, and later attended the University of Washington, where she was a member of Theodore Roethke's last class, and the University of Iowa. She has taught at St. Lawrence University, Kirkland College, and Syracuse University. Her books of poems are* Instructions to the Double *(1976),* Under Stars *(1978), and* Willingly *(1984).*

(Photo by Patricia Ellis)

Borrowed Strength

I woke up this morning with snow coming down outside and am now at my desk in the attic on Maryland Avenue in Syracuse, New York. There's old snow on the ground, and the wind's billowing the plastic sheeting that's stapled to my neighbor's windows. I've been told kindly, but firmly by the editor of this anthology that he's got to have this essay soon. There will be consequences. I imagine the worst—my poems left out—although neither the editor nor I have intended it to come to this. In the past I've worked well against deadlines, have written for the movies and for newspapers. But today I am empty on the subject of my poems. I'm like an archeologist studying an ancient map designating the burial place of the muses in the mouth of an active volcano. I don't want to go in.

Downstairs I hear a *Life* journalist interviewing Raymond Carver about his life and the fiction he writes. The journalist has been here two days, and he is so nice, so winning, I've said several revealing things I now wish I hadn't said. I know—I don't know, but I feel— he's going to use these things against me, against us. The little red light on his tape recorder was on, I noticed, even after he'd said we were, of course, talking "off the record." But somehow the need to be genuine, even at the risk of being taken advantage of, compels me to reveal.

Now I'm talking about poems and what I do there—trust and reveal. Some of the poems printed here are about ten years old. But although I've changed a good deal, I see I am still on the same journey, trying to make a music to accompany my life, and sometimes, if I'm lucky, to reach others.

To write is to brave the emptiness, to have patience toward the rushing in of fullness also, when it comes like Lorca's *duende* demanding your stamina and lifting you up until you do what you couldn't do. On the wall above my typewriter I've tacked some self-instructions, some clues as to why I'm writing poems and not writing ads or mending silos or operating heavy machinery with some road crew in North Dakota:

> The meaning of my existence is that life has
> addressed a question to me. Or, conversely, I
> myself am a question which is addressed to the
> world, and I must communicate my answer, for
> otherwise I am dependent upon the world's answer.

Jung said this and I copied it out in my handwriting and tacked it up. The ink has faded and the paper has curled and yellowed—it has been there that long. Emily Dickinson knew all about how poems keep one from being excluded from the world in the large spiritual sense. She wrote of her own poems: "This is my letter to the World / That never wrote to Me—" And the world didn't write to her then, though it does now every time a mind crosses one of her poems. Sometimes, when things are just right, the world doesn't write to poets, but *with* them.

When I remember Emily Dickinson's 1,775 poems I want to be used as fully as she was. Her gift gives me heart, though it humbles me too. At these times I feel I know what another of my messages on the wall means:

> It is immensely important that great poems get
> written. But it makes not an iota of difference
> who writes them.

Ezra Pound said that. I know I'm writing toward an ultimate disappearance. I am trying to go there willingly, that is, in such a way that the choosings and efforts toward speech use me well, use me up, yet replenish so that something of value lingers a while in the poems. The title of my third book is *Willingly* or *will*-ingly. It's my will, my legacy.

I don't do this alone. I've borrowed strength and love from so many, living and dead, near and far. There is at the back of my mind a view of the Straits of Juan de Fuca where I was born, that magical lane of the Pacific between Washington State and Victoria, British Colombia. It is a source of inexplicable energy to rest my mind there. Similarly I bring before me the presences of poets I admire, both living and dead: Michael Burkard, Madeline DeFrees, Stanley Kunitz—chief among those living. The ledger from the dead is constantly shifting, but I think of those steadily with me now: Louise Bogan, Theodore Roethke, Anna Akhmatova, W. B. Yeats, Federico García Lorca, Emily Dickinson and Li Po. These are the host I travel with in mind and spirit.

On the wall I've tacked some photos. I glance at them from time to time in the spaces between my attention to the work at hand. In one photo my neice, Leslie, is standing in her green coat and red shoes near a huge stack of pumpkins. I love the signs of harvest when I look at this child and these pumpkins. At this moment I'm reminded of the Cinderella story and see those pumpkins as if they could become golden coaches or mice, signs of what the imagination makes possible; signs of humility and grandeur, the woman-child who escapes a life of cinders and toil, but not with the prince of anything but the imagination.

In another photo taken on a porch in the sun, my mother has just finished brushing her hair and is about to braid it again. There are little ripples from the last time it was braided. The white hair rays out over her pink sweater and she clasps her hands as if to compose herself toward her eventual absence. The Cherokee blood of my great-grandmother shows in her face. She is a courage point on my map.

There are two poets on the wall—Linda Gregg and Laura Jensen. Laura is wearing a lavender sweatshirt that says "Longhi's Mall" on it. Her blonde hair hangs down behind her and reaches over the back of her chair. We've been friends for the past fourteen years. We share poems, joke, write letters and meet up when I can get back to the Northwest where she lives and where I return as often as possible.

Linda Gregg's reddish blonde hair is flung over her face. She's in Greece sitting on a flat stone and wearing a striped skirt and what looks like a white muslin top. Next to this photo of Linda is another she sent of her kitchen in Greece. There's a shelf in the foreground with stones, or maybe eggs on it. To the right of the shelf is a pair of child's scissors hanging by a finger loop. Under that there's a bottle of wine, or maybe it's vinegar. I love both of these photos because they tantalize. What is Linda thinking about there in the warm sun of Greece under all that hair? Is that an egg or a stone on the shelf? Wine or vinegar? Linda and I don't see each other very often, and we don't write much, but our spirits seem available to each other, an access that helps me locate high motives in this life of writing poems.

Someone looking at this little collection might call it: "Three Women With Beautiful Hair and Child With Pumpkins." Why all this attention to hair? Maybe because it signifies the sensual or something to do with the word *freedom,* the power of women's minds and hearts made visible, a calm outflowing of grandeur and humility. When I say "humility," of course I don't mean bowing and scraping. I mean the way a woman's energy persists in strength and rises to claim honor against adversity, even if she has to wait centuries, as with the women I met in China.

On my desk there's a snapshot of a man at a race track near El Paso, Texas. He's holding up a winning ticket and grinning. That's Ray Carver. We took his winnings and went over into Juarez, Mexico, that night with friends and ate shish kebabs and baklava in a Greek restaurant.

"The soul selects her own society." For some reason that's what I think when I look at the photo of Ray. He's downstairs now, with the

man from *Life* who wants to get his secrets. I could tell that pleasant
journalist mine in a hurry: I don't do this alone.

Black Money

His lungs heaving all day in a sulphur mist,
then dusk, the lunch pail torn from him
before he reaches the house, his children
a cloud of swallows about him.
At the stove in the tumbled rooms, the wife,
her back the wall he fights most, and she
with no weapon but silence
and to keep him from the bed.

In their sleep the mill hums and turns
at the edge of water. Blue smoke
swells the night and they drift
from the graves they have made for each other,
float out from the open-mouthed sleep
of their children, past banks and businesses,
the used car lots, liquor store, the swings in the park.

The mill burns on, now a burst of cinders,
now whistles screaming down the bay, saws jagged
in half light. Then like a whip
the sun across the bed, windows high with mountains
and the sleepers fallen to pillows
as gulls fall, tilting
against their shadows on the log booms.
Again the trucks shudder the wood framed houses
passing to the mill. My father
snorts, splashes in the bathroom,
throws open our doors to cowboy music
on the radio, hearts are cheating,
somebody is alone, there's blood in Tulsa.
Out the back yard the night-shift men rattle
the gravel in the alley going home.
My father fits goggles to his head.

From his pocket he takes anything metal,
the pearl-handled jackknife, a ring of keys,
and for us, black money shoveled
from the sulphur pyramids heaped in the distance
like yellow gold. Coffee bottle tucked in his armpit
he swaggers past the chicken coop,
a pack of cards at his breast.
In a fan of light beyond him
the Kino Maru pulls out for Seattle,
some black star climbing
the deep globe of his eye.

Complicity

The limbs are caught in each other
outside my window where the saw-men
have entered the tree. Dead limbs
pile up on the shadows.
Now a saw goes up on a rope
and the ground man steps back
for what falls. I tell him my father
rigged spar trees in the west.
I need a reason to watch
this tree come down.

He uses his weight on the rope
like a saw, then backs off.
The chainsaw snarls and jaws.
Over him, the tree and the wind: sawdust
over my house.

If a tree goes down among others
it makes its whole length felt
as something lost and final, not
this slow dispossession
of parts. I have heard a whole tree cry out
in the clearings my father made.
But this tree snaps and shudders
and calms itself back
into silence.

From the street, the houses
seem to have stepped away.

In my window the likeness
of the tree goes on, the light
opening and gathering
over my desk, over what I cannot heal.

The Ritual of Memories

When your widow had left the graveside
and you were most alone
I went to you in that future
you can't remember yet. I brought
a basin of clear water where no tear
had fallen, water gathered like grapes
a drop at a time
from the leaves of the willow. I brought
oils, I brought a clean white gown.

'Come out,' I said, and you came up
like a man pulling himself out of a river,
a river with so many names
there was no word left for it but 'earth.'

'Now,' I said, 'I'm ready. These eyes
that have not left your face
since the day we met, wash these eyes.
Remember, it was a country road
above the sea and I was passing
from the house of a friend. Look
into these eyes where we met.'

I saw your mind go back through the years
searching for that day and finding it,
you washed my eyes
with the pure water
so that I vanished from that road

and you passed a lifetime
and I was not there.

So you washed every part of me
where any look or touch
had passed between us. 'Remember,'
I said, when you came to the feet,
'it was the night before you would ask
the girl of your village to marry. I
was the strange one. I was the one
with the gypsy look.
Remember how you stroked these feet.'

When the lips and the hands
had been treated likewise and the pit
of the throat where one thoughtless kiss
had fallen, you rubbed in the sweet oil
and I glistened like a new-made thing, not
merely human, but of the world gone past
being human.

'The hair,' I said. 'You've forgotten
the hair. Don't you know it remembers.
Don't you know it keeps everything. Listen,
there is your voice and in it the liar's charm
that caught me.'

You listened. You heard your voice
and a look of such sadness
passed over your dead face that I wanted
to touch you. Who could have known
I would be so held? Not you
in your boyish cunning; not me
in my traveler's clothes.

It's finished.
Put the gown on my shoulders.
It's no life in the shadow of another's joys.
Let me go freely now.
One life I have lived for you. This one
is mine.

Under Stars

The sleep of this night deepens
because I have walked coatless from the house
carrying the white envelope.
All night it will say one name
in its little tin house by the roadside.

I have raised the metal flag
so its shadow under the roadlamp
leaves an imprint on the rain-heavy bushes.
Now I will walk back
thinking of the few lights still on
in the town a mile away.

In the yellowed light of a kitchen
the millworker has finished his coffee,
his wife has laid out the white slices of bread
on the counter. Now while the bed they have left
is still warm, I will think of you, you
who are so far away
you have caused me to look up at the stars.

Tonight they have not moved
from childhood, those games played after dark.
Again I walk into the wet grass
toward the starry voices. Again, I
am the found one, intimate, returned
by all I touch on the way.

The Meeting

for Ken Schar

My name is not my own
and you are lost in the sameness
of yours: marriage, divorce,
marriage, the name changed
like a billboard at the side of my life.

That day I saw you last
you were wearing a white suit
in the mid-winter haze.
It was too big for you.
Your shoulders didn't belong.
I heard you: 'If you feel
the rightness of a thing, do it.'

Twelve years we've come
and not a word between us.
Last night you got off a bus
in my dream. Your body
seemed too small for itself. It was
hurt by something outside my sleep.
You took off your coat.
I could see the bones of your arms.
We didn't mention it.
You asked for something ordinary
and wrong, vitamins, I think.

You had your camera on your chest
like a complicated doorknob.
You didn't open.
My hands came back
to me. I was awake in that last café
where I did not say *brother*, where
I stood apart from your sorrow
in my great young indifference.

Tired lives had run you out.
You were going away. 'Let them
have their bastard courage!'
Your hands came back
to you. You touched me, that hand
out of the grave. Early
and late, this hour has closed
around us.

Tableau Vivant

They think it's easy to be dead, those
who walk the pathway here in stylish shoes,
portable radios strapped to their arms,

selling the world's perishables, even
love songs. They think you just lie down
into dreams you will never tell anyone.
They don't know we still have plans, a yen
for romance, and miss things like hats
and casseroles.

As for dreams, we take up where the living
leave off. We like especially those
in which the dreamer is about to
fall over a cliff or from a bridge that
is falling too. We're only too glad
to look down on the river gorge enlarging
under a body's sudden weight, to have the ground
rushing up instead of this slow
caving in. We thrive on living out
the last precious memories of someone escaped
back into morning light.

Occasionally there's a message saying they want
one of us back, someone out there
feeling guilty about a word or deed
that seems worse because we took it as
a living harm, then died
with it, quietly. But we know a lot about
forgiveness and we always make these trips with
a certain missionary zeal. We get back
into our old sad clothes. We stand again
at the parting, full of wronged tenderness and
needing a shave or a hairdo. We tell them
things are O.K., not to waste their lives
in remorse, we never held it
against them, so much happens that no one means.

But sometimes one of us gets stubborn, thinks
of evening the score. We leave them calling
after us, *Sorry, Sorry, Sorry,* and we don't
look back.

LOUISE GLÜCK

LOUISE GLÜCK *was born in New York City in 1943 and raised on Long Island. She attended Sarah Lawrence College and Columbia University. Her awards for poetry include grants from the Rockefeller Foundation, the National Endowment for the Arts, and the Guggenheim Foundation. She lives with her husband and son in Vermont, where she teaches at Goddard College.* Her poems are collected in Firstborn *(1969),* The House on Marshland *(1975), and* Descending Figure *(1980).*

(Photo by James Baker Hall)

Death and Absence

What strikes me is how far away all this work seems. Not only the poems that are literally remote, that go back twenty years. Once a poem is resolved, I lose the sense of having written it. I can remember circumstances, but not sensations, not what it felt like to be writing. This amnesia is most immediate and most complete when poems are written quickly, but in all cases it occurs. Between poems, I am not a poet, only someone with a yearning to achieve—what? That concentration again.

So I have no reliable consciousness of myself as a creator, and this makes for great anxiety. When I am working, I am completely absorbed in the work. When I am not working, I tend to be absorbed in that fact: preoccupied, depressed, mired in self. One of the efforts of my life is to cope with silence; my best discovery has been teaching. It is useful to have commitments in the world independent of the need to write. And, luckily, the exhilaration of analysis extends to include the work of others.

The oldest poem here is "The Racer's Widow," lines of which were written when I was about fifteen. The best lines, in fact, though at that time the subject was different. Occasion might be a better word, for reasons which will become clear. In its first embodiment, the poem described the last agonies of a deer. I didn't know very much about deer, but then I didn't know very much about racing, either. The problem with the poem was that its declared subject was a fraud: my interest did not begin with a deer but with a metaphor. From the first, I wanted to talk about death; also from the first I had an instinctive identification with the abandoned, the widowed, with all figures left behind. I'll come back to this; the point at the moment is that, in this early poem, the widow was a doe. So the poem, as a whole, was mystical to the point of absurdity. Yet something in the language seemed true and deep: the legs "like snow," and so on. My problem, for years, was that I didn't know what these lines might describe. This is, for me, often the case: miraculously, some word or phrase will detach itself from the language, taking on a kind of radiance, but the task of writing is a search for context. I don't remember how, four or five years later, I hit on the persona here. But I had begun to read modern poems, that much is clear.

"Cottonmouth Country" dates from this time, too—from about 1963. Because it was written quickly, I have no memory relating to its composition. I did go to Hatteras; there was an actual snake. But those events seemed utterly without importance; at the time, they didn't even turn into anecdote. They emerged, months afterward, not as potential but as completed metamorphosis. This is the process of dreams: small details and forgotten incidents surface there, releasing some latent significance.

Poems of this kind are, for me, fairly rare. The other poems must, through effort, be made to sound so whole. Much such effort is represented here, long intervals of frustration. The longer poems did not, always, take longer to write, but the two here raise a particular issue. Because in each case the subject matter is felt to be both personal and charged, these poems have sometimes been praised for their bravery, which is not my word, as though their writing put an end to years of evasion. I have a great appetite for praise, and would like to be considered brave, but the term as used in this case results from misperception. The poems were not written sooner because, in both instances, resonance was missing. The original experiences had to be not simply assimilated but converted. Bravery was never at issue: I tried, regularly, to make poems out of these situations since I recognized their possibilities. These poems, these many attempts, were frank but without mystery. The problem was tone: toward my sister, toward the syndrome of anorexia which for years shaped my life, I kept taking appropriate attitudes, when what was wanted had to be, in some way, unique. In any case, obsession is not courage.

I have always been, in one way or another, obsessed with sisters, the dead and the living both. The dead sister died before I was born. Her death was not my experience, but her absence was. Her death let me be born. I saw myself as her substitute, which produced in me a profound obligation toward my mother, and a frantic desire to remedy her every distress. I took it all personally: every shadow that crossed her face proved my insufficiency. Not proved, maybe, but suggested, as the birth of my younger sister suggested yet more concretely. I wanted to be child enough. At the same time, I took on the guilty responsibility of the survivor. Everything was wrong—it seemed wrong to forget the dead child, impossible to attend her. I knew these things, as articulate insight, twenty-five years ago. They did not become the material of poetry until, at thirty, I had a child myself. The wild, protective, terrified love I felt for my son—that maternal love which, in being obsessed with protection, is obsessed with harm—transformed itself, over three years, into an analogous act of mourning. "Descending Figure" is saturated with a mother's grief and fearfulness and a haunted child's compulsive compensation. It means, also, to *study* maternal love, which continued to seem to me appalling, though I felt it. Originally, the second section, which describes a hypothetical painting, began: "That embrace, I ask you / does it guard or restrict?" In the end, those lines were cut: they summarized what the poem had to suggest. Of the three, this section was written last, and with the greatest difficulty. I had pretty much given up hope of drawing together the two existing poems about my sister, and was working on, trying to infuse some energy into, an ironic little poem about sources of illumination: the painting was made up to accommodate what I wanted to say. It was a fruitless exercise, until I thought of the poem in connection with "The Wanderer" and "For My Sister." Once this idea presented itself, the inert, shallow lyric with its chest and winter stars, became an excitement, borrowing urgency from the poems it would link.

As the editor of this volume knows, it has taken me a long time to write these paragraphs. I don't trust my prose, except in letters. My stake in poetry is immeasurable, but, oddly, this fact, like some ideal of service, arrests egotism. I have no such vision in prose. And whereas a letter gives me someone to address, a public occasion of this sort makes focus impossible. But "vision" and "focus" miss the point, though they make plain what is missing: I thought once that poems were like words inscribed in rock or caught in amber. I thought in these terms so long, so fervently, with such investment in images of preservation and fixity, that the inaccuracies of the metaphor as description of my own experience did not occur to me until very recently. What is left out of these images is the idea of contact, and contact, of the most intimate sort, is what poetry can accomplish. Poems do not endure as objects but as presences. When you read anything worth remembering, you liberate a human voice; you release into the world again a companion spirit. Perpetual resurrection—

I read poems to hear that voice. And I write to speak to those I have heard.

The Racer's Widow

The elements have merged into solicitude.
Spasms of violets rise above the mud
And weed and soon the birds and ancients
Will be starting to arrive, bereaving points
South. But never mind. It is not painful to discuss
His death. I have been primed for this,

For separation, for so long. But still his face assaults
Me, I can hear that car careen again, the crowd coagulate on asphalt
In my sleep. And watching him, I feel my legs like snow
That let him finally let him go
As he lies draining there. And see
How even he did not get to keep that lovely body.

Cottonmouth Country

Fish bones walked the waves off Hatteras.
And there were other signs
That Death wooed us, by water, wooed us
By land: among the pines
An uncurled cottonmouth that rolled on moss
Reared in the polluted air.
Birth, not death, is the hard loss.
I know. I also left a skin there.

For My Mother

It was better when we were
together in one body.
Thirty years. Screened
through the green glass
of your eye, moonlight
filtered into my bones
as we lay
in the big bed, in the dark,
waiting for my father.
Thirty years. He closed
your eyelids with
two kisses. And then spring
came and withdrew from me
the absolute
knowledge of the unborn,
leaving the brick stoop
where you stand, shading
your eyes, but it is
night, the moon

is stationed in the beech tree,
round and white among
the small tin markers of the stars:
Thirty years. A marsh
grows up around the house.
Schools of spores circulate
behind the shades, drift through
gauze flutterings of vegetation.

For Jane Myers

Sap rises from the sodden ditch
and glues two green ears to the dead
birch twig. Perilous beauty—
and already Jane is digging out
her colored tennis shoes,
one mauve, one yellow, like large crocuses.

And by the laundromat
the Bartletts in their tidy yard—

as though it were not
wearying, wearying

to hear in the bushes
the mild harping of the breeze,
the daffodils flocking and honking—

Look how the bluet falls apart, mud
pockets the seed.
Months, years, then the dull blade of the wind.
It is spring! We are going to die!

And now April raises up her plaque of flowers
and the heart
expands to admit its adversary.

Jeanne d'Arc

It was in the fields. The trees grew still,
a light passed through the leaves speaking
of Christ's great grace: I heard.
My body hardened into armor.

                      Since the guards
gave me over to darkness I have prayed to God
and now the voices answer I must be
transformed to fire, for God's purpose,
and have bid me kneel
to bless my King, and thank
the enemy to whom I owe my life.

Descending Figure

1   *The Wanderer*

At twilight I went into the street.
The sun hung low in the iron sky,
ringed with cold plumage.
If I could write to you
about this emptiness—
Along the curb, groups of children
were playing in the dry leaves.
Long ago, at this hour, my mother stood
at the lawn's edge, holding my little sister.
Everyone was gone; I was playing
in the dark street with my other sister,
whom death had made so lonely.
Night after night we watched the screened porch
filling with a gold, magnetic light.
Why was she never called?
Often I would let my own name glide past me
though I craved its protection.

2   *The Sick Child*

—Rijksmuseum

A small child
is ill, has wakened.
It is winter, past midnight
in Antwerp. Above a wooden chest,
the stars shine.
And the child
relaxes in her mother's arms.
The mother does not sleep;
she stares
fixedly into the bright museum.
By spring the child will die.
Then it is wrong, wrong
to hold her—
Let her be alone,
without memory, as the others wake
terrified, scraping the dark
paint from their faces.

3   *For My Sister*

Far away my sister is moving in her crib.
The dead ones are like that,
always the last to quiet.

Because, however long they lie in the earth,
they will not learn to speak
but remain uncertainly pressing against the wooden bars,
so small the leaves hold them down.

Now, if she had a voice,
the cries of hunger would be beginning.
I should go to her;
perhaps if I sang very softly,
her skin so white,
her head covered with black feathers. . . .

The Mirror

Watching you in the mirror I wonder
what it is like to be so beautiful

and why you do not love
but cut yourself, shaving
like a blind man. I think you let me stare
so you can turn against yourself
with greater violence,
needing to show me how you scrape the flesh away
scornfully and without hesitation
until I see you correctly,
as a man bleeding, not
the reflection I desire.

Dedication to Hunger

1   *From the Suburbs*

They cross the yard
and at the back door
the mother sees with pleasure
how alike they are, father and daughter—
I know something of that time.
The little girl purposefully
swinging her arms, laughing
her stark laugh:

It should be kept secret, that sound.
It means she's realized
that he never touches her.
She is a child; he could touch her
if he wanted to.

2   *Grandmother*

"Often I would stand at the window—
your grandfather
was a young man then—
waiting, in the early evening."

That is what marriage is.
I watch the tiny figure
changing to a man
as he moves toward her,
the last light rings in his hair.

I do not question
their happiness. And he rushes in
with his young man's hunger,
so proud to have taught her that:
his kiss would have been
clearly tender—

Of course, of course. Except
it might as well have been
his hand over her mouth.

3   *Eros*

To be male, always
to go to women
and be taken back
into the pierced flesh:

        I suppose
memory is stirred.
And the girl child
who wills herself
into her father's arms
likewise loved him
second. Nor is she told
what need to express.
There is a look one sees,
the mouth somehow desperate—

Because the bond
cannot be proven.

4   *The Deviation*

It begins quietly
in certain female children:
the fear of death, taking as its form
dedication to hunger,
because a woman's body
is a grave; it will accept
anything. I remember
lying in bed at night
touching the soft, digressive breasts,
touching, at fifteen,

the interfering flesh
that I would sacrifice
until the limbs were free
of blossom and subterfuge: I felt
what I feel now, aligning these words—
it is the same need to perfect,
of which death is the mere byproduct.

5   *Sacred Objects*

Today in the field I saw
the hard, active buds of the dogwood
and wanted, as we say, to capture them,
to make them eternal. That is the premise
of renunciation: the child,
having no self to speak of,
comes to life in denial—

I stood apart in that achievement,
in that power to expose
the underlying body, like a god
for whose deed
there is no parallel in the natural world.

ALBERT GOLDBARTH

ALBERT GOLDBARTH *was born in 1948 in Chicago. A graduate of the University of Illinois and the Iowa Writers Workshop, he has published more than a dozen chapbooks and books of poetry, including* Opticks *(1973),* Jan. 31 *(1974),* Comings Back *(1976),* Different Fleshes *(1979), and* Original Light: New & Selected Poems 1973-1983 *(1983). The recipient of a Guggenheim Fellowship in Poetry (1983) and several other poetry awards, he currently lives in Austin, where he teaches at the University of Texas.*
(Photo by Betty Gottlieb)

Some Things I Believe, 8/16/83

For a long while white groups—rock groups—provided acceptable versions of black blues songs that were then marketable to a mainstream audience. These were "cover versions." Black groups did it too, tailoring their street material to more widely commercial ends. It still happens that blues or Christian or hillbilly originals surface in versions that are "covered" for acceptance. Now when Moses went to the mountains to hear the Word, God needed to speak to him through a medium—the bush. And even from this, Moses needed to turn his face, or be blinded. The bush was a cover version of glory. There *is* a radiance so great, its being glimpsed will scorch our seeing forever. There is a pain so intense, direct contact will cripple, irremediably. There is a joy so numinous, to know it is to lose touch with this world. There is a thought so new, so strange, it will make of the mind another thing completely. For these, the poem is a cover version. It lets that pain or that thought or that glory into our lives— acceptably, so that we can lift it and know it and set it down and return when we care to. And the poet is its singer, who knew the original before it had words.

*

I believe that's true, at least about a real poem, that shapes or saves or lights our lives as we return to it, year to year. (We all know there are other, lesser kinds of poems—the one-time reads.) But in some ways that's still a useless definition. So is Housman's famous prickle while he's shaving, or Frost's much-quoted lover's quarrel with the world. Can't these refer to a film? A symphony? A stock-car race for that matter, or a sunset? In the Austin, Texas phone book, chance of many kinds places Dennis Overy and Mary Ovum on the same page. This is wonderful in its own way, but it isn't a poem, a Bergman film is not a poem, nor is a black seal arrowing perfectly into the waters, no matter the synergy of its parts in graceful attunement. But Richard Wilbur writes poetry, and so does Kenneth Koch. Elizabeth Bishop. Diane Wakoski. Why is it that these people are poets, whose work sometimes seems to have so little in common, who may seem to share more with the script writer or the composer or the stock-car racer than with the poet across the colloquium table? How is it, that I could use words about words to describe the words of a poem, which is what a poem is—words—yet we would all prefer as its definition that seal snapping fat-swaddled sinuous length through the waves?

*

These are the questions this kind of essay-writing provokes. They have their attraction, but I try to avoid them. These paragraphs are testament to, more than anything else, my failure today in avoiding the extraneous activities poetry generates. Other poets do well at those activities, and often I'm grateful. That this anthology exists, that Bly edited *The Fifties*, that Merwin translates . . . But I've never wanted to start a magazine, or do renderings from the Portuguese, or attend a Breadloaf convening, or grant an interview, or churn out reviews, or a column for *The American Poetry Review*, or keep a daybook, or try a novel, or give my days to a reading circuit, or compile a dictionary of poetic terms, or judge a competition, or direct a summer workshop, or sit on grants committees. And I haven't, for the most part. Others do, and theirs is perhaps a greater generosity, or a greater need to have their private calling empower their social/political lives, or a greater desire to generate *resumé*-stuff—whatever. I'm not a "man of letters." I try to work every day on my poetry. That's that. Every day I hope to send another seal out there.

*

Grant me this: we're *in* a seal, taking a tour of its body. If I'm going to lapse into commentary today, grant me that. Overhead is an arch, the compact seal hips, and it contours its roundings of muscle like Stonehenge shaping the vast surrounding skies. The nerves are great cables, and branch, and finally thin to hundreds of miles of sparking hairs. Over here two tendons grapple each other, lovers, wrestlers, fat antagonists oiled up, and so they lift a flipper. Shaggy swags hang down the throat. The tiny gyroscopes of balance float in their absolute fluids. Blood pumps through its brambles. A break in a bone has its story—this is what archeology's all about. We could be lost for generations in bountiful bodyscape like this, and still not see the whole of its detail, every bone a baton for the dance, and every amino acid a strict configuration of partners. . . . Step out, and back a few yards, and it all becomes a single undulant streak in the water—whizz, zip, ffft.

*

That doesn't describe all of my poems. If it did, they might not be poems so much as the workings out of a formula. (Pope and Blake are both on my shelf, Williams wrote both *Paterson* and "This is Just to Say.") But it does describe some of my poems, I think, including the several Bill Heyen's picked here. They ask to be small worlds of details in an interesting clutter—tactile objects, eldritch facts, textured language, jazzy and unforeseen actions large and small—that are finally functional subcomponents of what was, all along and overall, a directed shapeliness. I stand back and I'm pleased enough, today at least. The barking I hear is a seal of approval.

*

Flipper, tail, arc and dive—that's to talk of poetry as if it were all form. But what content, what truth, do the whiskers pick up, quivering at the horizon-edge? Grant me the turning away from marinelife anatomy a moment. Paul Dirac, who in 1933 shared a Nobel Prize for, among other things, the predication of antimatter, has said, "It is more important to have beauty in one's equations than to have them fit experiment. It seems that if one is working from the point of view of getting beauty in one's equations . . . one is on a sure line of progress." And David Attenborough writes of showing some Dogon tribal elders "photographs of two different figures of horsemen." He asks them which is "the more beautiful, *la plus belle?*" They seem baffled. Much back-and-forth ensues: explanations, refinements, discussion among the elders. "Eventually a judgment was given. The second was better because it was more correct, because it spoke more accurately and eloquently of the ancient truths." The sciences often come to say, in their own language, something poetry has been telling us even longer, in *its*. The physicist and anthropologist here are remarking that same attachment Keats took from the urn, that beauty *is* truth, truth *is* beauty, the whiskers *are* the whisper of the world. That is all we need to know.

*

On the fringe of the ocean they're coming in—wounded, exultant, sleek and salted, the low sun broken to tiny points of fire over their bodies. It isn't that I'm a terrific student of seals, or think of them as my totem-creature—nothing like that. But recently I've seen some in the Houston zoo. They merely seemed a likeable, handy metaphor for things I cared to say here, and even those things are already changing, hesitant about themselves, feeling ungainly, superfluous, dumb, in flux. I'd rather be writing poems. I should be. I will be, just a few minutes from now. This last thing: in the Houston zoo, they swim their concrete ring of water, not wholly wild any longer, but intricate and simple none the less, in that marvelous way all living things are, and dynamically supple, in that way a seal is even once-removed from the fierce, pure origin-place. They're the version of that place we can accept without being blinded.

Distances

and closeness, and the line between. Three inches
of earth might pack time from the trilobite
to the first clean Jericho kilnwork . . .
Here's a man, in a tower. It's dark and
once a day they give him bread and clotted milk.
He *thinks* it's once a day—the dark is
unrelieved by notions like "night" or "morning."
He thinks it's been ten years. He scratches
stickmen on the stones, and tells them stories
of a world called Out. He's in. The stone is
three inches thick—not much, unless it's everything.

*

What I didn't understand about light was
stars. Their light hit Earth—that was a
condition of "star," as 8th-grade science had it.
There were hundreds of thousands—Mr. Andrews
pulled down a chart, and there were hundreds of thousands
of bodies up there, hurtling light at Earth . . .
Then why was outer space so dark? What
happened? I think that man in the tower
must be in such light, as we are
when we sleep—and everything shining travels
a space so strange we don't see it.

*

If it's true of hundreds of thousands of bodies it's
true of one. I think that I'm a carrying-case
for something—because it's dark inside, because
there are these breathing-holes over the surface . . .
I guess I'm talking about the mind. It sleeps around.
It spends a third of its time unfaithful
to the body. They didn't explain it in 8th-grade science
that way, but sometimes I think of consciousness
and flesh as two lovers, asleep. You know that
truth about bodies: their asses touching, their
backs to each other, their faces in separate directions.

*

It was 8th grade that I fell for Janice Netter, I
could take my place three inches from her in gym line and
it might as well have been all of archeology's
wafery layering intervening . . . Then Mr. Andrews
would talk about light, in a prism, and this
became an initial lesson in distance's subjectivity.
Say they finally arrive, from Out. They want to give him
a home with windows again, lovers, roasted goose.
It's been ten years. He clings to a stone and growls.
He doesn't want to leave his stickmen,
those he feels closest to.

All-Nite Donuts

A customer's blowing
smoke rings almost

heavy as the dough o's rising
out of the vat of grease.

Outside, the whores are whistling
their one note, lips thick

donuts strawberry-glazed.
Inside, the register will open its drawer

for a quarter and make its single cheep.
At midnight I thought it

ugly, all those lime and lavender
stools along the counter like a used

car salesman's breath mints.
Maybe it is. But somehow now, by

three, the special bloodshot view
of overdue eyes finds special beauty

in this neon and its attendant fly,
both fitfully buzzing.—Not a classic beauty,

no, the whores don't swivel slightly
toward a passing trick like flowers

toward the sun, it isn't a bit like that.
But all of our zeroes are here

made sweet. I dunk one in a mug,
I raise decaffeinated instant in a toast

to what's available, when we need it,
all night. Some guy goes by. The whores

curve slightly, like plastic spoons
being worked in a hardening cheese dip.

Pleasures

The view from the dungeon's barred slit is
a tree. It's fall. Another leaf swirls down,
exactly fits its shadow. And a prisoner
alone with a wall understands how his days
too are a kind of shadowboxing in which the
shadow wins. Not far away really,

the Emperor lifts a plum by silver plum tongs.
From his shoulder, a mechanical bird,
a lark, is singing—its garnet-and-emerald
throat by his ear like a barber's clippers humming
the wish to fly. Its eyes are onyx. A woman
and a milk bath in the chalcedony tub is

just the thing after plums! The mechanical
woman, today. Its parts are a purring
in honey. And, like a bottle of fine wine, it's
best kept on its back. The faucets
are the antlers of a golden deer whose golden rider,
a woods nymph, pours appropriately from her cold

and hot nipples. She holds a gold tray for the soaps.
Some mornings, real deer enter the grounds. The

Emperor feeds them apples the scullery-domo
sixteenths, and their breaths against his palm
are heavier and grainier than the fruit. So
many pleasures! The deer, so delicate!—though

they appear in poems with tiresome regularity:
their tremulous sides, their elegant bamboo gait,
etc. Why not more of the beveled isinglass
stare of this handtooled copper doe with the
musicworks inside? Or toasters! How
about a plane of morning light being fixed

in an oblong on the mirrory side of a toaster!
Even now, somebody's wavery face
in such a composition may be eloquent of what
survives past pain—and it floats,
on silver, like the exhalations of kneeling
deer one autumn, like unconscious prayer. How

about it? So many pleasures! Even
the loud smear of tripe being hosed down a gray
market gutter, even the small white bird
of milk on a child's upper lip, umbrella's
metal spider, crazy lace of blood in the eyelid,
labyrinth gnat-belly, flamesnap, darkness,

waking in darkness, being yourself in darkness through
despondency, even a man about to place his head
in his hands and he sees, against them, yes how his
face exactly fits its shadow. Now it's fall, and so
chill, and his life is something he can still hold and
rub his face in, real, and warm, and nubbled lovely.

"And Now Farley Is Going to Sing
While I Drink a Glass of Water!"

At the Vent Haven Museum in Fort Mitchell,
Kentucky, over 500 wooden
ventriloquist's dummies sit

in lit approximations of interrelationship,
stand in small posed groups no stiffer
than friends in half of the photos you own,
grotesque, exaggerated in overblown grimace
or underdefined like a slug, and some equipped
to whistle, spit, stick out their tongues, and some
just quiet, legs crossed in the hot June dusk, not
sweating exactly, just sitting, familiar, and yet
not exactly familiar. And at

the Houston Zoo, June air induces
two giraffes to amatory show. A glance,
like lightning bounced between
the spires of Chartres, shoots through
the gangly calm that otherwise attends them.
The day's all pollen. Sneezing, I almost miss
his great pink party favor
unrolling. Hitting at the height
of their articulate quiet, late-day light

along their yellow length makes little
more than dappled light of their bodies,
light given form, light turned substance
as if by no more than the gathering here
of a cloud of pollen. This is the way,
or almost the way, it feels—yes? or the way we
want it to feel: flesh
gone rarefied into a luminous floating the
bees of us wobble tipsily through
to the flowers of us. No wonder
we're fixed at the chainlink fence with something just
this side of recognition on our faces. And at

the Institute for Biochemical Engineering in Salt Lake,
in its hospital's basement, a test collection
of artificial hearts, opening, closing, on beat
in the water tanks, and the calves next door
with hearts already implanted; and at
the northeast end of Quarryworld, the ocher bricks
being dumped with the hundred high clinks
of glass bottles; and at the rich, black back of
Kathy W.'s garden, the single cucumber
dozing around the hum of its own thin green; and

at the Vent Haven Museum,
the wooden figures of humans, that aren't humans,

saying something for us.

The Accountings

1.
So, you want a lot of money.—The way
an old Jewish curse starts, out of the days
of my childhood, when people and sayings were one.
For the guys on the block, it was this: that
if you think of baseball scores while Doing It,
you won't get soft. But all I could think of was
Doing It itself—which meant another world
completely, as I lay in the dark of my parents' house
while they talked love and salaries, Eisenhower
dreamed golf, and far-off unobtainable women
touched themselves when I touched myself, in
mixed-up collages of lipsticked smiles and bras.

2.
No wonder we call them platelets! I want to set
a meal in my heart for everybody I've ever loved.
I want them to sit in those huge red vaulted
chambers, and banquetize themselves happy, and
talk to each other at once—my parents,
the first anthologized poets of my high school years,
and all of the women from 2nd grade's Miss Portney
to my flint-eyed spark-visioned lover-before-last,
under a roof, with enough, at last, forever. Not
that my current lover would understand; although
I think the wish is common: provision; and
the premise is true: the heart's time is simultaneity.

3.
Finally you learn you lose yourself in a moment
larger than you are—all those baseball scores go
floating uncontrollably in magic space. And then
the long "I love you"s with a forefinger lightly winding
sleepiness tighter on each other's skin. We lose

ourselves in each other's skin. There are so many
of us, two seconds of bird in the sky can be a hook that
drags in Ellen Kaufman's quiet anger and ample breasts,
a first selected Whitman, my parents' stern warm
epigram voices . . . and the kitchens of the heart are laboring
mightily to keep up. *May you get a lot of money.*
They meant there were griefs involved—though kept on saving.

The Form and Function of the Novel

My parents have come to town for my wedding.
Because of some way a shadow falls, or a hand
in conversation cuts air as if laboring, my father
reminds me increasingly of a man in a small
Canadian village, who manufactures racks
for drying lace curtains, who catches shadow in
that same way, and who moves his hands as if against
a current, in a book

I've been reading but leave, to shop
for cheese, bouquets and the wedding trousseau.
While we pick over veils and daffodils, life
according to narrative forces set in motion
continues: the backlands
moon slips up like a washed dish, and a rig
clops heavily toward the main street's tethering-rail.
His son's come home, for that sturdy Canadian

spring with the flowers like nailheads everywhere,
home from study in Europe, his son the biologist
talking Darwin and opera these last two years
over cognac in snifters like goldfish bowls.
They argue. The father is oafish, gruff, a
squared-off man whose lips move reading.
The son knows quiche and genetics. He's
embarrassed. Their words are ugly weather. I

see, although the son ironically can't despite
his interests, how the distance between them is
nothing, you hear me?, nothing, compared to the first
irrepressible land plants over 400 million

years ago stretching familially to the flax
in the lace that's hung in the front display case
under the sign with the father's name but *and*
Son freshly painted out. I think he's special

in his plainness and hurt. In this chapter he's
alone. It's night, he paces in the store he loves, and
so the moon through the fine white nets of his trade
makes him a complicated figure at last,
doilied over by dark and silver, eloquent, pensive, oblique . . .
"Do you think she'll like this one?" I turn.
He's holding a lace dress up to the late deep light
and it's all I can do to stop crying.

MICHAEL S. HARPER

MICHAEL S. HARPER *was born in Brooklyn, New York, in 1938. He was educated at City College of Los Angeles, California State University, the University of Iowa, and the University of Illinois, Urbana. His* Images of Kin: New and Selected Poems *(1977) adds new work to poems selected from six earlier books. "My travels," he has written, "made me look closely at the wealth of human materials in my own life, its ethnic richness, complexity of language and stylization, the tension between stated moral idealism and brutal historical realities, and I investigated the inner reality of those struggles to find the lyrical expression of their secrets in my own voice." He edited* Chant of Saints: A Gathering of Afro-American Literature, Art, and Scholarship *(w. Robert B. Stepto, 1979). His most recent volume of poems is* Healing Song for the Inner Ear *(1984). The winner of a Guggenheim Fellowship in Poetry (1976) and of several other prizes and awards, he is Israel J. Kapstein Professor of English at Brown University. (Photo by Layle Silbert)*

Don't they speak jazz?

I was fortunate enough to be born at home, delivered by my grand-father, and so there was much lore attached to my birth, much signi-fying because I was marked for his father. My parents weren't rich, but they had a good record collection, and they prohibited me from playing any of their 78's, a guarantee that I'd investigate in my own time, always when they were out of the house. After dusting the rec-ords, and making sure the needle was in place, the records in the appropriate order, I'd forget not to hum the songs I'd heard, and get caught with a smile. I also had the habit of riding the subway trains on what we called off-days, days when we took off from school, all the Jewish holidays in particular; I'd been riding the subways since I was five, but my parents didn't know it, and it took them three years to catch me. On that fateful day I was illegally riding after school, and passed my father as he went to work; I knew he'd seen me, though he never let on, and I decided to get on the next train and continue riding. At the next express stop I got off intending to turn around and go back home to the inevitable whipping when I heard tapping on a window of another train—it was my grandmother; she waved faintly with a hint of a smile. Music and trains! Coltrane. You learn most by getting caught doing the things you love; it leaves an im-pression.

I knew Bessie Smith and Billie Holiday from birth, but I was a horn man: President Lester Young; Coleman Superhawk Hawkins; Big Bad Ben Webster; Charles Chan Parker, alias the Bird; John William Coltrane, alias the Trane. There's a story that Trane was searching for a particular tone on his horn; he had what we thought was a per-fect embouchure, but his teeth hurt constantly, so he searched for the soft reed which would ease the pain. After searching for a year, each session killing his chops, he gave it up completely; there was no easy way to get that sound: play through the pain to *a love supreme*.

I wrote, secretly, in high school, buried in the back of some English class for fear I'd be asked to stand and recite a memorized poem: Donne or Shakespeare, or John Keats; luckily I tore up all these ef-forts, switched to prose and short dramatic forms until I was almost through college. I was working on the postal facing table, the middle-class equivalent to the pool hall; almost everybody in sight had ad-vanced degrees. It was there I learned about Tolstoy and *So What* Dostoevsky, as one of my partners used to call the Russian under-ground man; my partner had discovered Miles Davis. When I went to the Writers Workshop at the University of Iowa, I was the only blood in either fiction or poetry, and I was enrolled in both; several teachers asked me was I going to be another James Baldwin—one of the faculty members so obsessed with Baldwin he *knew* I'd known Mr. Baldwin—I had read his novels and essays, but hadn't met him personally. I began to specialize in retorts to affronts. You met Isaac Singer? You been hunting with Hemingway? But this kind of humor didn't go over very well. All the writers in the workshop at the time were victims of the New Criticism, the poets writing in rhyme and meter, the fiction writers reading James and Forster. I hung out with the football players; this was the era of Iowa's great dynasty. The best lineman on the team, Al Hinton, would creep over to my garage (most blacks had to live in the dorm) apartment behind one of the few black families in Iowa City, and ask me if I knew anyone who could teach him to draw. We were dancing to "Gypsy Woman" and playing tonk; I used to stay in the library until closing time, 2 A.M., to avoid the cold. My first and only poem on the worksheet in the poetry class was a poem dedicated to Miles Davis, "Alone," which I've since cut to three lines: "A friend told me / he'd risen above jazz. / I leave him there." Jazz was my bible. How would it be to solo with that great tradition of the big bands honking you on? Could one do it in a poem? I'd taken my survey courses, studied my Donne and Shakespeare, got hot at the Moor of Venice, "I have done the state some service and they know it," hotter at Prospero, me mad Caliban, and gone on to American literature, without Frederick Douglass, or DuBois, Johnson or Toomer. Richard Wright I remember most clearly because he was talked about in Brooklyn when I was a kid; I read all his books in one weekend because none of his books had ever been taken out of the school library. I took offense at O'Neill's Brutus Jones (as I'd despised Vachel Lindsay's "Congo" poem), and T.S. Eliot's remarks on the ending of "All God's Chillun Got Wings" (neither play large enough for the torso of Paul Robeson), and searched for the cadence of street talk in the inner ear of the great musicians, the great blues singers. This brings me to church. My mother was Episcopal, my father Catholic, I was a Baptist because of the great singing; each Sunday I had to *hit the meter* (put money in the collection box), hit the holy water, and take the subway to 52nd St. to catch Bird play. One morning, just after 9 A.M., Bird came out a side door, his ax in a triply-reinforced Macy's shopping bag; "Boy, how come you not in church?" he asked, but I was quick, told him I'd been, and took up his horn case, the handles raggedly stringed. He took us, three or four kids, all under ten, to the subway station, changed a quarter, gave us each a nickel, told us not to sneak on the train going home, and disappeared uptown.

I have images of musicians at their best and when they were down and out; their playing seldom faltered—the other musicians wouldn't tolerate anything less than a journeyman job, a little extra inspiration. My people were good storytellers; some of my personal kin walked north and west during the Civil War from North Carolina, South Carolina and Virginia; one ancestor came from Chatham, Ontario, Canada. I was surprised to find their images in books, not Stowe's *Uncle Tom's Cabin*, the play version differing greatly from the text of the novel, but Douglass' 1845 narrative, written by himself; Douglass' rhetoric, the notion of each slave having on his person an articulate pass, was my ticket to freedom.

I have gotten letters from "friends" praising my knowledge of history; I learned a little terminology from a zoology teacher in Los Angeles who had us count somites in his worms; he told me I shouldn't study because I'd never get into medical school; pick up a broom and forget the microscope. He, of course, was being scrutinized for future reference. As a new critic once wrote, "Nigger your breed ain't metaphysical," and of course I'm not; the poet, Sterling Brown, whose record I heard in the library in San Francisco fifteen years ago ("the strong men, coming on / the strong men, git stronger"), coined an infamous retort—"Cracker, your breed ain't exegetical."

I wrote about my "Grandfather" because he was a hero in the highest sense, though he sometimes waited tables in white clothes; he taught me to study Sugar Ray's left-hook technique, how to step inside someone's sense of time, of theater, off the stage and in the arena, and floor-show to one's own tune. Ellison called it *antagonistic cooperation*; Wright called it the switchblade of the movie screen. Language and rhetoric are essential power; why else were the slaves prohibited from reading, from learning to pen their own sagas? Most great art is finally testamental; its technical brilliance never shadows the content of the song: "Deliver the melody, make sure the harmony's correct, play as long as you like, but play sweet, and don't forget the ladies."

Some final notes on the blues: always say *yes* to life; meet life's terms but never accept them; "Been down so long that down don't worry me / road so rocky won't be rocky long"; as Johnny Hodges must have said to Duke on tour: *you run them verbs* (in the key of G), *I'll drive the thought* (the rabbit on his own rainbow). A coda on the American audience: it is vast, potentially; "I wish you'd buy more books," said Huck to Tom—meanwhile Jim was bringing his family to freedom. The landscape of the poem is the contour of the face reading the Declaration of Independence; how many white Jeffersons are there in this country, anyway? When I interviewed for my present duty at Brown University, all that slave trade money come back to haunt me once again, a man yelled out from the genteel back of the room that I was an impostor, borrowing from musicians; couldn't I do something about my accent? People were embarrassed for him, he was quickly ushered out, and the East Side returned to normal, good old Providence with its old money and the Mafia flair. I remembered that Douglass had been run out of Providence to New Bedford after an abolitionist meeting and it's rumored that John Brown (the fanatical one) came all the way from Oberlin, Ohio, to meet the best gunsmith in town, a black infantryman from the Black Regiment of Rhode Island. "Straight, No Chaser," said the musician; he must have meant the street corner and the library; this has been a riff in honor of my ancestors, with some lies thrown in, a little stretching of the truth to make the point. One more lie to make the audience sweet: when I was in South Africa in 1977 on an American Specialist Program, all by myself, I landed at Jan Smuts airport in Johannesburg at about 2:30 A.M.; I was carrying Sterling Brown's *Southern Road* and Robert Hayden's *Angle of Ascent* and some of my own, one book with Coltrane's image on the cover. I was first addressed in Afrikaans, but not being *colored*, I answered in American, "I'm from Brooklyn; you ever heard of Jackie Robinson?" It took me awhile to get through customs; I was staying at the Holiday Inn right at the airport so all I had to do was wait for the little van picking up customers. I stood there for a few minutes, a few whites not far away; when the driver, a black South African, approached, I got ready to board, I was first in line; the driver held up his hand to me, telling me to wait, boarded all the white passengers, and drove off. I stood there taking names, so to speak. When the driver returned, he apologized for not taking me in the van with the other passengers. He wanted to know where I was from and then he said—"What language do you speak when the white people aren't around?" I said, "English," and he said, "No, no." What language did I speak when the white people weren't around— the second time he asked I changed my response to "American." "Brother," he said, "when blacks are among themselves, don't they speak *jazz*?" I nodded, *right on*, brother. Send more Afro-Americans from the States; bring your record collections. The battle of the big bands begins.

We Assume: On the Death of Our Son, Reuben Masai Harper

We assume
that in 28 hours,
lived in a collapsible isolette,
you learned to accept pure oxygen
as the natural sky;
the scant shallow breaths
that filled those hours
cannot, did not make you fly—
but dreams were there
like crooked palmprints on
the twin-thick windows of the nursery—
in the glands of your mother.

We assume
the sterile hands
drank chemicals in and out
from lungs opaque with mucus,
pumped your stomach,
eeked the bicarbonate in
crooked, green-winged veins,
out in a plastic mask;

A woman who'd lost her first son
consoled us with an angel gone ahead
to pray for our family—
gone into that sky
seeking oxygen,
gone into autopsy,
a fine brown powdered sugar,
a disposable cremation:

We assume
you did not know we loved you.

Reuben, Reuben

I reach from pain
to music great enough
to bring me back,
swollenhead, madness,
lovefruit, a pickle of hate
so sour my mouth twicked
up and would not sing;
there's nothing in the beat
to hold it in
melody and turn human skin;
a brown berry gone
to rot just two days on the branch;
we've lost a son,
the music, *jazz*, comes in.

Dear John, Dear Coltrane

> *a love supreme, a love supreme*
> *a love supreme, a love supreme*

Sex fingers toes
in the marketplace
near your father's church
in Hamlet, North Carolina—
witness to this love
in this calm fallow
of these minds,
there is no substitute for pain:
genitals gone or going,
seed burned out,
you tuck the roots in the earth,
turn back, and move
by river through the swamps,
singing: *a love supreme, a love supreme;*
what does it all mean?
Loss, so great each black
woman expects your failure
in mute change, the seed gone.
You plod up into the electric city—

your song now crystal and
the blues. You pick up the horn
with some will and blow
into the freezing night:
a love supreme, a love supreme—

Dawn comes and you cook
up the thick sin 'tween
impotence and death, fuel
the tenor sax cannibal
heart, genitals and sweat
that makes you clean—
a love supreme, a love supreme—

Why you so black?
cause I am
why you so funky?
cause I am
why you so black?
cause I am
why you so sweet?
cause I am
why you so black?
cause I am
a love supreme, a love supreme:

So sick
you couldn't play *Naima,*
so flat we ached
for song you'd concealed
with your own blood,
your diseased liver gave
out its purity,
the inflated heart
pumps out, the tenor kiss,
tenor love:
a love supreme, a love supreme—
a love supreme, a love supreme—

Love Medley: Patrice Cuchulain

"Stirrups, leggings, a stainless
steel slide, a dishpan, sheet,
a thread spool, scissors,
three facemasks, smocks, paper
overshoes, a two-way mirror, dials":
the head and left arm
cruise out, almost together,
and you drop into gloves,
your own ointment
pulling your legs
binding your cord; the cheesed
surface skin, your dark
hairless complexion, the metallic room,
orchestrate and blow up your lungs,
clogged on protein and vitamins,
for the sterile whine of the delivery
room and your staff of attendants.
It is free exercise when the cord's
cut; you weigh in for the cleanup
as your mother gets her local
for her stitches: boy, 6 lbs 13 oz.

As you breathe easily, your mother's
mother is tubed and strapped,
hemorrhaging slowly from her varices;
your two dead brothers who could
not breathe are berries
gone to rot at our table:
what is birth but death
with complexity: blood, veins,
machinery and love: our names.

Last Affair: Bessie's Blues Song

Disarticulated
arm torn out,
large veins cross
her shoulder intact,

her tourniquet
her blood in all-white big bands:

Can't you see
what love and heartache's done to me
I'm not the same as I used to be
this is my last affair

Mail truck or parked car
in the fast lane,
afloat at forty-three
on a Mississippi road,
Two-hundred-pound muscle on her ham bone,
'nother nigger dead 'fore noon:

Can't you see
what love and heartache's done to me
I'm not the same as I used to be
this is my last affair

Fifty-dollar record
cut the vein in her neck,
fool about her money
toll her black train wreck,
white press missed her fun'ral
in the same stacked deck:

Can't you see
what love and heartache's done to me
I'm not the same as I used to be
this is my last affair

Loved a little blackbird
heard she could sing,
Martha in her vineyard
pestle in her spring,
Bessie had a bad mouth
made my chimes ring:

Can't you see
what love and heartache's done to me
I'm not the same as I used to be
this is my last affair

Debridement: Operation Harvest Moon: *On Repose*

The sestina traces a circle in language and body.

Stab incision below nipple,
left side; insert large chest tube;
sew to skin, right side;
catch blood from tube
in gallon drain bottle.
Wash abdomen with phisohex;
shave; spray brown iodine prep.

Stab incision below sternum
to symphis pubis;
catch blood left side;
sever reddish brown spleen
cut in half; tie off blood supply;
check retroperitoneal,
kidney, renal artery bleeding.

Dissect lateral wall
abdominal cavity; locate kidney;
pack colon, small intestine;
cut kidney; suture closely;
inch by inch check bladder,
liver, abdominal wall, stomach:
25 units blood, pressure down.

Venous pressure: 8; lumbar
musculature, lower spinal column
pulverized; ligate blood vessels,
right forearm; trim meat, bone ends;
tourniquet above fracture, left arm;
urine, negative: 4 hours; pressure
unstable; remove shrapnel flecks.

Roll on stomach; 35 units blood;
pressure zero; insert plastic blood
containers, pressure cuffs; pump chest
drainage tube; wash wounds sterile
saline; dress six-inch ace wraps;

wrap both legs, toe to groin; left arm
plaster, finger to shoulder: 40 units blood.

Pressure, pulse, respiration up;
remove bloody gowns; scrub; redrape;
5 cc vitamin K; thorazine: sixth
laparotomy, check hyperventilation;
stab right side incision below nipple;
insert large chest tube; catch blood drain bottle . . .

Grandfather

In 1915 my grandfather's
neighbors surrounded his house
near the dayline he ran
on the Hudson
in Catskill, NY
and thought they'd burn
his family out
in a movie they'd just seen
and be rid of his kind:
the death of a lone black
family is *the Birth
of a Nation,*
or so they thought.
His 5'4" waiter gait
quenched the white jacket smile
he'd brought back from watered
polish of my father
on the turning seats,
and he asked his neighbors
up on his thatched porch
for the first blossom of fire
that would burn him down.

They went away, his nation,
spittooning their torched necks
in the shadows of the riverboat
they'd seen, posse decomposing;
and I see him on Sutter
with white bag from your

restaurant, challenged by his first
grandson to a foot-race
he will win in white clothes.

I see him as he buys galoshes
for his railed yard near Mineo's
metal shop, where roses jump
as the el circles his house
toward Brooklyn, where his rain fell;
and I see cigar smoke in his eyes,
chocolate Madison Square Garden chews
he breaks on his set teeth,
stitched up after cancer,
the great white nation immovable
as his weight wilts
and he is on a porch
that won't hold my arms,
or the legs of the race run
forwards, or the film
played backwards on his grandson's eyes.

Nightmare Begins Responsibility

I place these numbed wrists to the pane
watching white uniforms whisk over
him in the tube-kept
prison
fear what they will do in experiment
watch my gloved stickshifting gasolined hands
breathe *boxcar-information-please* infirmary tubes
distrusting white/pink mending paperthin
silkened end hairs, distrusting tubes
shrunk in his *trunk-skincapped*
shaven head, in thighs
distrusting-white-hands-picking-baboon-light
on this son who will not make his second night
of this wardstrewn intensive airpocket
where his father's asthmatic
hymns of *night-train*, train done gone
his mother can only know that he has flown
up into essential calm unseen corridor

going boxscarred home, *mamaborn, sweetsonchild*
gonedowntown into *researchtestingwarehousebatteryacid*
mama-son-done-gone/me telling her 'nother
train tonight, no music, no breathstroked
heartbeat in my infinite distrust of them:

and of my distrusting self
white-doctor-who-breathed-for-him-all-night
say it for two sons gone,
say nightmare, say it loud
panebreaking heartmadness:
nightmare begins responsibility.

ROBERT HASS

ROBERT HASS *ws raised in San Francisco, where he was born in 1941. His undergraduate degree is from St. Mary's College in Moraga, California, his M.A. from Stanford University, where he held Woodrow Wilson and Danforth fellowships. His first book,* Field Guide *(1973), won the Yale Series of Younger Poets competition, and* Praise *(1979) won the William Carlos Williams Award from the Poetry Society of America. His most recent book is* Twentieth Century Pleasures: Prose on Poetry *(1984). In 1984 he received an award from the American Academy and Institute of Arts and Letters and a five-year grant from the John D. and Catherine MacArthur Foundation. He lives with his wife and three children in Berkeley, California.*
(Photo by Robert Selden Smith)

Poetry and Place: A Note

I don't know exactly how poetry civilizes the earth, but it civilizes the earth. I don't know what would be changed if Wordsworth at the age of thirty-two had not, one morning, stood on Westminster Bridge in the early fall and seen

> Ships, towers, domes, theatres, and temples lie
> Open unto the fields, and to the sky;

or if, on the outskirts of Chang-an, the great T'ang capital that is now the modest industrial city of Xian, Tu Fu, who lived to see T'ang civilization torn apart, had not, at a pretty picnic on a canal in June, watched a storm gather:

> And it rained, soaking the festive little party.
> The squall rose and beat against the boat.
> The girls of Yueh in their soaked scarlet skirts,
> The girls of Yen weeping tears of mascara;

and I don't know how we would see the Sierra Nevada, what those mountains would be to us, if that Scotsman from Wisconsin, John Muir, had not chosen to live down Calvinism by hiking the passes with the essays of Emerson in his kitbag:

> By the side of Canyon Creek you find the rose and homely yarrow, and small meadows full of bees and clover. At the head of a low-browed rock, luxuriant dogwood bushes and willows arch over from bank to bank, embowering the stream with their leafy branches; and drooping plumes, kept in motion by the current, fringe the brow of the cascade. From this leafy covert the stream leaps out into the light in a fluted curve thick-sown with sparkling crystals, and falls into a pool filled with brown boulders, out of which it creeps grey with foam-bells and disappears in a tangle of verdure like that from which it came.

Maybe it is that the poetic imagination takes hold of things so completely without altering them. All the rest of the fever of man-the-maker is packed into Wordsworth's list. How many of the impulses of the city he manages to evoke in that one line—ships for speed and commerce and the hunger for foreign places; towers for defence, for the old Norman dream of the city, for worship and the expression of power; domes for power and worship and public administration and the Jacobean idea of a Greek civility; theaters for art and sexuality and the enactment of dream under lights; temples for worship and for commerce and for law. It is remarkable the way Wordsworth opens up all that anthill busyness and makes it seem vulnerable and innocent, like the openness of a child's face or sexual openness, as if the oldest goddess of fertility who created both wealth and cities were still a presence in the world in 1802 when the first steamboats appeared on the Thames:

> Ships, towers, domes, theatres, and temples lie
> Open unto the fields, and to the sky;
> All bright and glittering in the smokeless air.
> Never did sun more beautifully steep
> In his first splendour, valley, rock, or hill;
> Ne'er saw I, never felt, a calm so deep!
> The river glideth at his own sweet will:
> Dear God! the very houses seem asleep;
> And all that mighty heart is lying still!

The Houses of Parliament will burn down and a landmark clocktower take their place; Trafalgar Square will redefine the center of the city, and these events will not alter London more radically than this vision of it. In ways that scholars can trace through poetry and painting and photography, the vision stays. It has become an aspect of the place.

This happens to places in different ways and it is difficult sometimes to know when we are experiencing place apart from the history of sensibility that has played over it. I was in Lyon recently, a city where I had never been before. The first thing I did was wander into a park and I had already been instructed how to see it. Chestnut trees, policemen on bicycles, a gazebo-like restaurant serving Rhone wine and beer and sandwiches, wooden tables and chairs on a sweep of raked gravel. Impressionist painting had made it seem not just a place but a view of life in which sunlight and holidays and having pouting lips or a terrific moustache counted for a lot. On a weekday afternoon, wonderfully mild in late October, there was only one other customer at the outdoor cafe, an older man with glasses and close-cropped hair; he was drinking wine and reading a paperback book with a look of amused and concentrated loathing; a park attendant swept fallen sycamore leaves; high school kids—boys and girls—strolled by in leather jackets; in the distance, through the trees, swans on a reedy lake. I thought I knew exactly where I was.

And the hotel. It was in the middle of a new housing development called on the realtor's huge billboards—if I needed to be jerked into the twentieth century, this did the trick—*le district de Nouveau Tonkin.* The hotel was on a street called *Rue John Ford.* The view from the window was desolating: glass and unfinished concrete, row on row of cramped angular highrises, cement courtyard between them, an occasional manic and unappetizing play area for children constructed out of bright-colored plumber's pipe, not a soul in sight. It did not look like any American city but it seemed familiar and the sensation it produced in me was like a memory compounded of clarity and anguish. After a few minutes, I realized that the feeling came from the films of Antonioni, maybe from the paintings of de Chirico. I had already been taught that there is a gauntness in the sterility of new urban landscapes that is spiritual. I think that is the word for it. It merges in my mind with the faces of actors and actresses, Marcello Mastrionni, Jeanne Moreau, passive faces, empty of feeling but not of depth. The function of art, a Russian formalist critic said, is to free us from the automatism of perception. It is surprising how fast art itself becomes part of that automatic response.

This makes me value the individuality of a poem. Of course, poets also cast the lights and shadows of sensibility on things. I tend to see Boston with Robert Lowell's double vision of the spruce, modest Federalist ideals of the past and the glutted violence of the imperial present and to walk the streets of Manhattan sometimes in a Frank O'Hara haze, as if in the bedlam of the streets someone I liked was going to show up at any moment and we were going to go off and do something amusing. And I experience those moods, like the moods of impressionist and existentialist films, as a kind of pleasant infiltration. But the specific weight of the words in a particular poem has another effect. Yeats in a public park in Dublin, "That is no country for old men," and the amazing thing the old man says looking at the young, "Once out of nature, I shall never take/My bodily form from any natural thing." Eliot's London, "I had not thought death had undone so many," with its muted tenderness and shock, with the sense of it costing him to see what he is seeing. Or Kenneth Rexroth in the late thirties in San Francisco, trying out a Chinese line in English on a city that poetry had hardly touched:

> The tide is out and the air is full of the smell of the ocean,
> The newly-arrived mockingbirds are awake
> In the courtyard behind the houses.
> I pass a frosted refrigerated window
> Where five disembowelled white hares

Hang on their furred hindpaws from a five-spoked rack.
The unlit florists' windows are full of obscure almond blossoms.
I have been sitting at Sam Wo's drinking cold aromatic
liquor . . .

This last is valuable to me, I suppose, as the question of place interests me, partly because I grew up in California at a time when schoolbooks were still printed in Boston and New York and the putatively normal children about whom I read did things like put on boots to play in the snow and go on car trips with their parents into landscapes of lime-green foliage, and red barns and white clapboard Congregational churches. Rexroth's poem, like the poems of Wordsworth and Eliot and Yeats, exists for me not as a mood but as a given music of words by a particular writer at a particular moment in his life. It has a weight that my own inward recitation of it notices and measures. I don't see North Beach and Chinatown through Rexroth's eyes, so much as I am aware of his presence. And that is the way a poem inhabits place, not as a color cast over it, but as a resident spirit.

I think that is why most self-conscious efforts to create a national or a local literature do not succeed very well. They are likely, for one thing, to be too committed to describing the virtures of place and by extension the virtue of the writer, which is why, in our time, most of the self-conscious poetry of place ends in complacency and moraliz-ing. I don't think that poetry can be married to place; it will refuse the domestication. It needs to be more open-eyed than that and it is bound to see that, in the end, living in a place is not a virtue but a necessity. Poets can, however, marry their lives to places for longer or shorter times, and there is a chance that, if they write out of those lives, they will have made the places where they lived clearer and more human by their presence.

San Pedro Road

Casting, up a salt creek in the sea-rank air,
fragrance of the ferny anise, crackle of field grass
in the summer heat. Under this sun vision blurs.
Blue air rises, the horizon weaves above the leaden bay.
Rock crabs scuttle from my shadow in the silt.

Some other day the slow-breathing, finely haired mussels
on the shore, under rocks, buried thick-clustered in black mud
would be enough, blended in a quick formal image
with butter, tarragon, a cool white Napa Valley wine.
Today in the ferocious pointless heat I dream,
half in anger, of the great white bass,
the curious striper, bright-eyed, rising to the bait,
flickering in muddy bottoms, feeding the green
brackish channels where yachts wallow in the windless air.
My hands are tense.
                    A carcass washes by, white meat,
spidery translucent bones and I think I understand,
finally dumb animal I understand, kick off boots, pants, socks,
and swim,
              thrashing dull water to a golden brown,
terrorizing the depths with my white belly, my enormous length,
done with casting, reeling in slowly, casting . . .

After the Gentle Poet Kobayashi Issa

New Year's morning—
everything is in blossom!
I feel about average.

A huge frog and I
staring at each other,
neither of us moves.

This moth saw brightness
in a woman's chamber—
burned to a crisp.

Asked how old he was
the boy in the new kimono
stretched out all five fingers.

Blossoms at night,
like people
moved by music

Napped half the day;
no one
punished me!

Fiftieth birthday:

From now on,
it's all clear profit,
every sky.

Don't worry, spiders,
I keep house
casually.

These sea slugs,
they just don't seem
Japanese.

Hell:

Bright autumn moon;
pond snails crying
in the saucepan.

Measure

Recurrences.
Coppery light hesitates
again in the small-leaved

Japanese plum. Summer
and sunset, the peace
of the writing desk

and the habitual peace
of writing, these things
form an order I only

belong to in the idleness
of attention. Last light
rims the blue mountain

and I almost glimpse
what I was born to,
not so much in the sunlight

or the plum tree
as in the pulse
that forms these lines.

In Weather

1
What I wanted
in the pearly repetitions of February
was vision. All winter,
grieved and dull,
I hungered for it.
Sundays I looked for lightning-
stricken trees
in the slow burning of the afternoon
to cut them down, split
the dry centers,
and kindle from their death
an evening's warmth
in the uxorious amber repetitions *excessively fond of or submissive to a wife*
of the house. Dusks
weighted me, the fire,
the dim trees. I saw
the bare structure
of their hunger for light
reach to where darkness
joined them. The dark   *sexual*
and the limbs tangled
luxuriant as hair.
I could feel night gather them
but removed my eyes from the tug of it
and watched the fire,
a smaller thing,
contained by the hewn stone
of the dark hearth.

2
I can't decide
about my garbage and the creatures
who come at night to root
and scatter it. I could lock it
in the shed, but I imagine
wet noses, bodies grown alert
to the smells of warm decay
in the cold air. It seems a small thing
to share what I don't want,
but winter mornings the white yard
blossoms grapefruit peels,
tin cans, plastic bags,
the russet cores of apples.
The refuse of my life
surrounds me and the sense of waste
in the dreary gathering of it
compels me all the more
to labor for the creatures
who quiver and are quick-eyed
and bang the cans at night
and are not grateful. The other morning,
walking early in the new sun,
I was rewarded. A thaw turned up
the lobster shells from Christmas eve.
They rotted in the yard
and standing in the muddy field I caught,
as if across great distances,
a faint rank fragrance of the sea.

3
There are times
I wish my ignorance were
more complete. I remember
clamming inland beaches
on the January tides
along Tomales Bay. A raw world
where green crabs
which have been exposed
graze nervously on intertidal kelp
and sea anemones are clenched and colorless
in eddying pools
near dumb clinging starfish

on the sides and undersides of rock.
Among the cockles and the horseneck clams,
I turned up long, inch-thick
sea worms. Female,
phallic, ruddy brown, each one
takes twenty years to grow.
Beach people call them *innkeepers*
because the tiny male lives inside
and feeds on plankton
in the water that the worm
churns through herself to move.
I watched the brown things
that brightness bruised
writhing in the sun. Then,
carefully, I buried them.
And, eyes drifting, heart-
sick, honed to the wind's edge,
my mind became the male
drowsing in that inland sea
who lives in darkness,
drops seed twice in twenty years,
and dies. I look from my window
to the white fields
and think about the taste of clams.

4
A friend, the other night,
read poems full of rage
against the poor uses of desire
in mere enactment. A cruel music
lingered in my mind.
The poems made me think
I understood
why men cut women up. Hating
the source, nerved,
irreducible, that music hacked
the body till the source was gone.
Then the heavy cock wields,
rises, spits seed
at random and the man
shrieks, homeless
and perfected in the empty dark.
His god is a thrust of infinite desire

beyond the tame musk
of companionable holes.
It descends to women occasionally
with contempt and languid tenderness.
I tried to hate my wife's cunt,
the sweet place where I rooted,
to imagine the satisfied disgust
of cutting her apart,
bloody and exultant
in the bad lighting and scratchy track
of butcher shops
in short experimental films.
It was easier than I might have supposed.
o spider cunt, o raw devourer.
I wondered what to make
of myself. There had been a thaw.
I looked for green shoots
in the garden, wild flowers in the woods.
I found none.

5
In March the owls
began to mate. Moon
on windy snow. Mournful,
liquid, the dark hummed
their cries, a soft
confusion. Hard frost
feathered the windows.
I could not sleep.
I imagined the panic
of the meadow mouse,
the star-nosed mole.
Slowly at first, I
made a solemn face
and tried the almost human wail
of owls, ecstatic
in the winter trees, *twoo, twoo.*
I drew long breaths.
My wife stirred in our bed.
Joy seized me.

6

Days return
day to me, the brittle light.
My alertness has no
issue. Deep in the woods
starburst needles of the white pine
are roof to the vacancies
in standing still. Wind
from the lake stings me.
Hemlocks grow cerebral
and firm in the dim attenuation
of the afternoon. The longer
dusks are a silence
born in pale redundancies
of silence. Walking home
I follow the pawprints of the fox.
I know that I know myself
no more than a seed
curled in the dark of a winged pod
knows flourishing.

The Feast

The lovers loitered on the deck talking,
the men who were with men and the men who were with new
    women,
a little shrill and electric, and the wifely women
who had repose and beautifully lined faces
and coppery skin. She had taken the turkey from the oven
and her friends were talking on the deck
in the steady sunshine. She imagined them
drifting toward the food, in small groups, finishing
sentences, lifting a pickle or a sliver of turkey,
nibbling a little with unconscious pleasure. And
she imagined setting it out artfully, the white meat,
the breads, antipasto, the mushrooms and salad
arranged down the oak counter cleanly, and how they all came
as in a dance when she called them. She carved meat
and then she was crying. Then she was in darkness
crying. She didn't know what she wanted.

Late Spring

And then in mid-May the first morning of steady heat,

the morning, Leif says, when you wake up, put on shorts, and that's it for the day,

when you pour coffee and walk outside, blinking in the sun.

Strawberries have appeared in the markets, and peaches will soon;

squid is so cheap in the fish stores you begin to consult Japanese and Italian cookbooks for the various and ingenious ways of preparing *ika* and *calamari*;

and because the light will enlarge your days, your dreams at night will be as strange as the jars of octopus you saw once in the fisherman's boat under the summer moon;

and after swimming white wine; and the sharing of stories before dinner is prolonged because the relations of the children in the neighborhood have acquired village intensity and the stories take longer telling;

and there are nights when the fog rolls in that nobody likes—hey fog, the Miwok sang, who lived here first, you better go home pelican is beating your wife—

and after dark, in the first cool hour, your children sleep so heavily in their beds, exhausted from play, it is a pleasure to watch them,

Leif does not move a muscle as he lies there; no, wait; it is Luke who lies there in his eight-year-old body,

Leif is taller than you are and he isn't home; when he is, his feet will extend past the end of the mattress, and Kristin is at the corner in the dark, talking with neighborhood boys;

things change; there is no need for this dream-compelled narration; the rhythm will keep me awake, changing.

A Story About the Body

The young composer, working that summer at an artist's
colony, had watched her for a week. She was Japanese, a
painter, almost sixty, and he thought he was in love with
her. He loved her work, and her work was like the way she
moved her body, used her hands, looked at him directly when
she made amused and considered answers to his questions.
One night, walking back from a concert, they came to her
door and she turned to him and said, "I think you would
like to have me. I would like that too, but I must tell
you that I have had a double mastectomy," and when he
didn't understand, "I've lost both my breasts." The rad-
iance that he had carried around in his belly and chest
cavity—like music—withered, very quickly, and he made
himself look at her when he said, "I'm sorry. I don't
think I could." He walked back to his own cabin through
the pines, and in the morning he found a small blue bowl
on the porch outside his door. It looked to be full of
rose petals, but he found when he picked it up that the
rose petals were on top; the rest of the bowl—she must
have swept them from the corners of her studio—was full
of dead bees.

WILLIAM HEYEN

WILLIAM HEYEN *was born in Brooklyn, New York, in 1940. His undergraduate degree is from SUNY at Brockport, where he now teaches, and his graduate degrees from Ohio University. He was a Fulbright lecturer to Germany (1971-72) and a Guggenheim Fellow (1977-78).* He edited A Profile of Theodore Roethke *(1971) and* American Poets in 1976 *(1976). The American Academy and Institute of Arts and Letters awarded him the Witter Bynner Prize, given annually to a younger American poet, in 1982. He has published seven volumes of poetry, most recently* Long Island Light *(1979),* The City Parables *(1980),* Lord Dragonfly: Five Sequences *(1981), and* Erika: Poems of the Holocaust *(1984).*
(Photo by Layle Silbert)

Glad to Be a Fool

It seems to me now that the poems in my first book (*Depth of Field*, 1970) were written by someone who wanted to know everything those poems were saying and doing. I labored over each one, strained to control its rhythms and rhymes, tortured its thought. I chose subjects—they didn't choose me—that seemed to me to be the stuff of Poetry. Sometimes I yearned for the Grand Statement. I wanted, too, to render my subjects in an inviolate language, one that held all its own answers so that *readers*—I was not thinking much about *listeners* back then—would not make me out to be foolish or insensitive. I was in my own heart wide-open and vulnerable, and did not want to be hurt. My strategies, in fact, seemed to work. Seldom was heard a discouraging word. People seemed to think that I was smart and that I knew what I was doing.

"Birds and Roses Are Birds and Roses" and "Existential" are typical of that first book. I still care for these poems. They come from what I was at the time, are what I could do at the time, and they helped me, draft after draft as they came into being, to learn about compression, austerity, the economics of line movement. Their individual lives may be strict, restricted, essentially closed, and I may have come to believe more in uncertainty and mystery than these poems do, but they still insist on their own implosions in ways I can't deny or condemn.

But I've come to feel, as Archibald MacLeish once said, that our best poems—both those already written and those not yet committed to paper—somehow go on writing themselves. They have lives of their own beyond our time-bound abilities to know them completely. It may be that those things that get into a poem subconsciously are the things about it that will make it hardest to get rid of. Poets are not editorialists who know beforehand precisely what it is they have to say. They do not know just what is behind the pressure they feel to write and the pleasure and/or pain of the process itself. My earlier twelve-liners wanted to be diamonds, but I am now glad to be a fool when it comes to knowing much about the long subconscious foreground, the life source and self-generating vitality of any poem that hopes to matter. . . .

Over a week or two a few Augusts back I'd find myself feeling depressed about something. I'd be gardening and close to tears, or I'd be riding my bike along the Erie Canal here in Brockport and feel my throat tightening. I'm not usually this way, and I couldn't locate what was wrong. Then I realized that it was only summer's end, that my children were growing up too fast and would soon be leaving home, that I was getting older and mourning for myself and the "golden-grove unleaving" around me as in Hopkins' "Spring and Fall." I'd survive. The sadness passed.

I wrote "Ram Time" during those days. I didn't know, as I began to tell of how Wenzel slaughtered a ram, that I would have him blood the animal and then lift it *again* until "even its last / heartdrops swelled / out of the cut." During my boyhood I'd known a farmer by the name of Wenzel, but I'd never seen him kill a sheep this way. I didn't know I would slow the poem down in the several ways I did. Even the momentary theme of blood-guilt is just a diversion, I think, and the poem is not at all about this. I didn't know I would keep the boy in the fold, or have my speaker talk about stopping time. He knows as he speaks that if and when he finishes the story, has the boy carry the pail of blood to Wenzel, thirty years of his own life will have gone by. Maybe he protests a little, telling us he'll have held the boy in ram time for as long as he wanted, saying "Believe me, / I'm almost ready to let go," but he does seem to accept himself, his identity, his life that "goes on."

What happened, then, was that without my knowing it a subject had chosen me and I was writing about something deeply important in my own life during the writing. "Ram Time" is an extremely personal poem, but not an autobiographical one. It was about a year before I made the connection—I was reading a journal I keep—between "Ram Time" and the melancholic I'd been at the end of that summer. I wrote that poem because I had to. Its form developed by way of feelings decades deep in me. Objectified as it is, containing a world within itself, it nevertheless came out of real and present life. It goes on resolving itself. I somehow managed to write a poem—I want to understand such a complex process only imperfectly—that was mine and not mine at the same time. In part, it belonged only to itself, moved according to its own laws and necessities. Writing it, I had to be free in ways I was not free when writing the poems that went into my first book.

"Poem Touching the Gestapo" is from *Erika* (1984), a book of some fifty poems about the Holocaust. The poems find many different strategies for getting themselves said. This one is an outpouring, once and for all, of myriad abominations of the Third Reich, a naming. The poem seems to me to be a vomiting-forth, an attempt to regurgitate everything at once. In its movements, in its desire somehow to touch the Gestapo itself, it has a life of its own, one I cannot now censor. . . . I wrote "The Children" after a dream, the ending of which I couldn't later recall. It may be the most affirmative poem I've ever written.

"Mother and Son" had two main sources, though I don't remember which was first. I had the dream of my mother younger than I'd ever seen her, and I'd read Mark Strand's beautiful "My Mother on an Evening in Late Summer."

"The Berries," from its opening dependent clause, makes a rhythm and music that seem to me to be mine. Somehow, it slows down as I say it. Its images of ice- and berry-light, its three tenses (present, past, and a further past remembered during present and past), move toward a single word, "except," and a faith true to the poem's own thoughtfulness. I never say it but that I lose myself inside it during the saying. It is a poem, in part, about the gift that poetry itself is for us.

Birds and Roses
Are Birds and Roses

I have come to rely
on the timeless in the temporal,
on the always faithful inner-eye,
on detail that deepens to fond symbol.

But all morning the sun found
feathers scattered under a bush
where roses had fallen to the ground.
The remains of a thrush.

I would flesh this one bird's feathers,
resume its quick eye and lilting trill.
But these were not the mystics' flowers:
their bush cast a shadow like a bell.

Existential

Half seeing and half smelling a scrap
of bacon, an eel blunts its nose on wire,
but finally steers into the cone of water
given shape by the trap.

Eats, and begins to define the rigid walls
of its cell. Burrows its mud floor, but bares
the same wire. The eel hovers, stares,
circles and settles.

It hears its gills feel the waters flow.
Waits in its cage. It can't or won't remember
the small way out it entered, or does know
and doesn't care, or neither.

Ram Time

Wenzel knelt to his tied ram,
stretched its neck,
made the quick cut,

grasped ear- and shoulder-wool,
directed the dying animal's bloodfall
into a pail,

the most blood I'd ever seen,
as it poured, then slowed,
then dripped.

Then Wenzel lifted the limp ram
until its flow began again.
This time,

after even its last
heartdrops swelled
out of the cut,

he carried the ram away
over his shoulders,
its head lolling backwards,

its eyes glazed, all
four hooves in his hands. . . .

I am the boy who stands in that grass,

witness, and will soon
probably carry the pail of blood

to Wenzel in his barn,
but want to wait, here,
for some reason, now,

thirty, or a hundred years,
or two, more or less, later. From this far,
the pail could be filled with milk

brimming white as washed eggs,
white as—but no, there's no
mistaking it. Some

will stick, in fact,
to the boy's hands
when he lifts the pail

to carry the blood to Wenzel.
But now, here, for just this long, only
half knowing why,

he waits in the fold.
I can almost taste the beautiful

life's blood of the dead ram,
see how it will crest
from side to side,

how he will carry it,
how the sun itself will shine on it,
how Wenzel will thank him

and tousle his hair. . . . Meanwhile,
it's not impossible to stop time,
or let it drain away,

as I will. Even when I'm dead,
I'll have held the boy here
in ram time

for as long as I've wanted. Believe me,
I'm almost ready to let go.
I look up ahead

past fold and meadow
to the barn where
Wenzel is waiting.

My life goes on.
The boy lifts the pail.

Poem Touching the Gestapo

> *Behind the apparently iron front of Teutonic organization, there was a sort of willed chaos.*
>
> Edward Crankshaw

> *The system of administration [at Auschwitz] was completely without logic. It was stupefying to see how little the orders which followed one another had in common. This was only partly due to negligence.*
>
> Olga Lengyel

You now, you in the next century, and the next,
hear what you'll almost remember,
see into photos where he still stands, Himmler,
whose round and puffy face concealed visions,

cortege of the condemned winding toward Birkenau,

and how to preserve Jews' heads in hermetically sealed tins,

der Ritter, knight, *treuer Heinrich*,

visions of death's head returning in Reich's light,
the Aryan skull ascending the misformed skull of the beast,
the Jew, Gypsy, lunatic, Slav, syphylitic, homosexual,

ravens and wolves, the Blood Flag, composer Wagner
whose heart went out to frogs, who, like Martin Luther,
wanted to drive Jews "like mad dogs out of the land,"

Heydrich dead but given Lidice,
Mengele injecting dye into Jewish eyes—
Ist das die deutsche Kultur?—
this vomit at last this last
cleansing and an end to it,
if it is possible, if I will it now,

Lebensborn stud farms, *Rassenschande, Protocols
of the Elders of Zion, SS* dancing in nuns' clothes,

Otto Ohlendorf, who left his Berlin desk to command
Einsatzgruppe D and roam the East killing
one million undesirables in less than two years' time,
lamenting the mental strain on his men,
the stench of inadequate graves,
corpses that fouled themselves in the gas vans,

the graves rupturing, backs, backs of heads, limbs
above ground as they are here, if I will it now,

the day-in, day-out shootings of Jews, some attractive,
brave, even intelligent, but to be dealt with
in strict military order, not like at Treblinka where
gas chambers were too small, and converted gas vans' engines
sometimes wouldn't start, the thousands already
packed into the showers for history,
their hands up so more would fit, and smaller children
thrown in at the space left at the top,

and we knew they were all dead, said Hoess of Auschwitz,
when the screaming stopped,

Endlosung, Edelweiss, Lebensraum, Mussulmen, Cyklon B,

"and his large blue eyes like stars," as Goebbels wrote,
and the Fuehrer's films of conspirators on meathooks,

we cannot keep it all, an end to it,
visions of loyal Heinrich, what engineer Grabe saw at Dubno,
he and two postmen allowed to watch, the vans arriving,
a father holding his boy and pointing to that sky,
explaining something, when the SS shouted and counted off
twenty more or less and pushed them behind the earth mound,

Stahlhelm, Horst Wessel, Goring in a toga at *Karinhalle,*
redbeard Barbarossa rising,

that father and son, and the sister remembered by Grabe
as pointing to herself, slim girl with black hair,
and saying, "twenty-three years old,"
as Grabe walked behind the mound and saw a tremendous grave,

the holy orders of the *SS,* Lorelei, the Reichstag fire,
Befehl ist Befehl, Anne Frank in Belsen, jackboots, Krupp,

bodies wedged together tightly on top of one another,
some still moving, lifting arms to show life,
the pit two-thirds full, maybe a thousand dead,
the German who did the shooting sitting at the edge,
his gun on his knees, and he's smoking a cigarette,
as more naked victims descend steps cut in the pit's clay,
clamber over the heads of those already dead there,
and lay themselves down. Grabe heard some speak
in low voice, . . . listen . . .
before the shooting, the twitching, the spurting blood,

competition for the highest extermination counts,
flesh sometimes splashed on field reports,
seldom time even to save skulls with perfect teeth
for perfect paperweights,

his will be done, and kill them, something deeper dying,
but kill them, cognac and nightmares but kill them,
Eichmann's "units," the visions, the trenches
angled with ditches to drain off the human fat,

the twins and dwarfs, the dissidents *aus Nacht und Nebel,*

Professor Dr. Hans Kramer of the University of Munster
who stood on a platform to channel new arrivals—
gas chamber, forced labor, gas chamber—and later,
in special action, saw live women and children thrown into pits
and soaked with gasoline and set on fire—
Kramer, a doctor, who kept a diary filled with
"excellent lunch: tomato soup, half a hen with
potatoes and red cabbage, sweets and marvellous vanilla ice,"

while trains kept coming, families with
photograph albums falling out of the cars, the books

of the camps and prisons, the albums imprinting the air,
as here, we close our eyes, and the rain falling from photos
onto the earth, dried in the sun and raining again,
no way to them now but this way, willed chaos,

visions deeper in time than even the graves of the murdered
daughter who tells us her age,
in the round face of the man with glasses and weak chin,
Himmler, *Geheime Staats Polizie*, twisting his snake ring,

as now the millions approach, these trucks arriving with more,
these trains arriving with more, from *Prinz Albrecht Strasse*,
from the mental strain on Ohlendorf's men,
from the ravine at Babi Yar, from the future,
from the pond at Auschwitz and the clouds of ash,
from numberless mass graves where Christian prayer and Kaddish
now slow into undersong, O Deutschland, my soul, this soil
resettled forever here, remembered, poem touching the Gestapo,
the families, the children, the visions,
the visions . . .

The Children

I do not think we can save them.
I remember, within my dream, repeating
I do not think we can save them.
But our cars follow one another
over the cobblestones. Our dim
headlamps, yellow in fog, brush past,
at the center of a market square,
its cathedral's great arched doors
I know, now, this is a city
in Germany, two years
after the Crystal Night. I think ahead
to the hospital, the children.
I do not think we can save them.

Inside this dream,
in a crystal dashboard vase,
one long-stemmed rose unfolds
strata of soft red light.
Its petals fall, tears, small
flames. I cup my palm to hold them,
and my palm fills to its brim,
will overflow.
Is this the secret, then? . . .
Now I must spill the petal light, and drive.

We are here, in front of the hospital,
our engines murmuring. Inside,
I carry a child under each arm,
down stairs, out to my car.

One's right eyeball hangs on its cheek
on threads of nerve and tendon,
but he still smiles, and I love him.
The other has lost her chin—
I can see straight down her throat
to where her heart beats
black-red, black-red.
I do not think we can save them.

I am the last driver in this procession.
Many children huddle in my car.
We have left the city. Our lights
tunnel the fog beneath arches of linden,
toward Bremerhaven, toward
the western shore.
I do not think we can save them.
This time, at the thought, lights
whirl in my mirror, intense
fear, and the screams of sirens.
I begin to cry, for myself, for the children.
A voice in my dream says
this was the midnight you were born. . . .

Later, something brutal happened, of course,
but as to this life I had to, I woke,
and cannot, or will not, remember.
But the children, of course, were murdered,

their graves lost, their names lost,
even those two faces lost to me. Still,
this morning, inside the engine of my body,
for once, as I wept and breathed deep,
relief, waves of relief, as though the dreamed

rose would spill its petals forever.
I prayed thanks. For one night, at least,
I tried to save the children,
to keep them safe in my own body,
and knew I would again. Amen.

Mother and Son

The failing Long Island light
filters through catalpas along our driveway.
It must be May—the trees' white blossoms
do drift down around her, petal after petal
catching a glint of sun before
dying into ground-shadow. My mother,
now younger than I ever knew her,
looks toward me. I am not there
in body, but somehow as an eye
among the blossoms and heart-shaped leaves.
I have never seen such longing before.
She could fall among the dead petals here,
after her moment of light, and disappear
before I'm born. . . . I worry that thought
and think to speak to her. What could I say,
if I could? This is up to her.

I have awakened again, with one more after-image:
my mother's decision there in that true dream
waited for all the blossom lamps to blacken.
Then, drawing her shawl tighter around her shoulders,
she walked inside to fifty years of women's work
done each day undone. What should they have known,
the husband and children? She lived among them
almost as a stranger. . . . Only once did one
follow her far enough to read her eyes.

He could not speak to her there
where the Long Island light still holds her,
somewhere, in that driveway, wherever that light is now.
If you die before me, try to find her.
It will be a May evening, petals
glinting the last sun. Tell her, if you can,
that I have seen her there, and know.

The Berries

My wife already there to comfort,
I walked over icy roads
to our neighbor who had lost her father.
The hard winter starlight glittered, my breath
formed ascending souls that disappeared,
as he had, the eighty-year-old man
who died of cancer.

In my left coat pocket, a jar
of raspberry jam. . . . I remembered
stepping into the drooping canes, the ripe
raspberry odor. I remembered bending over,
or kneeling, to get down under the leaves
to hidden clusters. . . .

Then, and on my walk, and now, the summer berries
made/make a redness in my mind. The jar
presses light against my hip, weight
to hand to the grieving woman. This gift
to her, to me—being able to bear
the summer's berry light like that, like this,
over the ice . . .

When I was a boy, the Lord I talked to
knew me. Where is He now? I seem to have
lost Him, except for something
in that winter air, something insisting on being
there, and here—that summer's berries, that mind's
light against my hip, myself kneeling again
under the raspberry canes.

FAYE KICKNOSWAY

FAYE KICKNOSWAY *was born in Detroit in 1936, and grew up in Detroit and Los Angeles. Thinking of herself in the third person she writes: "The two cities, as well as the space between them seen from automobile windows, are major influences on her work and the choices she has made in her life. It was her family's desire that she be an artist; she went quiet instead, finally coming to the page in words. She was a student at Wayne State University and at San Francisco State College, the drive between Detroit and the Pacific Ocean having shifted north. She has done drawings for all but one of her books and exhibited in galleries, one museum show, and juried shows." Her books include* A Man Is a Hook. Trouble. *(1974),* Nothing Wakes Her *(1979),* Asparagus, Asparagus, Ah Sweet Asparagus *(1981), and* She Wears Him Fancy in Her Night Braid *(1983). Viking/Penguin will publish another collection in 1985.*
(Photo by John J. Richards)

Aside

There was a "Gracie," backwoods raw with missing teeth and lots of heavy jewelry. She was married to a short, alcoholic, Native American factory worker who was the uncle of a very good friend of mine. Her name was not Gracie, it was something more elaborate, and I am surprised that I can not remember her real name because I do remember thinking it so strange I would never forget it. I called her Gracie in the poem because of what the word "grace" signifies: to have Grace in one's soul as well as to have grace as a physical attribute. The song "Amazing Grace" also influenced me in naming her.

Gracie talked a lot. I was impressed with her teeth and how she held her head when she talked: she tilted it back and to the side. The gesture made of her face a caricature of steeple-shaped black nostrils and red-lipsticked, skinny lips puckering and stretching around a mouth which had stumpy, black teeth or no teeth at all. Her speech was country, almost sounding faked in its thickness. She had the hillbilly accent people make fun of.

She scared me. There was a force of personality, a dumped-down meanness to her which was all caged up and bewildered and lamenting. I believe now, at this distance, I heard a little of my own mother in her, that "I've-been-cheated-poor-me" voice that wants to be all fists and teeth and get even for how starved life has become. My mother's voice was the first female voice to energize me: I did not want it coming out of me. It not only came out of Gracie's mouth, where it had an intensity full of enough fire to do physical damage, but I heard that particular female voice whenever I walked down the stairs and out the front door. It was everywhere, like the noise of traffic or mosquitoes. I could white-it-out, not pay attention to it until someone like Gracie pinned me awake in front of it and cautioned me that she had been the most beautiful, succulent, virgin-female flesh God had ever created for the world to ruin.

I heard my father in her talking, too, his hillbilly tongue he wanted most in his life to disown, feeling embarrassed by it and cheated: he believed that if he had sounded more northern, he would have had the world like a fig between his teeth.

I met Gracie very briefly when I was twenty-one and did not write her down until I was either twenty-eight or twenty-nine. There were three deaths in my family: my younger brother in September, my father in November, and in February, my grandmother. The last death was the most painful. My grandmother was a doer, had no patience with sitting around and feeling sorry. She was a painter whose work never got farther than her own walls. And she was magical: what was in her house, her yard, thrived. The neighborhood children brought her injured animals to heal. There were stories, spoken matter-of-factly, that when she was a girl on the farm in Ohio she had been a beekeeper and could whistle swarming bees out of the air and into hives.

I hated that she was dead. One of my pleasures had been, each early spring, walking with her through her yard as she touched and greeted each of her plants, welcoming them back. She was seventy-two when she died and reverent and excited and totally engaged with what was around her. Unlike Gracie, who sat all folded-up and nasty.

The poem "Gracie" uses the sestina form but is not a sestina in the strictest sense. The first six end words are the end words throughout the poem and all six words appear in the tercet; however, the poem is one stanza short of the required seven stanzas and the end words do not appear in their proper end positions. When I sat down to write about Gracie, I let her talk. I noticed certain words repeated: chicken, bonnet, home. I tinkered with her as prose, but her speech on the page did not have the timing prose has, and I knew she was a poem. I forced her into quatrains and lost what had triggered the poem: my sense of her grieving for the girl she had been. The Gracie who had spoken to me about herself was the future of the "Gracie" of my poem, the future she unwittingly comes north to become. The real Gracie, grotesque and bitter, was not the voice of the poem. I pulled out the recurring words and wrote them down. Then I attached them to phrases. I looked at the story she was telling. The poem took four days and many drafts to complete.

"Mr. Muscle-On" is a real person, too. Once, in fact, I knew three of him at the same time; each had a woman in his life he completely terrorized. I think of the poem as a portrait, photographically accurate right down to his mother, before whom he was meek and submissive and Momma's sweet, sweet boy.

"In Mysterious Ways" is irreverent and as tongue-in-cheek as those sly old nursery rhymes.

"The Horse" came about because of a photograph by Walker Evans and is one of the very few poems I have written by hand, preferring the noise and combat of my old, upright Royal typewriter to a pen and paper. The poem began as one large, impenetrable block; I took it apart phrase by phrase until I was able to solve it.

"There Is No" was the fifth section of a poem the other four parts of which no longer exist.

Gracie

I mean, I'm a no shoes hillbilly an' home
is deeper in the map than Kentucky or Tennessee an'
all I been raised to do is walk the chicken
yard, spillin' grain from ma's
apron, maybe once a week wear a bonnet
into town. I have red hair an' white skin;

men lean on their elbows lookin' at me. Ma's
voice tells me, "Don't breathe so deep," an'
the preacher says how happy I'll be when I'm dead. Skin
touchin' skin is evil. I'm to keep inside the chicken
yard, no eye's to see beneath my bonnet.
Farm boys suck their cheeks an' call, "Come home

with me, I'll give you your own chicken
yard an' take you proudly once a week to town." Home
ain't enough. As I spill grain from ma's
apron, I see city streets hung with lights an'
a dark room with a window lookin' on the bonnet
of the sky. Voices stroke at my skin

through its walls. When the grain's gone from ma's
apron, I hang it on its hook by her bonnet.
I figure to be my own fare North an' leave home.
My legs are crossed under a counter. I smell chicken
fry. A man leans on his elbows; his eyes drink my skin.
In a dark room, my dress undoes my body an'

I lie with him. His hot mouth comes home
on mine. I expect to hear the preacher's or ma's
voice yellin' at me, but the only voices in the wall's skin
are strange an' soft. I have beer an' chicken
for breakfast. All day I wear his body like a bonnet.
My stockin's are run. The streets are hung with lights an'

he sleeps. I stand by the window an'
look into the night's skin, fancy home an' the chicken
yard, ma's apron an' my head cool in its bonnet.

Mr. Muscle-On,

talking his cock, talking
his legs straight across the planet.   every
step gives flowers, onion and garlic.
he piss big

as an elephant.   make shit in balloon race.   good
for you.   carries his eyes like tiny baskets
of thistles and snakes.   walks pre-occupied
through your body.   takes

large bites of your hair and your hands.   needs
you.   got so much cold in him, kills stars.   mr.
walking straight up.   mr.
meat factory.   mr.
kill them cows with a single beat of mah heart
baby.   momma, o

momma, rain coming from her mouth all over his face, spit
like you make a dog your dog, mouth
to mouth, holy joining, momma—the tit factory—holy holy,
the centerfold alive like a picture show in every drop of cock
juice.   momma, miss doughnut of 1942.   miss show her knees
for the war effort, open toe wedgies wet
as his dreams, spit them rivets
in them airplane blues: momma.   a real

pair.   boobies up his ass where it feels
so good, shes
his motorcycle, his cold metal tit, where it counts, right
between the legs.   fascinating.   balling

through traffic, wide screen, panavision, technicolor cum
backing up his kundalini,
snotting from his nose, dayglo
women with fluorescent tongues sucking it off
his face.   should

charge them cash for what they get.   better
than whiskey. mr. holy-virgin, vulture man. mr.
balls big as dishpans man.   got

hands like helicopter blades, comes
quiet to your body, his mica blood 20 degrees
below zero.   normal range.   unchanging.   says
hydrochloric words.   webs you with them.   look out.
pulls his cock out of his ass and rams it
down your throat.   gets mad at you his cum dont crack
you open, kill you dead on the spot.   mr.

white powder man, bad
dreams like arm pit steam—your
burden—snort him up, he'll keep you

down, o!
what a ride, the heliograph of your heart
goes dead, cranberry juice—chilled—at 4:30 a.m.,
in texas, a menu saying, 'thanks, call
again', is whats left of you, put
back by the salt, pepper, napkins, and ketchup.   momma
did good

by her boy, got little jars of his insides
on the kitchen stove where she can eat
on them and know hes safe.   momma dont allow no
birthday from her gut, shes all swole up
just thinking him back where he belongs.
mr. dildoe.   mr. silver bullet.   mr. keep clean
for her.   easy

does it when youre a transplant, when your face
is wallpaper with no wall behind it.
anything that comes to hand might fit.   and he
dont know no better.   momma got him dead
asleep.   hes the metal claw she operates

and she figures you as food.   look out; her
old cunt chews
like it still had teeth.

In Mysterious Ways

Condoms keep catching at the river's
skirt. And some girl, swimming

in New Jersey—a virgin who doesn't know what
it's all about, has no explanation
for anything—gets bitten
on her trunks by one of them
that's filled out
like a little fish. And it's a Miracle
a *real* Miracle,
what pops her belly out.
But no one
believes her; no one.

The Horse

He'd rent the horse and it sounding like it had asthma
and its legs shivery
and its back dropped so far your feet dragged
on the ground when you sat on it
even if you was the youngest,

he'd rent it,
touching it on its side all the way down to its tail
and back up to its neck,
picking its feet up, squinting into its face,
prying open its mouth: horse,

it was after all
a horse
and all he needed was what it was
harnessed to the plough for a couple of afternoons,
he had a hand cultivator but it was hard,
slow work; that horse,

I always waited for it to die the way it shook
and wheezed,
and he'd hit it with the harness straps
and swear at it and say he could surely do it faster,
and it would pull and rattle at the harness
and he'd have his sleeves rolled up
and be hauling back on the plough,
pulling against the horse, and the ploughshares
would dig

into the dirt
and get stuck, and he'd have the harness wrapped
around him and in his hands as well as the plough

handles, his feet braced and his legs stiff,
his hat pulled deep on his forehead,
cussing his luck for having thought to do it
this way when he had good strong kids
could pull better, the horse too old

and sick to care, and him sweatier, and finally
so mad he wasn't mad at all,
his lips tight and disappeared right off
his face and his arms lumpy with his veins
all knotted out in his skin
and his shoes unlaced and full of dirt,

him more buried and turned over than the earth,
stiff-legged and measuring nothing with his eyes
like he had done when he began,
not looking
at where the sun stood in the sky and how long

it would take to do this much and then
that much and by mid-afternoon,
if he was lucky, maybe this part here
and that would leave over there and back behind that
little U in the trees to do.
Nothing. His eyes

straight ahead and on the horse's backside,
blinking the sweat loose sometimes
but mostly letting it settle and roll down
his eyes, not looking anywhere,
turning the horse around,
pulling on the plough, loosening it,
holding onto the animal and turning it all
around
to walk back up again, dipping the ploughshares
and pushing them
so that they were into the ground
and could claw it up
and out and him

as tired by the time she made him quit
as the horse had been when he had started,
giving him water and looking at him suspicious
and cautious of his mood
and what she could do to make it better
so he wouldn't be mad supper was late
when we got home, and him saying

if that horse died
on his land, the man who owned it
had better come and clear it off
and pay him back his money
and money besides for the time lost
looking at his goddamn dead horse,
whatever possessed him to think he needed
to use it, anyway.

He'd say it as he untied the harness straps
from around his back and arms and hands,
looking down at it like he hadn't never seen it
before and didn't know maybe
it belonged on trees
or should be thrown in the water
or used in the house somehow in the winter
near the stove, it so heavy and useless,
he spoke

so flat and low with no heat in his voice,
it all burned out of him by the sun
and the work he'd done and have to do again
tomorrow and probably, by the looks of it,
the next day, too,

and he'd heard there were better ways to live,
better ways, with only looking at the fields
from automobile windows as you drove
along beside them
and pointed out the window
and wondered what that hillbilly was doing,
and he was tired
of being the hillbilly
and tired
of being tied to this useless hide

of dog food all the days of his life,
and to this small patch of land—
worthless was what it was—
and he'd drink

from the dipper and us crowded together
back where he couldn't reach us with the harness straps
if he should try, looking
at him and at her, knowing she'd handle it,
she'd even out his temper before we took the horse
back and headed for home ourselves.

And as we went back
and it darkening
his mood toward the horse
changed
and he wasn't so sour toward it, it did the best
it could, old and lame
and sick as it was. The air

was cooler
and his body and legs weren't so knotted up
nor his arms,
his sleeves rolled down, his hat
pushed back on his head, the day
didn't hurt so much thinking about it
as we walked in the slow dark
toward home.

There Is No

There is no silk nor worm to spin it.

There is no hallway
no dark
no rain
no grape or rose or hill.

There is no otter
nor ocean nor sand.

There is no onion
nor tongue.
There is no stocking

no wagon or horse
or ploughman.

There is no book
no noise in the stairwell
no neighbor
hanging wash.

There is no dream
no biscuit
nor spring nor winter air.

There is no candle
nor door closing
nor music.

There is no swan or sparrow.

There is no broom
or dust.

There is no moon
no pocket nor fence nor window.

There is no fog
no mountain grove nor fire

nor still lake.
There is no boat
nor oar nor cat
nor cargo
nor men
in caps
waiting.

PAUL MARIANI

PAUL MARIANI *was born in 1940 in New York City. His undergraduate degree is from Manhattan College, his graduate degrees from Colgate University and City University of New York. Since 1968 he has taught at the University of Massachusetts, where he is now Professor of English. "I have already spent half my life," he has written, "working out the ramifications of accepting theologically, philosophically, aesthetically, the fact of incarnation."* He has published A Commentary on the Complete Poems of Gerard Manley Hopkins *(1970),* William Carlos Williams: The Poet and His Critics *(1975), and* William Carlos Williams: A New World Naked *(1981). His books of poetry are* Timing Devices *(1979) and* Crossing Cocytus *(1982).*
(Photo by George Newton)

Breaking Bread

I need poetry in the way I need the things which sustain me day by day. Principal among these, I know, is language. Like the language I hear my wife using when she is in the kitchen telling me about her job teaching four- and five-year-olds. Or the language of my sons, the way they kid each other and me, the kinds of jokes they make, the way they play with words. Or the way they can strike at the heart of the matter and call a thing by its proper name. Or the language of friends, sometimes in letters, or on the phone, but best when I can sit and have a beer with them and talk about anything in the world. Frost understood something of this when he said that the words (he was thinking of the words of a poem, but words for all that) could be a momentary stay against confusion.

We all know that any number of agencies and institutions and businesses have designs on us and use language for the power they can have over us. When I was young I had a friend who lied to me for years. Slow to understand, it never occurred to me then that a friend could do that. But when we were older and he was studying to become a lawyer, he told me that for him language meant power, the power of getting your own point across. After all, who the hell really knew the truth about anything anyway? I could see his point, but shortly afterwards it struck me in looking back over our friendship that he'd already been doing just that for years: lying to me when it suited his purposes to do so. And while I guess I could understand his doing that, I could no longer see him as my friend. I suppose it was a question of language and its uses.

You don't have to read very many of my own poems to begin to understand that the words which make up the poem amount to a sacred text for me. When I was seventeen, I went away to Beacon, New York to study for the priesthood. By the time I was eighteen, I knew I wanted to get married . . . or that is the way I put it to myself. You understand what I mean. Ritual is still very important to me. So is discipline, sacrifice, helping the less fortunate—breaking bread and sharing it I guess you could call it. But the most important thing for who I am as a person is the power words have for good. Poetry is just such a good and so important to me that I have come in the past few years to want most of all to define myself as a poet. Please understand that I do not say this lightly. So when someone at eighteen or twenty or even thirty says to me, "I am a poet," I don't know whether to laugh or simply dismiss what he or she has just said as a faulty use of language. I guess it's the same with marriage or the priesthood or any profession. My father used to say you weren't really married until after you had a couple of kids. But I think now you are not married until you realize what marriage means: the choice—in good times and bad—to stick by the person you said yes to all those years ago. When you have been married long enough you will know what I mean.

The same is true of the poet. You work at the craft long enough, you wrestle with it, you go through long dry spells when nothing seems to work, and you wait, the way a hunter has to wait in the dark for long hours sometimes and maybe even days and weeks before (if he is lucky) the prey comes into sight. And then you have to be ready to respond to the critical moment with everything you have learned. In the meantime, you can do all sorts of other things while you are a poet. You can be a doctor (or a lawyer even) or a writer or a teacher or a book salesman or an engraver or a translator or a mother or a father or even a priest. But you will know yourself at the heart of the matter to be a poet in the way a priest is always aware of his being a priest whatever else he is doing. For if you are a poet, you must be constantly listening to the language, listening to those around you who are actually using the language, even as you listen to the presences of those masters who have preceded you and whom you must imagine yourself as passing muster for.

Once, about nine years ago, the Italian poet Giovanni Giudici stayed with me as a guest in my home for a few days. He talked in halting English and I in even more halting Italian about poetry and finally I screwed up enough courage to show him a sheaf of my poems I had until then kept hidden. He looked at them and then, later, unexpectedly, said to me: "Paul, it is time for you to stop being an altar boy and ascend the steps to become a priest." He did not have to explain that metaphor to me. A year or so later I prayed very hard (Hopkins would call this telling secrets, but so be it) that I might have the courage—and the skill—to do what I by then realized was the most important thing I could ever do: write poetry which my own exacerbated critical intelligence could live with and which might celebrate my passage through this time and place. How well that prayer was answered is for others to say. For me, it is enough to realize that at that point—almost imperceptibly—I crossed my own great divide and that—for better or worse—I can never go back now.

Coincidentally, it was also then that my parents split up after seven kids and thirty-five years of marriage. Something, I guess my whole youthful world, died then. And even though I had been married for more than a decade and had three sons of my own when the split came, I know I mourned when the cramped quarters in Mineola which we'd called home for twenty years was sold and the seven kids, one by one, left Long Island for good. On the other hand, that "death" of a family freed me to write about what was most important to me, though until then I had not admitted such a thing to myself. I mean the sacredness of human relationships, no matter how insignificant those relationships appear to the outsider, and the concomitant realization that language has the ability to kindle again what would otherwise have been only a dying memory, like an old signpost on one of the old two-lane highways we travelled in our youth. I guess it was a way, too, of going back over the things that had shaped me—and I would bet many of us—and then of making a propitiation of sorts. It was a way of saving *something* even as I had to learn to finally let it go.

With others of my poems, I have tried to look at what we call the larger issues: political issues like the bomb and gas warfare and assassinations and the war that is still going on all over the world between men and women, fathers and mothers and sons and daughters, a war which has had many more casualties than those we hear about over Sakhalin Island or in Beirut or El Salvador, as important as it is for us to be aware of those places of suffering as well. Worldsorrow is more than just a theory, I think. Great-hearted Virgil for one seems to have known there were tears for these things as well.

And then there is my self-conscious preoccupation with the language itself, with the words—with every last article and preposition—which go to make up each line and stanza and poem. How hard, Williams has told us, to keep to the edge of the advance, how easy to slip back into the old molds. Nine times out of ten, it is hard, damn hard, for me to write poems. Often, I suppose, I would prefer doing almost anything else than wrestle with words in the necessary isolation it takes to make a poem work. I am a naturally gregarious person and would prefer to spend my time with others. But if I followed my own inclinations, I could never get said what I know I must say before I die. Sometimes when I am with others, I can't believe the things I say, things which are more often than not banal or stupid or inadvertently harmful. I would almost prefer to say nothing, except that that too would be taken as anti-social behavior. I want to tell people that I love them, those I know and those I don't, and I want to tell them I care, in the way we say that good craftsmanship shows someone that the craftsperson cared about the thing he made and the person he made it for.

I try to make poems. I want people to understand them, and I want them to be able to go back to those poems time and time again and still find that the poem holds up and will not break in half the way bad workmanship so often does. I don't care how long it takes them to understand that I have been waiting for them in the poem. But after

they have examined the line breaks and the syntax and the metaphors
running through a poem and say, yes, that's a living language, that
sounds like someone talking, that sounds like a real person, an Amer-
ican speaking in the last few years of the second millenium, I hope
they will see something of themselves as well and say, well, that's how
it is sometimes, I suppose. I can understand that. If they can do that,
they will have a living text, a sacred text because whatever is human is
finally holy. But they will have a text written not in Mallarméan Latin
but in the vulgate, in the bread of a common language. I have not
forgotten those who like resonance in their poetry, who might want to
think about language as a memorial act or language as a transubstan-
tiation of the bread of experience into art. But first I want to feed the
hungry, myself included.

Golden Oldie

One of those golden oldies from the fifties
is filling up the whole inside of the station-
wagon and though it is January and iceruts
make moving difficult the one two

onetwothreefour moves me back
with my special girl at someone's wedding, my chair
pushed back against the table, keeping rough
time with a smooth spoon, olive pits

and gravy stains on the lined tablecloth,
cigarsmoke making my eyes water,
while a local threepiece band, over
the drift of chatter, the loud laugh, the one

two jiggle jiggle of the middle-aged couples
on the dancefloor, plays that same sweet tune.
No one can listen to such music and still
sit still. Even my mother and father

who have been at it ever since they left
the church have called a truce. With one arm

he helps her up and they glide together out
onto the center of the floor. You can't help

watching as they move together as one to the one
two and onetwothreefour—dragonflies skimming
over the still warm water like blue
whirrs caught in that golden light a little

boy remembers. And though the dance end
and each drift off the dancefloor, one here
one there so that the house shrink
back and suddenly grow old and the children

wither and so my mother's voice slur
into the receiver growing dim and dimmer
as the snow drifts up against her room
and my father scrape like an old record caught

in an old rut, saying I've got to make
a living to keep the house together what
can I do? one two, still, here, now,
they are keeping perfect time, my father's broad

back stretching his darkblue jacket, shiny
with the years, his capable mechanic's arm around
his young wife's waist, thick with seven kids
and God knows how many miscarriages. Now

everyone is watching them glide gracefully
across the floor. Even I am beside myself
as we cheer them on. They can dance
on and on as long as the music lasts.

The Girl Who Learned to Sing in Crow

Narcotic plash of water from the kitchen sink,
the easter blue of early morning lifting through
the open window behind the sink, those buttercups
plucked by their young and hairy stems from the border
along the rusting fence, plucked and grouped together
in her own grape jelly glass, placed just so

on the worn formica sill as in a frame. My sister's still
life, caught in this tableau gesture of doing once again
those breakfast dishes like the little mother
she used to think she was, as she sang long and softly
like the solo alto that she might have been at Mass,
like in fact a blind canary. How she sang then
with all the bright abandon of her ten and tender
years, sang then long and soft and sweetly, though
her brothers, toughened and ashamed of so much sweetness,
mocked and mimicked her in counter-song, *Caw-caw*.

No need at this great distance to rehearse the pressures
there to stun and stunt a voice. The truth is that even now
I cannot bring myself to put it down on paper. Call it
the pockmarked havoc of our growing up. Jesus, call it
whatever name you bloody please. It's all behind us anyway
and that voice is riddled through with pain. And which
of us will take the blame for the silence which says so well
how we treat our women? Who will count the costs?
As, item: how we mock them for the same courage
we ourselves have gasped after each in our locked
and airless rooms. As how we sacrifice their hopes to men
we sense are stronger than ourselves, slapping back
and rump in bawdy fellowship. So that, as sweet day
yields to day we still catch glimpses of a scrawny girl
learning how to split her tongue and caw. Hell,
we know it happens all the time. We know
just as they do it's the song birds make good eating.

The Ring

Only after, wading waist deep
through the black waters of the duck pond,
did he feel its absence first: the slight
pressure on the small finger of his right
hand gone. He would have lost it, then,

in tumbling from the peak of the covered
bridge in the shoot-out re-enactment
staged in the brilliant outdoors light

for those seven hundred spellbound
daycamp kids. He would have lost it

in the mud pushing up for air, the fall
and death of the Outlaw convincing to the kids
and to himself for the minute he was under.
Sport enough for a watermelon sort
of afternoon. But this was deadly earnest.

Forget the macho saga of the West, his boss
swinging that pearl-handled gun of his,
forget his foreman father shouting
from the stand of willows above the pond
to load the garbage truck before the dump

in Oceanside closed down. Instead he'd turned
back to the little pond, scattering
the quacking ducks, diving under time
and time again to claw at stringy weeds
and slimy rocks as he sifted for the little ring.

And so, long after the kids and counsellors
were gone and night had drifted in and he had
to give it up and tell her, though day by day,
painting fence or cleaning up the trash, he kept
staring at the pond, puzzling where the little thing

could be. Twenty years and more and that girl
his wife now and mother of their three tall sons
and still it troubles him, that highschool ring,
Mary Louis, Class of '59, a thing
worth maybe sixty bucks (if that)

at the present gold exchange, an accident
as both of them had come to understand. Forget it,
she had said, and that seemed that. . . . Except
as sign, except as something lost in that
mock-heroic falling from a height

into the duckslime water, a *prefigura*, sign
circling on itself. He might have shrugged it off,
this husband and this dedicated father, after all

the mediating years. Except, that is,
for the bent figure he sees wading wet and cold

out into the water with the evening shadows
coming on. For the hundreth and the thousandth
time he watches as the figure holds its breath
and he feels his heart begin again to pound
as he goes under one more time. His eyes

tear and his fingertips are raw
from clawing as he circles still again,
searching for the thing he cannot name
inside the little ring which would surely
hold the answer if only he could find it.

News That Stays News

I don't know but it might have been
the summer of '58, July, time thickening
or thinning the way heavy fog will on a slick
country road, the headlights spattering
as if they'd hit a wall. What I do remember
though as if it were yesterday is my father

down in the engine room under the pool
at Baumann's Summer Day Camp trying to fix
the leaking chlorine tank and fiddling
with the valves and meters, me standing
on the metal grid ladder over him my hand
on the drum door and then the thick yellow gas

seeping up to catch him staggering sideways
like some Bowery drunk gagging for air as he made it
up the steps his green mouth retching so that
he was straight out for two days. All I caught
was a mouthful of the stuff and that left me
weak-kneed and my lungs rasping, enough of a taste

so that it still smells every time I dive
into a motel pool. It was mustard gas killed
my mother's father and don't let anyone tell me

different, though it took fifteen years to do the job,
the cloud hugging the shelled ground as it rolled
in over that no-man's land with the dawn breeze

before it hunkered down on those trapped there
in the trench without their masks. Gas. Gas.
Outlawed in the twenties and then so many times again.
And now, after the Army has at last admitted
to the effects of Agent Orange on our own boys
(to say nothing of what we did to tree and Cong),

the other side is seeding its own rain of terror,
yellow spoilt-grain toxins rocketlaunched by Jeep
and helicopter into Laos and Kampuchea, Yemen
and Afghanistan, dumbstruck villagers including
pigs and babies, left to drown in their own blood,
faces gone black from that internal strangulation,

so that I sit on the edge of my easy chair before
the T.V. screen and pound the arm rest
with my clenched right fist, again, again, until
my sons start up, one from his comic book the other
from his world history homework, each wondering
what all this new commotion is about.

Then Sings My Soul

Who can tell a man's real pain
(or a woman's either) when they learn
the news that they must die? Sure
we all know none of us is going anywhere

except in a pineslab box or its fine
expensive equal. But don't we put it
off another day, and then another and another,
as I suppose we must to cope? And so

with Lenny, Leonardo Rodriguez, a man
in the old world mold, a Spaniard
of great dignity and a fine humility,
telling us on this last retreat for men

that he had finally given up praying
because he didn't want to hear
what God might want to tell him now:
that he wanted Lenny soon in spite

of the hard facts that he had his kids,
his still beautiful wife, and an agèd
mother to support. I can tell you now
it hit us hard him telling us because

for me as for the others he'd been
the model, had been a leader, raised
in the old Faith of San Juan de la Cruz
and Santa Teresa de Avila, this torreador

waving the red flag at death itself,
horns lowered and hurling down on him.
This story has no ending because there is
still life and life means hope. But

on the third day, at the last Mass, we were
all sitting in one big circle like something
out of Dante—fifty laymen, a priest, a nun—
with Guido DiPietro playing his guitar

and singing an old hymn in that tenor voice
of his, and all of us joining in at the refrain,
Then sings my soul, my Savior God to Thee,
How great Thou art, how great thou art,

and there I was on Lenny's left, listening
to him sing, his voice cracked with resignation,
how great thou art, until angry glad tears
began rolling down my face, surprising me. . . .

Lord, listen to the sound of my voice.
Grant Lenny health and long life. Or,
if not that, whatever strength and peace
he needs. His family likewise, and

his friends. Grant me too the courage
to face death when it shall notice me,

when I shall still not understand why
there is so much sorrow in the world.

Teach me to stare down those lowered horns
on the deadend street that shall have no alleys
and no open doors. And grant me the courage
then to still sing to thee, *how great thou art.*

WILLIAM MATTHEWS

WILLIAM MATTHEWS *was born in Cincinnati in 1942. He holds degrees from Yale University and the University of North Carolina at Chapel Hill. He has taught at Wells, Cornell, Sarah Lawrence, and the Universities of Colorado, Iowa, Washington, and Houston. "Just as an architect uses walls to organize space," he has said, "I use the words of a poem to organize silences. . . . These mute events are closely linked to the silences and strange landscapes in the natural world. That natural world, to an American, is large, often melodramatic, and strange—even in the most settled regions, where I have spent most of my life." He has published many volumes of poetry, including* Ruining the New Road *(1970),* Sleek for the Long Flight *(1972),* Sticks and Stones *(1975),* Rising and Falling *(1979),* Flood *(1982), and* A Happy Childhood *(1984).*
(Photo by Arlene Modica)

Generations

I don't know who the other poets in this anthology will be, but if they, like me, are around forty, then we're beginning to belong to a generation, in the full sense of that word, for the first time. Earlier, we were of course more generated than generating. Understandably, since as James Wright used to say, "it takes a long time to live," we made our poems to find out what we were made of. The answers turned out not to be surprising: our families, our experience, our reading, our courage, our failures and losses and what accommodations we made with them. But we needed to make them *our* answers; writers are stubborn that way, like most people.

In every generation of poets there is far more talent when the generation is thirty than there is achievement when the generation is sixty. It's interesting to wonder why this should be so. John Logan's essay "On Poets and Poetry Today" (1971) offers a suggestive psychological hypothesis.

The body of work a poet makes, argues Logan, is the body of the opposite-sex parent. Thus, for Sylvia Plath, the colossus was the body of her father. His argument works even better for male poets (this fact and something rather creakily mechanical about the psychoanalytic vocabulary he uses are liabilities to his hypothesis), for in recreating the upper half of the mother in their early work, they can express their nostalgia for the breast and motherly nurture. To recreate the lower half of the mother is more difficult work.

> But oftentimes the poet would rather die than face the sexuality of the mother (and hence, of the parents together), which keeps him separated from her in tragic fashion. He chooses death over the tragic encounter, remaining a lyric poet, holding onto his melancholy for dear life. . . .

We could also note that every poet is given, by life, and far earlier in life than a beginning poet is old enough to be a beginning poet, a large chunk of the material necessary for making a body of work: childhood, coming into sexual life, the recognition of mortality, etc. Such material doesn't need to be discovered; in fact, it forces itself upon us. And since it is made up of rites and passages central to us all, good poems shaped from such material are likely to find ready sympathy and assent from readers. Some of the appeal of such poems is how they unite us, like stories told by schoolmates or army buddies— stories that stress common experience and suppress the many distinc-

tions between schoolmates and army buddies that will, outside school
or the army, provide them very divergent experiences.

For if we seem to grow up in ways more or less like each other, by
contrast our lives as grown-ups are very disparate, idiosyncratic,
handmade, not always easy to understand. One could list the same
adjectives to describe fully made bodies of work by mature poets. We
read them because they illuminate our lives, but what we recognize in
them is not our own confirmed experience, but how Marianne
Moore's work, let's say, could have been fashioned only by Marianne
Moore. We recognize the world we share with her in her poems, but
we recognize, too, that only she could have shown us the world that
way, and that without her our world would be smaller. This is an
almost wholly opposite reaction to the one we have reading rites of
passage poems by younger poets, in which we recognize ourselves and
say, more or less contentedly, "what a small world."

It isn't that the poet's later work will have a less intimate relation to
the poet's experience, I imagine, but that the imagination—which fed
at first almost wholly on experience—widens as well as it deepens, and
finds more and more sustenance in its own creations. What we get
from fully matured poets is not a life—someone who comes after
writes that—but a body of work, which, by a cruel and paradoxical
compensation, grows strong and thoroughly articulated as the poet's
own body degenerates. Of course the poet's body does that no matter
what.

What lies before us we can only know by going there, it's banal to
say but important to remember. This prediction seems germane: our
most difficult and interesting work, and with luck our most joyful
work, is only now beginning.

The Search Party

I wondered if the others felt
as heroic
and as safe: my unmangled family
slept while I slid uncertain feet ahead
behind my flashlight's beam.
Stones, thick roots as twisted as
a ruined body,
what did I fear?

I hoped my batteries
had eight more lives
than the lost child.
I feared I'd find something.

Reader, by now you must be sure
you know just where we are,
deep in symbolic woods.
Irony, self-accusation,
someone else's suffering.
The search is that of art.

You're wrong, though it's
an intelligent mistake.
There was a real lost child.
I don't want to swaddle it
in metaphor.
I'm just a journalist
who can't believe in objectivity.
I'm in these poems
because I'm in my life.
But I digress.

A man four volunteers
to the left of me
made the discovery.

We circled in like waves
returning to the parent shock.
You've read this far, you might as well
have been there too. Your eyes accuse
me of false chase. Come off it,
you're the one who thought it wouldn't
matter what we found.
Though we came with lights
and tongues thick in our heads,
the issue was a human life.
The child was still
alive. Admit you're glad.

Bring the War Home

In its tenth year we realize
the war will always live with us,
some drooling Uncle Cockroach
who won't die.
Why should he? We don't want to.
He's our obvious secret,
an insect in amber,
a bad marriage the kids
won't believe we fought
for their sakes.
It's too late for them to take
their country back, its three-legged
dogs and seedlings and medical
techniques you couldn't learn
in three decades of peace.
They're ours—didn't we
save their lives?
And we are theirs.
Our guilt is the heroin of Vietnam,
the best smack on the streets.

Taking the Train Home

1.
Dusk grew on the window.
I'd listen for the click
of the seams in the rails
to come at the same speed
the telephone wires sagged
and then shot upward to the pole.
All night I slept between
the rails, a boy on a stretcher.
When I'd wake up outside
Chillicothe I felt like a fish.
Alfalfa and cows peered in
as I went by in my
aquarium, my night
in glass. Dawn flew against

my window the same way
a fly swarms by itself
against the heat of a bare
light bulb, like a heart attack.
I'd be home soon, 7:15,
all out for Cincinnati.

2.
It's Sunday and I'm only four
and my grandparents are taking
me to Sharonville, to the roundhouse.
Pop drives. The part in the white crest
of his hair is like a compass needle.
Non sings. From the back seat
I lean between them, I can
feel the soot, the cinders
like black popcorn under my feet.
The roundhouse ceiling is charred
by sparks, and grime
smears its highest windows.
Coalcars smolder on sidings
while the engine turns
away from its arrival.

I was going to live in a roundhouse
when I grew up, a lighthouse.
Every morning the moon
would steam in over the sea
and turn around.
The table would be set for breakfast
before I went to bed,
my little tower of pills
beside the juice glass.
My hair would be white, like Pop's,
and by its light the ships,
long pods of sleep and fuel oil,
coffee beans, brooms
with real straw,
by the light of my hair
ships would sleep into port
and germinate.

3.
In my dream I'm only four
again, Pop is alive.
He walks slowly—emphysema.
I've eaten something
metallic, something
I don't understand.
I circle away from him
to vomit among roadside weeds.
I force it up.
It's like gruel, with roofing nails
for lumps.
I love this dying man.
I look up and he bobs over a wave
in the road, he's swimming
out to sea. I begin
following but my legs are too short,
death is my father,
this is my body
which will fall apart.
I'm sleeping on the ocean.
I'm asleep on a train
outside Red Lion, Ohio.
I don't know; I can't tell,
but it seems to me
that if I could watch my body sleep
it would glow,
growing its antibodies
to eternal life,
growing the lives we give away
when we wake.

In Memory of the Utah Stars

Each of them must have terrified
his parents by being so big, obsessive
and exact so young, already gone
and leaving, like a big tipper,
that huge changeling's body in his place.
The prince of bone spurs and bad knees.

The year I first saw them play
Malone was a high school freshman,
already too big for any bed,
14, a natural resource.
You have to learn not to
apologize, a form of vanity.
You flare up in the lane, exotic
anywhere else. You roll the ball
off fingers twice as long as your
girlfriend's. Great touch for a big man,
says some jerk. Now they're defunct
and Moses Malone, boy wonder at 19,
rises at 20 from the St. Louis bench,
his pet of a body grown sullen
as fast as it grew up.

Something in you remembers every
time the ball left your fingertips
wrong and nothing the ball
can do in the air will change that.
You watch it set, stupid moon,
the way you watch yourself
in a recurring dream.
You never lose your touch
or forget how taxed bodies
go at the same pace they owe,
how brutally well the universe
works to be beautiful,
how we metabolize loss
as fast as we have to.

Living Among the Dead

> *There is another world,*
> *but it is in this one.*
> Paul Eluard

First there were those who died
before I was born.
It was as if they had just left
and their shadows would

slip out after them
under the door so recently closed
the air in its path was still
swirling to rest.
Some of the furniture came from them,
I was told, and one day
I opened two chests
of drawers to learn what the dead kept.

But it was when I learned to read
that I began always
to live among the dead.
I remember Rapunzel,
the improved animals
in the *Just-So Stories*, and a flock
of birds that saved themselves
from a hunter by flying in place
in the shape of a tree,
their wings imitating the whisk
of wind in the leaves.

My sons and I are like some wine
the dead have already bottled.
They wish us well, but there is nothing
they can do for us.
Sebastian cries in his sleep,
I bring him into my bed,
talk to him, rub his back.
To help his sons live easily
among the dead is a father's great work.
Now Sebastian drifts, soon he'll sleep.
We can almost hear the dead
breathing. They sound like water
under a ship at sea.

To love the dead is easy.
They are final, perfect.
But to love a child
is sometimes to fail at love
while the dead look on
with their abstract sorrow.

To love a child is to turn
away from the patient dead.
It is to sleep carefully
in case he cries.

Later, when my sons are grown
among their own dead, I can
dive easily into sleep and loll
among the coral of my dreams
growing on themselves
until at the end
I almost never dream of anyone,
except my sons,
who is still alive.

Unrelenting Flood

Black key. White key. No,
that's wrong. It's all tactile;
it's not the information
of each struck key we love,
but how the mind and leavened
heart travel by information.
Think how blind and near-
blind pianists range along
their keyboards by clambering
over notes a sighted man
would notice to leave out,
by stringing it all on one
longing, the way bee-fingered,
blind, mountainous Art
Tatum did, the way we like
joy to arrive: in such
unrelenting flood the only
way we can describe it
is by music or another
beautiful abstraction,
like the ray of sunlight
in a child's drawing
running straight to a pig's ear,
tethering us all to our star.

HEATHER McHUGH

HEATHER MCHUGH *was born in San Diego in 1948 and raised in southern Virginia. A graduate of Radcliffe College and the University of Denver, she has been a MacDowell Colony fellow and has won an NEA grant. She has taught at Antioch College, Stephens College, SUNY at Binghampton, and the University of Washington, where she is currently Milliman Writer-in-Residence. She is the translator of D'Après Tout:* Poems by Jean Follain *(1981). Discussing a particular Follain poem, she says that it can "be read as an account of the act of poetry itself, moving from solitude to community through its audiences, altering their experience of the world." Her books of poetry are* Dangers *(1977) and* A World of Difference *(1981).*
(Photo by J. Mirskin)

Sound Off

I began to write because I was too shy to talk, and too lonely not to send messages. I come from parents with no history of kidding; what they raised, between the two of them, were voices. My own voice fell into broken English, wrecked études, odd body parts. I went to my room to compose myself, composing in the process counterparts, voices raised only in refrain.

All thought is fore- or afterthought, I think, but poems happen (Wordsworth notwithstanding) *in flagrante delicto.* As I look over this present sampling (some from before I reached majority) I sense the risks of having written poems since I was six: the risks of habit and of toying; risk the *enfant terrible* might turn out to be just *vieux terrible,* perfectly postcocious; risk of taking decibels for power, and deafening a listener to the intricate. But every writer's signature weaknesses suggest a signature strength: my hope's for force of feeling, in a force of form.

I see in this selection lots of sex and song, in which two impulses I've always found the greatest occasions for human boundlessness, the biggest jumps for joy, the deepest powers to reconcile. Sex and song could breach the reticences of episcopal decorum, quake the English gardens, burn the bush. Maybe only people who get too good at crawling finally have to strut so bad; maybe only the one who memorized somebody else's catechisms and who knew by heart the hundred prepositions, develops the devilish urge to ask the nun what the positions are (say 69, and missionary). "I remember Rodin / telling me one day with a cocky air / (we were at Chartres, taking the train) / that, being too pure, the cathedral provoked / winds of disdain." (Rilke's French, my translation). Schooling made me the quiet queen of yeses and nos, the little professor of right and wrong. Today I struggle with that legacy—the academic knack for revising the mess of the real world out (since the real world will not fall on only one hand or the other) and the trouble of real love, too (neither all nor nothing, my pet bailiwicks, but more importantly, more negotiably, some some). The trouble with mind, says Bierce, is it only has itself to know itself with. Raised on brain waves, making odes to diodes, deriving my sense of consequence from sequence, stuck on time, I plowed myself a rut of thought it's hard to climb from (etymology of delirium): the rut of easy twos, exclusive twos, marked by beginning and end, impress of poet and priest, though the world be one and numberless.

For opposites are intimates—occurring, not in nature, but only in the heady realm of simple absolutes (my old quicksand of stomping-ground). The superpowers (call them Good and Evil) are so similar they frame each other's thoughts; the thumbs we call opposable are twins. God save us from our righteousness, the languages of brutal black and white, while all the world turns gray.

Poems are not proper. They are not proper to. They are not proper to the self, particularly. In a house, I look for windows, because I look for what is not its own most fond and most consuming subject, and because I love what holds light (= lets light through). In a land, I look for water; in a word, for what moves.

Nor, as Aldous Huxley says, am I captain of my soul. I am only its noisiest passenger.

Squeal

She rides the last few minutes
hard, pressing her heels
in the stirrups, keeping
what she can concealed, a stone
hidden in a fist. But she's grown
too big, the room too cramped,
the body too well lit
with wet. A man has got a hand
in her again, he wants to pick
her pocket, leave her flat.
The room begins to heave, the white
elastic walls of senses wow,
the words well up, the skin
begins to give and give until the sheet-
rock splits, the last uncommon
syllable is leaking from her lips:
her body breaks in two. Spectators
grin. The sex is speakable.
The secret's out.

Gig at Big Al's

There is a special privacy on stage.
Wearing little, then less, then

nudity's silver high-heeled shoes,
I dance to myself: the men

posed below at tables
with assessors' gazes and the paycheck's
sure prerogatives are dreams
I've realized, my chosen

people, made-up eyes, my fantasies.
I pull down dark around the room.
I turn on sex's juke two-step.
I set foot on the spotlight's

isolated space and grease
my hips and lick my legs. With a
whiplash of gin in the first row anyone
can beat around the bush, can buy

my brand of loneliness, all possible
circumlocutions of crotch. No one
can touch me, by law
I cannot touch myself. So none

of it is public, not until
in one side door
on his soft shoes
my lover comes to watch.

Having Read Books

It is dangerous to stand in early fall
under apple trees in a field.
In the backyard they shoot
fruit. It is dangerous to jack
the old car up in its old barn, and the baled
hay rotting overhead in its stall
is more dangerous than books. You come
right through the door into my house
with that seedy look, those eyes
green-gardened with intelligence, and some
deep danger in the way that you are learned.
I have stood under the trees,

borrowed time in the barn
and breathed grease,
and I am not about to turn
careful today. Grabbing your arm,
dragging you outside, without
thought, I take
the risk of you in the hay's rot.

Message at Sunset for Bishop Berkeley

How could nothing turn so gold?
You say my eyelid shuts the sky;
in solid dark I see stars
as perforations, loneliness
as blues, what isn't
as a heavy weight, what is
as nothing if it's not ephemeral.

But still the winter world
could turn your corneas to ice.
Let sense be made. The summer sun
will drive its splinters straight
into your brain. Let sense be made.
I'm saying vision isn't insight,
buried at last in the first
person's eye. You

should see it: the sky
is really something.

Brightness

Before history,
before you counted,
March was a day that went
lazing through slow
grades of gold.

The schoolyard wall

stood out so sharp
in some lights it could cut;
the sky kept cool
reserves of gauze and tincture.

Then a day was all you had.
You thought it huge.
And those forsythia—
so many whips about
to snap out yellow sound you felt

no one could sum them up.

Meantime

In the days when everyone said
oh boy and gee, when women
were stoled and muffed
and men would be men,
the hurricane her seventh birthday

was her first idea of sex—
that undomesticated power no one
could withstand, whose outskirts
bedraggled the trees. She suffered
an infatuation. Many ladies later,

she'd recall the proper name for this,
but in the meantime, something
had to be made of boys, who kept
cropping up. Windmill of ankles
and wrists, she had to turn

thirteen.

The Fence

Suddening one day by myself
I took my girlhood off and came

to understand the slugfests
of the forked and haloed boys.

I fell in love, by accident
and by design: its physics
was mishap. Every feather
of our burning wings was fixed

in Fibonacci series; every bush
was script with lash and spine.
It all made sense! My animals
danced, my spirits were artless,

I ran between them,
drumming the uprights of the fence.

Form

We were wrong to think
form a frame, a still
shot of the late
beloved, or the pot thrown
around water. We wanted
to hold what we had.

But the clay contains
the breaking, and the man
is dead—the scrapbook
has him—and the form of life
is a motion. So from all this
sadness, the bed being touched,

the mirror being filled,
we learn what carrying on
is for. We move, we are moved.
It runs in the family.
For the life of us
we cannot stand to stay.

Breath

What I want from God, feared to be
unlovable, is none of the body's
business, nasty lunches
of blood and host, and none

of the yes-man networks,
neural, capillary or electric.
No little histories recited
in the temple, in the neck and wrist.

I want the heavy air,
unhymned, uncyclical,
the deep kiss—absence's.
I want to be rid of men,

who seem friendly but die,
and rid of my studies
wired for sound; and ready for the space
in which all names for worship

sink away, and earth recedes
to silver vanishing, the point
at which we can forget

our history of longing
and become
his great blue breath,
his ghost and only song.

I Knew I'd Sing

A few sashay, a few finagle.
Some make whoopee, some
make good. But most
make diddly-squat. I tell you this

is what I love
about America—the words it puts

in my mouth, the mouth where once
my mother rubbed

a word away with soap. The word
was cunt. She stuck that great
big bar in there until there was
no hole to speak of, so

she hoped. But still I'm full
of it—the cunt, the prick,
short u, and short i, the words
for her and him. I loved

the things they must have done,
the love they must have made
to make an example of me.
After my lunch of Ivory I said

vagina for a day or two, but knew
from that day forth which word
struck home like sex itself. I knew
when I was big, I'd sing

a song in praise of cunt. I'd want
to keep my word, the one with teeth in it.
And even after I was raised, I swore,
nothing, but nothing, would be beneath me.

SANDRA McPHERSON

SANDRA McPHERSON *was born in San Jose, California, in 1943. After graduating from San Jose State College, she studied at the University of Washington in Seattle. She has received grants from the Ingram Merrill Foundation, the National Endowment for the Arts, and the Guggenheim Foundation, has taught at the University of Iowa and the University of California, Berkeley. Her collections of poetry are* Elegies for the Hot Season *(1970),* Radiation *(1973),* The Year of Our Birth *(1978),* Sensing *(1980), and* Patron Happiness *(1983). She lives with her husband and daughter in Portland, Oregon, where she teaches and freelances.*

(Photo by Henry Carlile)

A Little Help from Your Subjects

I like to read poems first with my senses, not with my analyzing intellect. So "Poppies" starts with a color. That poem is one of my earliest fully realized writings. I was maybe twenty-two when I wore a loud orange raincoat up from California to attend school in Seattle; it used to be one of my favorite colors. A year later I was married and working on this poem. Poppies must not be picked in California; they are the state flower. But in Washington they were fair game. Now I would never pick wildflowers, but in 1967 I wanted to observe them close at hand. In three days the poppies went through the surprising motions described in the poem. Afterward I developed the theory that the subject of your poem helps you by writing at least half of the poem.

In "His Body" this theory was certainly proved. I did the observation and the poem was quickly written—in half an hour as opposed to the usual period of one month to three years. I also wrote it with the energy of conviction that men's bodies had not been poetically documented as much as women's bodies. This was new territory. I would like to see other poems explicitly describing bodies, by other poets. In the seventies, I think, "body" became an easy magic word in hundreds of people's poems, but I don't like the word alone like that: I want particulars.

Camping in the San Juan Islands off Washington, I saw a dead crow being consumed by many small consumers, like shoplifters in a meat market. "Letter with a Black Border" was the second in a series of letter-form poems I developed around 1970 and continue to write variations on. I could sandwich a letter of different content in between opening and closing stanzas telling a separate story. Every detail did not have to "fit." "Open Casket" develops this form again, several years later. When writing the parts in "Letter" about the crow, I felt frightened, especially by the final image of the motorcade of mourners. The "filling" comes from details I had seen while exploring other parts of the West—the Whitman memorial in eastern Washington and a battlefield in the Big Hole country of Montana.

"Centerfold Reflected in a Jet Window" uses another relative of mine, my late paternal grandmother, in the last stanza. I began the poem with no preconceptions about how it might end. What interests me about its manner of composition is this: it is possible to begin a poem which has no end because the material "right" for the ending hasn't happened yet. I had not lived the ending yet, only the beginning and middle (both roughed out on the plane whose window was reflecting the *Playboy* centerfold in the hands of the man in front of me). When my grandmother died, I pictured her flying alongside heaven and I thought of her familial affection as the third love story in the poem. The metal shoulders were the hangers in her closet, still wearing her dresses after her death.

Her husband's funeral twenty years earlier is the subject of "Open Casket." I was twelve; it was my first and only open casket funeral. Seeing down into death, I thought, was like being in the glass-bottomed boat I took also as a child in Monterey Bay. Coincidences were the green-filtered colors of tidal animals and the unreal hues the faces of the dead are painted. The penultimate word "vacation" took on the second meaning of vacating the living body in this context. Many California memories came back with the exploration of the funeral's relationship to the boat: bus journeys, field trips, and the colors of each one. As if I were looking through a window into the home movie of my memory . . .

When Elizabeth Bishop died unexpectedly in 1979, I wanted to preserve some memories I had of her. My husband and I met in the first class she ever taught, winter term 1966, University of Washington. We once had a conference in her apartment. She had brought only a few possessions up from Brazil. Her prize one was a black madonna. I was pleased to be able to layer the poem "For Elizabeth Bishop" with descriptions of the globe because she so liked to travel, liked maps, etc. The objects tell most of the story. They are trustworthy and suggestive objects; they contain ideas but are a whole lot more attractive than ideas.

The background to "Wings and Seeds" is the discovery of the identity of my birthparents when I was thirty-seven years old. Adopted at birth, I was raised by a caring family and seldom thought about searching for my original parents. But in my thirties I began to wonder if that mysterious man and woman thought like me. So I searched. Our meeting was a comfortable and fascinating one. It seems one can be by heredity a birdwatcher. My birthmother, my daughter, and myself all came from accidental pregnancies. I liked that very much and discovered that it permitted the meeting of opposites in the last two lines of "Wings and Seeds."

When amused or moved by my own poems, I don't feel like the author of the elements that have the power to touch me as a reader. I feel instead that things speak for themselves. But I still must elect our plain American vernacular Queen for a Day, clothe her in graceful sentences, teach her to speak with the freshest vocabulary. I must give her a day away from idiomatic boring chores and let her have a night in which she is the enchantment.

Poppies

Orange is the single-hearted color. I remember
How I found them in a vein beside the railroad,
A bumble-bee fumbling for a foothold
While the poppies' petals flagged beneath his boot.

I brought three poppies home and two buds still sheathed.
I amputated them above the root. They lived on artlessly
Beside the window for a while, blazing orange, bearing me
No malice. Each four-fanned surface opened

To the light. They were bright as any orange grove.
I watched them day and night stretch open and tuck shut
With no roots to grip, like laboratory frogs' legs twitching
Or like red beheaded hens still hopping on sheer nerves.

On the third afternoon one bud tore off its green glove
And burst out brazen as Baby New Year.
Two other poppies dropped their petals, leaving four
Scribbly yellow streamers on a purple-brimmed and green

Conical cadaver like a New Year's hat.
I'd meant to celebrate with them, but they seemed
So suddenly tired, these aging ladies in crocheted
Shawl leaves. They'd once been golden as the streets

Of heaven, now they were as hollow.
They couldn't pull together for a last good-bye.
I had outlived them and had only their letters to read,
Fallen around the vase, saying they were sorry.

His Body

He doesn't like it, of course—
Others, who don't wear it but see it, do.
He's pale, like a big desert, but you can find flowers.
No, not entirely pale:
Between shin and ankle the twin sun marks;
And where his shirt (now draped from a chair back)

Was, he contrasts with dark hands
And neck/face
Like a rained-on street where a car has just been driven
Away.
Don't picture a beer paunch.
And he is a smooth animal, or soft where he isn't smooth,
Down to his toadskin testicles.
He lies prone on clean bedsheets.
There is a single light in the room.
Now run your hand down his back, its small, and up
The hips and over. Their sheen's like that
On blue metal music boxes made to hold powder.
But the rest of him is sprouted with black down-going hair,
His whiskers in so many foxholes,
Eager to out.
Are they in any order?
Age has so far
Remained locked inside.
I'm not a doctor
And glad not to have a doctor's viewpoint.
I'm glad I haven't the petite,
Overwhelmed sight of an antibody.
And yet I'm not just anybody perusing his body—
I have a reason to like it better than I like other bodies.
Someone else can praise those,
Each lonely and earthly, wanting to be celestial.

Letter with a Black Border

Black centipedal bugs
Round the corner of a feather,
Turning their bodies like silverfish—
Otherwise they might be buses
Disappearing down a dark street.
To them it is crow city,
Pinions that may last as long as a building.

   I could mail this letter there.

   I was going to send you the green trees
   But they were shaking.

I wanted to give you the wheat fields of Washington
But the Whitmans were massacred.
And the rattlers took everyone
The long way home.
And the squirrels ran down
Like snow in spring.
All of the rivers had battles;
I wanted to send you the trees
That hid the heroes.

The wild mint sends its own purple message
On runners.

Along an elegant white rib one vermin goes
Like a hearse over the bridge
In the city.

Its lights are on
But you do not know
A single one of the mourners.

Centerfold Reflected in a Jet Window

There is someone naked flying alongside the airplane.
The man in the seat in front of me is trying to hold her.
But she reflects, she is below zero, would freeze the skin
off his tongue.

Beside me also someone is flying.
And I don't say, "Put on your sweater."
And I don't say, "Come back in this minute,"
though she is my daughter.

And there is an old woman riding inside the earth.
Metal shoulders wear her dresses.
She believed she would be an old woman flying alongside heaven
because she loved, because she had always loved.

Open Casket

To see the anemones, urchins, and crabs
take the Pacific Grove
glass-bottomed boat.
The colors are extraordinary
for the glass rejects the surface
of crumpled brine
and substitutes a clear view of
each thing's design
in water-oiled harmony
of movement and pigment.

So much cooler
than riding the bus
between Santa Barbara and San Jose,
the poor leaving the rich
to go back where we belong.
Leaving and entering towns
by undersized roads,
passing through dark bean fields
worked below the hard dust
of hills, subsisting on coffee
cream, we read the depot literature
of miraculous healing,
in the night heat only a jeweler's window
filled with amethysts
frosts over.

Or San Jose to Sacramento,
reading the Gospel of John
in a little red pocket version,
going to slide along the floors
of the gold and white capitol,
all the state's children gathered under one roof
and made to think of poppies and mountains.
Certainly too many people—
each someday living
beyond another, being
ready to write a book like John's
to the friend who comes back.

White salts and rusts and mires
where the rivers used to be . . .

Thin wildflowers
and our colored pencils in the grass . . .

But in Monterey Bay,
in the brine the sun has turned
gray, blue, and green at once
like the window of a Greyhound bus,
there's a way to see down in.
How close the slightly unreal colors come,
the spines' red-violet and the blue-black
of shells. It is summer and
vacation there.

for EWM d. 1956

For Elizabeth Bishop

The child I left your class to have
Later had a habit of sleeping
With her arms around a globe
She'd unscrewed, dropped, and dented.
I always felt she *could* possess it,
The pink countries and the mauve
And the ocean which got to keep its blue.
Coming from the Southern Hemisphere to teach,
Which you had never had to do, you took
A bare-walled room, alone, its northern
Windowscapes as gray as walls.
To decorate, you'd only brought a black madonna.
I thought you must have skipped summer that year,
Southern winter, southern spring, then north
For winter over again. Still, it pleased you
To take credit for introducing us,
And later to bring our daughter a small flipbook
Of partners dancing, and a ring
With a secret whistle.—All are
Broken now like her globe, but she remembers
Them as I recall the black madonna

Facing you across the room so that
In a way you had the dark fertile life
You were always giving gifts to.
Your smaller admirer off to school,
I take the globe and roll it away: where
On it now is someone like you?

Wings and Seeds

Hiking a levee through the salt marsh,
My birthmother and I. She is not teaching
Me to read and write but to believe
The hummingbird mistrusts its feet,
Weak below its feisty wings.

We trample brass buttons and chamomile,
As if to concern ourselves no more
With clothing and tea.
We twine hands, we trade heavy binoculars.
The clouds are coming from far out on the sea
Where they'd only the fetch to ruffle.

Separately our lives have passed from earthy passion
To wilder highliving creatures with wings.
With our early expectancies
Did we come to think ourselves a flight of nature?

Terns flash here, four dolled-up stilts in a pool,
Dozens of godwits a thick golden hem on the bay—
You'd think we too knew how to find
Our way back to this home ground.

I was a child of pleasure.
The strong pleasurable seeds of life
Found each other.
And I was created by passion's impatience
For the long wait till our meeting.

JUDITH MINTY

JUDITH MINTY *was born in Detroit in 1937. She has degrees from Ithaca College and Western Michigan University.* Her first book, Lake Songs and Other Fears, *won the United States Award for 1973 of The International Poetry Forum.* Her other books of poetry include Yellow Dog Journal *(1979),* Letters to My Daughters *(1980), and* In the Presence of Mothers *(1981). Though, as she once wrote, she has "lived in/loved one place most in my life"—the lake country of northern Michigan—to earn her living she has had to become one of the many wandering poets of her generation. She has taught at the University of California at Santa Cruz, Syracuse University, Thomas Jefferson College at Grand Valley State Colleges, Central Michigan University, Humboldt State University, and elsewhere.*

(Photo by Ann Minty)

About "Orchids"

"Orchids" was written over a five-year period, from 1976 to 1981. Here are two journal entries that, I think, relate to the poem:

12-8-76. Though I sailed on his boat a few times, I barely knew him, and I've come to the funeral more to comfort K_____ than anything else. She was closer to her father than any of his sons were and her back is the straightest in the front pew. She's as stoic as he was.

These are my townspeople. I can greet everyone here by name. This church fills with thick notes from the organ, statues and stained glass, painted angels on the ceiling. I remember the tilt of his head, the squint of his eyes, as he lined up telltales on the jib and set his course in the wind.

I haven't received communion since I married. My own parents grow old in Detroit. His coffin is covered by a pall and the priest sprinkles holy water on it. The altar boys pass with the cross and the paschal candle. The censer swings. I genuflect. I strike my breast and the Latin words return: *et cum spiritu tuo.*

One winter, my father flooded the whole backyard for a skating rink. Summers, we'd go camping in the Blue Moon trailer. He showed me how to mark trails in the woods—spruce, crooked stump, rock. "Learn to walk without snapping twigs," he said.

9-28-80. Today I visit my friend R_____ who has cancer. She's shared this bedroom for twenty years with her husband. She's sleeping when I enter, curled up like a child in her adult crib. Today she wears a crocheted bonnet; there's no need for the wig anymore.

I sit close to the bars of her bed. She hears my voice and stirs and opens her lovely eyes. I'm not sure she recognizes me, but she smiles. Months ago, she stood fiercely against this illness and wouldn't let it push her around. Weeks ago, she came to my house and we drank tea together. Today is different. It's too hard. Now she can't speak. She doesn't want to move. I try to keep my voice from quivering; I want to be as strong as she is. I tell her that the pines outside her window are beautiful. I tell her about finding a puffball and some boletes. She's smiling. I would like to touch her hand, but it's hidden under the yellow blanket; so I talk some more, about the goldeneyes nesting in the reeds at her shoreline.

I would like to hold my friend in my arms. I would like to pick up this frail body that doesn't belong to her, lift her from this damned bed and carry her—out of this room and down to the lake where water moves in its secret rhythms. I would like to breathe her back to health again.

Instead, I tell her about when I was a child—how I got up early and waited in the woods for deer to pass on their way to the river. I tell her they came, though I'm not sure that's the truth. But I'd like her to smile again. I'd like her to smile, if she can.

The End of Summer

1.
The old bitch labrador swims
in heavy circles. Under water
her legs run free without their limp.
She stretches brown eyes toward me,
snorting, and the stick I throw
stirs gray memories of ten Octobers,
ducks that fly at the sun and fall.

2.
On the Pere Marquette River, salmon
quiver upstream from the lake, return
to alpha. At the dam
they leap and throw themselves
through currents, stretch
and spend themselves
against the torrent from the falls.

3.
All week the sky has filled
with orange petals. Butterflies
floating in cycles toward milkweed,
monarchs freed from their chrysalis,
waiting for the wind's current
to die. The beach
is covered with torn wings.

4.
Fire, off the merganser's hood.
This summer he nested

in our channel, drifted
with the half-tame mallards. His sharp bill
stabs water to catch bread I throw.
But he belongs by the sea. I want him
to fly now, before October and guns.

Wounds

> *Daughters of Jerusalem, do not weep for me,*
> *but weep for yourselves, and for your children.*
> —Luke, ch. 23

She has been bleeding
for ten days in Mexico.
Ashamed to speak of it, she follows
the coastline with him
and covers her wound,
stops it up
like a crack in a seawall.

Smiling, touching his hand, she
pretends there is no sickness
in her belly, in that ocean
where I swam. She walks
the shore with him,
drives through dusty towns
and climbs cathedral steps.

She prays to the child and weeps
for nails in hands and feet.
Today in the kitchen, "Oh Christ,"
I cut my finger. I bound it
to stop the bleeding
and told my daughter
it was nothing.

In my sleep I am crying. Nightmares
cannot be stopped up.
There is a child
in a boat. The boat
is sinking, slipping

into the water. There is no one
to hear. The water is red.

Prowling the Ridge

You, husband, lying next to
me in our bed, growl
like a wild dog or wolf
as you travel the woods
of your dream.
I feel your legs running
from or after some

thing. Now you turn
and curl toward the moon.
Away from me, you
prowl along ridges, hunt
with the pack. You rest
your paws on wild fur, bare
teeth to raw meat.

If I reach out and touch
the curve of your haunch,
brush my hand over your skin,
I can tame you
back to this room, to this wife
still outside
your blanket of sleep.

But it's your dream
I burn for, the other
place and time.
Wolf, leave tracks now. Quick.
Let me follow your scent.

Burning Against the Wind

You must burn against the wind, always, and burn slowly.
—Henry David Thoreau

1.
In this falling of seasons,
I hunch against the wind toward forty.

2.
Since morning
the brown squirrel, dead
on the road,
tail lifting
in the draft of cars, innards
singing from his mouth.

3.
At the lake, gulls
turn their backs
to the sunset, feathers
set against gale winds.

4.
Ships go down
in October, the beginning
of storms from the north.
They cast off, the proud bows head west
and run before broken seas.

5.
A blanket
breaks over my lawn.
Slow falling, this sewing of patches
on my green bed.

6.
Sailors
call for mother
as waves fold over them.

7.
Fox fire glows on the hill
out of old wood, long seasons.

8.
Leaves curl in
toward the flame, eyes
of tiny animals,
children's voices crying in the night.

9.
If I open my coat, will you
kiss my breasts warm,
help me lean against this wind?

Making Music

Tuesday afternoons in the cave of our basement
my mother, like an organist,
sat in front of the old white mangle,
her music heaped in a wicker basket beside her.
I saw the flash of fur under her arm

as she lifted a sheet, folded it twice, and with her knee
moved the pedal that made her instrument go.
I watched wrinkles feed into the mangle, heard a hiss
as heat met dampness of muslin, smelled soap under scorch,
saw clean hymns flow out of the roller.

I have no talent for music, am not my mother.
Two hours by car from Kalamazoo to Muskegon
I sit behind the wheel, direct my instrument
along a white line, around curves, over rises;
my pedal maintains a tempo of seventy miles an hour.

Headlights rest on the fur of dead animals, and my wheels
roll over them: rabbits, cats, squirrels
pressed into the sheet of highway. It is a long drive home.
The hum of my motor blends with the thump of bodies
and the static rock beat out of the radio.

The Legacy

No need to dial the doctor. I have
already heard that it flows in the genes,
floats on invisible electric currents
perhaps, from mother to son
to daughter, the mother again.

I have been to that old barn, looked
up through the dusting sunlight
from loft to splintered rafter; have almost
seen the rope, the empty space full with her
sagging skirt and dangling legs.

I have listened, but they never speak
her name, that grandmother
shrouded in dust, the grave
marked with whispers that sin begets sinner.
I have ceased to pray to the Virgin.

No matter. Yesterday I saw fire
in a cat's eye, touched the coarse mane
of a wild horse, at last set my house
in its strange order. At night
clouds form in front of the pale moon.

Orchids

1.
Service for townsman, old sailor
whose face I barely recall, except
as it raised
to catch telltales on the jib.

I rise with incense and candle flame
to alleluias rolling in waves.
A long time, Father,
since I faced
linen touched to chalice, breaking of wafer.

I can't help
the hand-stitch at my breast, this genuflection.

2.
We float like dreams in our funeral clothes, third car
behind the hearse, this time the uncle
who was mean and crotchety,
surgeon whose fingers finally
twisted so crooked he couldn't hold his cigar,
who never shut off the television
and let conversation fall to his wife.

Past elms, old houses
turned into offices, past storefronts blinking OPEN,
past the black man on Peck Street,
hat over chest, standing
with head bowed until we all roll past.

3.
Up North near Cross Village
in the divided cemetery, I step over
a wire fence
to low graves and bend to Chippewa names.
This is the paupers' side.

When the earth goes soft, falls
under my feet,
I think I will sink down to them
except for the crow that shrieks,
beating wings under my ribs.

4.
They roll the drawer shut on her
and I hear a woman
crying. The voice is glass shattering
on the mausoleum floor.

My chair scrapes. I stand
like stone for this suicide. My daughter
unfurls inside my belly
to take hold of her aunt's name.

5.
My own aunt saw her dead mother once
in a moth
battering its wings against the kitchen door.

Last year, when her heart stopped in California, she found me
sleeping in a hotel room in Michigan.
In the dream, we held hands. Her pulse
fluttering against my thumb.

6.
There is no end to this, reader.
My friend was a warrior, yet even she quit.

I sat with her before she left
but we couldn't make the journey together. Her breath
was fragile as an orchid's petal,
she was already floating in air.

ROBERT MORGAN

ROBERT MORGAN *was born in Hendersonville, North Carolina in 1944, and grew up on a farm in the Blue Ridge Mountains of that state. He attended North Carolina State University and the University of North Carolina at Chapel Hill and Greensboro, has worked as a farmer and housepainter, and has taught at Salem College in Winston-Salem, North Carolina. "I believe in the anarchic and creative soil," he once said, "and stick to the fringes of society, out where it comes into collision with nature, in the chaotic backwashes and countereddies." Now professor of English at Cornell University, he is the author of* Zirconia Poems *(1969),* Red Owl *(1972),* Land Diving *(1976),* Trunk & Thicket *(1978),* Groundwork *(1979), and* Bronze Age *(1981).*
(Photo by Nancy Morgan)

The Cubist of Memory

You begin with a vision of making something glorious, then fumble for a way of realizing that unheard music. I remember staring across the Green River valley in western North Carolina toward Cicero Mountain when about fourteen and thinking that the summit seemed woolly and domed as a mastodon heaving itself out of the west into morning. I wanted to make a 'poem' as grand as the mountain, as voluptuous as its flanks, as remote and lofty, yet fertile with springs and cliffs and mold-fed vegetation. January seepage over the peak cliff froze and glistened like a single diamond eye. Until I studied piano at nine or ten and learned to read notes, I often heard music in my thoughts while looking out on ridge or pasture, or jerking up weeds, or sitting in prayer meeting. The long compositions I made up mentally were based on hymns and snatches of organ and orchestral music heard on my grandfather's radio. Every fact and landscape and time seemed to have its melodic correlative.

After a long circuit through science and math—those were 'beat the Russians' years—I came back to music through story-telling. I drafted many stories and pieces of novels in my late teens at Chapel Hill, and even published some of the former. Then I decided that Southern fiction had been done already; but Southern poetry was nearly nonexistent. I would go off in an unknown direction, away from Faulknerian rhetoric toward plainness, compactness, simplicity. I wanted a clean transparent music, more like Webern than Beethoven, nonmetrical, experimental, 'classical.' To help free myself from myself—from ego, ambition, self-consciousness—to get on with the work, I tried to be true to objects, and to the verbal objects that measured and enacted world and thought. I wanted poems terse and precise, yet as encompassing as mathematical proofs.

When my sister brought her freshman anthology home from Bob Jones University I read in it the opening section of "Song of Myself" and was astonished and exhilarated that one could leap in a sentence from the soul to a single spear of grass. I also found there Stevens' "Domination of Black" and remember a similar elation at the colors, and the comparison of leaves turning like the fire with the gathering of planets. The combination of intimacy and distance was unforgettable. But my prose squibs and haiku and images never became poems, the breath of poems, until I realized that poems were voice, were telling sentences. In 1964 I was reading *Four Quartets* and noticed how lean and sumptuous Eliot's sentences were, great sentences accordioned into lines.

"Cedar" was written in the summer of 1970 when I was exploring the most elemental kinds of poems. I began a series on metals, and finished one called "Copper." I would choose the name or image of something common and try to describe it accurately, and then evoke the associations brought to mind. "Cedar" was more successful than most, I think, because I got the sound right. The longer, sustained sentences integrate the levels of reference and metaphor. As I remember, the seed of the poem was the idea of likeness and unlikeness, wood becoming music, sap becoming scent, the finite expanding infinitely. All senses echoed, as Baudelaire said, and all images and memories were kin. All were in some fantastic way equal: beauty and ugliness, absence and presence, the significant and useless. The ear knows long before the mind whether a poem or passage is working. It is music that tells the meaning. But also, it is the meaning that makes the music. The tune of poetry comes more from what is said, and how quickly it is said, than from stresses and rests. Economy tends to create melody. My dream was to write a maquette-sized poetry, of bonsai complexity and detail. Each poem was a new beginning of perception, an atom of recognition, explosive in its transfers of bond and structure.

"Pumpkin," written January 18, 1972 during my first year at Cornell, shows the same preoccupation with description. Starting out to render pumpkins buried under weeds I came upon the planets rising. I have been asked why the title is singular, and have no good answer, except to say "Pumpkin" was the working title and seemed to evoke the essence of the thing, something more mythic than 'pumpkins.' I like the feeling of homemadeness in a poem, the thing jotted and joined from materials at hand. A poet can travel light because his medium is the landscape and language he travels through, which mirror those he carries within.

"Face" (1974) shows a growing interest in the use of conversational tone and narrative. Coming to Cornell and talking daily with students and colleagues changed, apparently, my sense of cadence. I could write in longer units. Where before my poems had seemed to be spoken against the silence of all eternity, they began to sound more like someone talking on a given afternoon. I had been especially terrified, when young, of Jesus coming again and taking all but me to heaven. It was not Blake's tiger I had in mind, but Eliot's "Christ the tiger." I am only now realizing the importance of hymns and gospel songs to me, both their words and music: for the sense of far-off heaven, of revival, sadness, submission, of ecstatic promise of resurrection. The central figure of our culture is that promise of rebirth. The stuff of poetry is compost, human as well as vegetable, verbal and cultural; but it is the prospect of rising from the rot and ruin that empowers the statement and embodiment of the words.

In the mid-1970's I not only discovered narrative in verse, and the wealth of loric material in my family memories, but also rhymed forms and balladic horror and compression. The best of these experiments were probably "Wedding Party" and "Mountain Bride." The latter is based on a story I heard my grandfather tell by the fireplace. I thought he must have known those Revises, since there were Revises in our community. But when I read the poem at UNC-Asheville a member of the audience mentioned that John Ehle had told the same story in one of his novels, and later I found it was a widely known folktale. I hope I have added something to it by condensation, selection of detail, and form.

"Buffalo Trace." Among my favorite writers are Bartram, Wilson, Audubon, Michaux, Lewis and Clark. I like the sense that the continent has been written on by glaciers, earthquakes, floods, buffalo, Indians, and hunters. The soil is haunted by the Cherokee and Iroquois, extinct giant animals, ice tracks, frontier preachers. Looking for new ground to clear we find Old Fields, scrublands opened by fire or ice storms or Indian hoe-farmers. All is in fragments, and the recognition and gathering of those shards is the cubism of memory and imagination that implies the whole. All the best poetry is fragments joined in new ways, the broken edges sharp enough to cut as well as refract light and attention. At our best we recognize that we are just members of the chorus of language, that our voices, when most our own, are in concert with speakers past and present, with facts and their metaphorical fables.

Reflecting the rivers and oceans of buffalo were the streams and inland seas of birds, the passenger pigeons. No image in all the early travel reports evokes the pristine grandeur of the interior more than the descriptions of those extinct hosts. When writing the poem "Passenger Pigeons" I could think of no modern equivalent, except air traffic, and TV and radio signals.

In my earliest memories our house is filled with the flotsam and leftovers of World War II. I played with chevron patches, messkits, gas masks brought back by my uncles. The bureau drawer held rationbooks, and in the buttonbox were several paper penny tokens from 1943. But over all the paraphernalia and talk was the spoken and unspoken presence of my Uncle Robert who had been killed in a B-17 in 1943, the year before I was born. He cast a shadow almost as large as the Biblical figures' over my play and daydreams. The pigeons in the barnloft had been his, the collection of arrowheads in the attic, the toolboxes and paintset; even my name had been his. I constantly felt the difference between his reported goodness and generosity and my own fear and mischief. He had been an athlete, a martyr, an artist, and I had no choice but to rebel, then follow.

I began writing "Lightning Bug" in 1969, but was unable to find an appropriate ending. Finally the phrase, 'the edge of the orchard country,' came to me this year (1983). It suggested redolence, proximity and distance, a projecting of attention out to the horizon of trees and stars. Suddenly the poem felt complete, and I could let it rest.

We love poetry in part because it is useless. In an age when everything seems to have its price and schedule, poetry is without deadlines or market value; it is undenominated by party or church or special-interest lobby. Its playfulness both serves and is subversive to causes we solemnly admire. Poetry's power is very real, though indirect. A great poem can affect the lives of all, whether they read it or not. As poetry is based on the gold standard of experience, so experience is keyed to the bedrock of the best expression. My understanding of tradition is that our language and age are writing us, in ways we can't always see. An individual may have nothing better to contribute than a radical, humble attention that both startles and reassures.

Cedar

Smell the recorders buried here.
Music lies in the wood
as in the cat's entrails, in ore.
Faint musk of old arrows, canoe ribs.
Wood still giving
its breath, radioactive—releasing
a subtle verb for years
to fill whatever room or closet it lies in
till it's dark, inert
as the wood of cathedral carvings.
Weather leaches the glow
and withes of cool air plunder the fibers. The heat
is drunk off.
The wood reveals in lessening quanta the spice
from a country no one has seen,
leaking from a broken limb expanding to nonexistence.
But inside the scent's strong as light; it repels

the moth as two ends of a magnet
shun meeting.
For they are from the same country, the smell
lunar, musty, an ember so cool
you can hold it in your hand, and the moth
burning out of the dark, its semiquaver
weak as a photograph emerging in the darkroom pan.

Pumpkin

By fall the vines have crawled out
twenty yards from the hill
coiling under weeds.
The great cloth leaves have shriveled
and fallen. No sign of a harvest.
No way to tell where the pumpkins are scattered
except wade into the briars and matted grass,
among hornet nests and snakes,
parting the brush
with a hoe. Or wait
a few weeks longer till the weeds dry
up, burned by frost,
and huge beacons
shine through
like planets submerged and rising.

Face

The story went that once someone, an unbeliever,
looking into the clouds saw among the luminous
caravan of shapes and smokes, the usual sheep

and outcroppings of battlevapor, signals, choo-
choos, stretching fish, when suddenly in
one great chunk of the sky the Lamb himself,

the face of longhaired Jesus, looked sadly down
at him. Struck down on his way from that moment
he believed. Having a camera he snapped the

quickly dissolving icon. Advertised on radio
and at revivals that photo sold thousands. Looking
at the black and white you never found the image

at first, but when it came rushing out of the
wisps and puffs hardening into a perfect likeness
the recognition was beyond all expectation chilling.

For months I kept eyes ahead or to the ground out
of horror, feared looking back I would see
the Tiger clawing through eastern azure.

Mountain Bride

They say Revis found a flatrock
on the ridge just
perfect for a natural hearth,
and built his cabin with a stick

and clay chimney right over it.
On their wedding night he lit
the fireplace to dry away the mountain
chill of late spring, and flung on

applewood to dye
the room with molten color while
he and Martha that was a Parrish
warmed the sheets between the tick

stuffed with leaves and its feather
cover. Under that wide hearth
a nest of rattlers,
they'll knot a hundred together,

had wintered and were coming awake.
The warming rock
flushed them out early.
It was she

who wakened to their singing near

the embers and roused him to go look.
Before he reached the fire
more than a dozen struck

and he died yelling her to stay
on the big four-poster.
Her uncle coming up the hollow
with a gift bearham two days later

found her shivering there
marooned above a pool
of hungry snakes,
and the body beginning to swell.

Buffalo Trace

Sometimes in the winter mountains
after a little snow has blown in the night
and nothing's alive in eye-range
but the clouds
near peaks frozen clean
in the solstice sun,
the white finds a faint depression
to stick in out of wind
and makes visible for the first time
through woods and along the slopes
to where it nicks the rim
perceptibly, a ghostpath
under brush and broomsedge,
merging in the pasture with narrow
cowtrails but running on through fences
and across boundaries, under branches
in tattered sweep out to the low
gaps of the old migrations
where they browsed into the summer mountains
then ebbed back into the horizon
and back of the stars.

Passenger Pigeons

Remembering the descriptions by Wilson
and Bartram, and Audubon and other
early travelers to the interior, of the sky
clouded with the movements of winged pilgrims
wide as the Mississippi, wide as the Gulf
Stream, hundred-mile epics of equidistant wings
horizon to horizon, how their droppings
splashed the lakes and rivers, how
where they roosted whole forests broke down
worse than from ice storms, and the woods floor
was paved with their lime, how the settlers
got them with ax and gun and broom
for hogs, how when a hawk attacked
the endless stream bulged away
and kept the shift long after
the raptor was gone, and having read how
the skies of America became silent, the fletched
oceans forgotten, how can I replace
the hosts of the sky, the warmblooded jetstreams?
To echo the birdstorms of those early
sunsets, what high river of electron, cell and star?

Cow Pissing

First the tail begins to stiffen
at its root. The thick base rears and
a warp runs out the length of the
appendage to the dirty hank
and the whole is lifted slightly
to the side, exposing the gray
puckered pussy. But it's how the
back arches up that startles, how
she humps as though bracing against
and backing into something hard,
pressing to release a valve or
tip a cask open. And the stream
that starts comes as though from a hose
not round but flattened by her lips.

Shot on the pasture dirt the jet
wears out a basin that overflows
into tracks and sprays gold mist on
hooves and grass, shivering rainbows.
When the blast lessens and scalds down
to tatters and drips and is done
she whips the tail a few last times to
knock off the last drops and walk on
to graze. The puddle glistens like
gold wine in the sun, and crackles
as it soaks into the splash track.
The grass sparkles many colors
where the growth will be less for the
libation a while, and then more.

Uncle Robert

M Sgt. Robert G. Levi 1915-1943
Serial No. 34119284
325th Bomb Sqdn.
92nd Bombardment Group
Eighth Air Force

In the little opening in the woods
your cot springs were a crisp red wool
on the moss. While we raked leaves
for the cowstall Grandma told me how
you came up here on summer afternoons
to read and paint and sleep after
working the hootowl shift at the cottonmill.
You must have meant to return to leave
your couch on the innerspring moss
on the mountainside.

          The metalwork you did
in the CCC—toolbox, a vase, buckets
thick as stoves—was scattered through house
and barn. I lost your flies and tackle
in the weeds above the garden, and stuck
your chevron patches to my flannel shirt.
In the messkit returned from England

I fried sand like snow, and found
the picture of your fiancée in the cedarchest.

It was hinted I was 'marked' somehow,
not only by your name, but in some way
unexplained was actually you. Aunts and cousins
claimed we favored and I spoke with your stammer.
Your paintings watched me
from your bedroom wall and mantel
and your poem clipped from the paper
yellowed among the rationbooks. I inherited
your Testament with its boards of carved cedar,
and the box of arrowheads you picked
from the dust of bottomlands on Sunday afternoons
like seeds and teeth of giants.

No one opened the steel coffin sent back
to see what bone splinters or rags
had been found where the B-17 novaed
above East Anglia. I touched the ribbons
and medals in the bureau, the gold buttons.
Your canoe lay in the barnloft for years
between the cornpile and the wall, heavy
with dust as the boat in a pyramid
and tracked by mice and swallows. The paint
and canvas curled away from the cedar slats.
I meant to use it someday but never dared:
it was not creekworthy without new skin
and too heavy for one to carry. I turned
it over and looked into the belly
and sat on the webbed seat, rocking
on the corn-bearinged floor. Once hornets
built in the prow what I imagined
was a skull with honey brains. On snowy days
I sat there and paddled across the wilderness
of loft dark. The summer before you left
you portaged to the river and back,
then carried the canoe up there.
Something was always scary about the craft:
each time I turned it over fearing to see
a body inside. It lay among the shucks

and fodder as though washed up by a flood
and stranded forever.

                        One day I found your bugle
in the attic, velveted with dust and lint.
The brass felt damp with corrosion,
the bell dented and dark as leather.
I took it out behind the house and,
facing west, blew into the cold mouthpiece
a hopeful syllable. The metal trembled
and blared like a sick steer, went quiet.
I poured all my body heat into the barrel
and a sour flatulence shook out and echoed
off the mountains. I made half-musical
squeaks and bursts till dizzy, aiming vowels
like watermelon seeds into the tube.
When the groans returned from Buzzard Rock
I thought they must be wails from the cove
for someone dead, and nothing I had sent,
or the ghost of a train lost in the valley
and relayed like an aural mirage from
the past still with us and talking back.

The flag that draped your casket was kept
folded in the trunk. They said
I had the high-arched 'Levi foot'
like you, and your quick laugh. I was told
you made your own marbles as a boy
by rolling branch clay into balls and baking
in the oven. Mama liked to take out
of cloth a clay statue of a naked man
face down in the dirt which you once
modeled and called "The Dying Warrior."
I marveled at the cunning work of leg
and tiny arm and spilling hair, and touched
your fingerprints still clear on the base.

Lightning Bug

Carat of the first radiance,
you navigate like a creature
of the deep. I wish I could read

your morse across the night yard.
Your body is a piece of star
but your head is obscure. What small
photography! What instrument
panel is on? You are winnowed
through the hanging gardens of night.
Your noctilucent syllables
sing in the millenium of
the southern night with star-talking
dew, like the thinker sending nous
into the outerstillness from
the edge of the orchard country.

JOYCE CAROL OATES

JOYCE CAROL OATES *was born in 1938 and grew up in the country outside Lockport, New York. She has degrees from Syracuse University and the University of Wisconsin. Currently on the faculty of the Creative Writing Program at Princeton University, she has won many awards, including the National Book Award, and is a member of the American Academy and Institute of Arts and Letters. She has edited several anthologies, and has published more than twenty volumes of fiction, plays, and criticism.* Invisible Woman: New & Selected Poems 1970-1982 *(1982) is drawn from five previous collections of poetry.*
(Photo by Jerry Bauer)

The Dream of the "Sacred Text"

One of the oldest stories we tell ourselves has to do with the dream of the "sacred text."

Sometimes in yearning, sometimes in despair, all writers tell themselves this story: language set down with such talismanic precision, such painstaking ardor, such *will*, it can never be altered; language that constitutes an indissoluble reality of its own—human in origin, more-than-human in essence.

Not *what* is being said, but *how*. For *what* is frequently given to us, *what* is inevitable: it is *how* that makes, or has the possibility of making, the text sacred.

How to explain to ourselves the motive behind this old, old impulse? Perhaps it has something to do with the child's belief in omnipotent thought; an early sense that dreams are not "merely" interior but might be shared by others close by. One wishes for permanence by way of the medium of language, a command that time stand still. What is curious is that the act of writing often satisfies these extraordinary demands. We immerse ourselves in it so deeply, "writing" in our daydreams, "composing" in our sleep, telling ourselves again and again *what* it is we were born to tell, time finally seems to warp or to fold back in upon itself. The true poet is always writing poetry, always sounding words, measuring cadences, hearing, feeling, attending to, taking the pulse of. . . .

Content yields to form, form to "voice." But no one knows what "voice" is; only when it is absent; when one *hears* nothing.

Where do you find the time, people ask, to write so much?—and it would strike the ear as a peculiar reply, perhaps even an insolent reply, if I asked in return: Where do you find the time to breathe so much?—to eat, to sleep, to *exist*? For some of us "writing" is as natural or anyway as irresistible and necessary as breathing; the feat isn't in doing it but in *how* it is done. Everyone included in this volume, surely, knows what I mean, though it's notoriously difficult to explain to someone to whom the very notion of a "sacred text" is incomprehensible.

(In reading, we are searching for sacred texts written by others *that we might read them*. Reading too is a highly mysterious and utterly private, even secret, activity: a rent in the fabric of time, so to speak, a sudden lifting of the veil that separates one consciousness from another. Sounding the talismanic language of another in our own ears, are we not participating in a reality exterior to our own?—preceding it and fated to outlive it? Unless the "voice" rings false, or there is no "voice" at all.)

For the poet, *each poem as it is being composed* is a part of the sacred text. Or it may appear to be *the* sacred text, summing up all that has gone before, supplanting it. For those of us who also write longer works—eight-hundred-page novels, for instance—poetry is the miracle of *finitude*, of *exactness;* it affords the pleasure of revision, and revision, and yet again revision, as longer forms cannot. We all know that to write a page over is almost inevitably to improve it; but how many times can eight hundred pages be rewritten?—how much can one indulge oneself, *what* being given, in elaborating upon *how?* The poem is by definition that which can always be rewritten another time, sounded yet again in the mind's ear, envisioned yet again in another formal arrangement. Hence the almost irresistible impulse to rewrite one's early work in assembling a "selected" or "collected" volume.

The melancholy secret at the heart of all creative activity has something to do with our desire to *complete* a work, to impose *perfection* upon it, so that, hammered out of profane materials, it becomes sacred: and no longer strictly personal. Yet the desire brings with it our exclusion from that phase of our lives. To begin a new work almost always involves extraordinary effort, but after a while—weeks, months, occasionally only days—it acquires its own rhythm, its own unmistakable voice; and begins, as we say so inadequately, to "write itself." Everyone who has ever written has experienced this curious phenomenon: by no means a perfunctory or mechanical activity, it has something to do with listening very closely, being silent and listening, subordinating oneself and *listening* . . . and being willing to go as slowly as "listening" demands. We tell stories to ourselves, we tell poems, we murmur half-understood fragments, snatches of language, dialogue, we force ourselves to become transparent so that something (a part of ourselves?—an alien force?) might be transmitted by way of us. All these efforts have to do with the dream of the sacred text, which we share.

Completing a poem, we are properly expelled from it. We should be eased out, forced to let go; we should not find it alarming that a door closes slowly behind us. And it really *does* close. A work of poetry or fiction may be many things to many people but to the author it is a monument to a certain self, a certain unrepeatable chunk of time: so many pulse-beats, so much effort.

So I found in bringing together a volume of selected poems (*Invisible Woman: New & Selected Poems 1970-1982*) that the "self" behind the poems was no longer what might be called "mine." I was now a reader, and a very critical and impatient reader. Either I must rewrite everything entirely in what I now perceive as "my" voice, or I must discard most of it, though it's no doubt the case—surely it *is* the case— that the "self" of the present tense will one day strike a future self as erroneous. So I discarded most of it . . . reprinting only a small selection of my earlier poetry, and rewriting that, to the extent to which it allowed itself to be rewritten. I suppose I am not a competent judge of my own writing at this stage in my life because I am so absorbed—as most of us are—in telling myself new stories, experimenting with new versions of *how,* modified versions of *what.*

It must be the case too that so many of us shrink from considering "old" work because the mere fact that it is old suggests that the yearning for the sacred text, operant then, was not (evidently) successful. *That* talismanic precision, *that* painstaking ardor, *that* will—doesn't it all look merely vulnerable now, from our vantage point of a "superior" maturity? It isn't even that we keep on writing to correct past errors and to make amends for the incompleteness of past efforts— we are simply too taken up by the storytelling of the present, the pursuit of today's sacred text, to be in a position to identify with yesterday's.

Knowing oneself after all posits a single self to be known, at a single point in time. And the very rhythms and cadences of poetry speak to selves, fluidity, movement, ever-unfolding revelations—the search for the elusive sacred text, *the* text.

Acceleration Near the Point of Impact

the needles are starved, brown
fire-hazards warned of in the papers
but the evergreen rises miraculous
red- and green-glassed ornaments
at its peak a hand-sized fluffed
angel

again the release of dirty snow
the melting rush of sewers
the church bells' ambitions
a Sunday of parades

rockets, ten-cent bombs
End of Summer Sales
bins of heaped-up bathing suits
their straps confused together
sandals and synthetic-leather backless shoes
with three-inch cork heels

and tactile November skies
by minutes and inches pushing us
into history

The Stone Orchard

Slowly, by day, in the cold sun of autumn,
the pears harden to green. To stone.

They are shrinking to stone,
to peevish greeny peace.

This is the logic of hatred:
they cannot ripen, or fall.

This is the logic of chastity:
the facial mask too tight to age.

Slowly, by day, with the sun as a witness,
the pears of the orchard turn to stone.
The trees ache. The old limbs sag.
Their discomfort is too curious to be tragic.

Who has warned us against this hard bitter taste?—
the small flat dead pleasure of stony fruit.
I love it, the bitterness,
the peevish chill.
The chastity of stone.

I stride through the stone orchard
immense with satisfaction.
I own this, and I own this.
The stony weight, the pitiless density.
The logic of hatred.

The Wasp

O the instrument draws close,
very close.
The wasp is silent.

Gowned and gloved and regal
the surgeon makes his perfect
incision, O watch.

Don't flinch: a deep inky hair
from the base of the skull to the parietal.
It cannot hurt, such thin trickling blood!

O the rubber fingers peel back the scalp,
the sticky scalp. Lie still.
When the bone is exposed the air hums.

O the wasp is now in a fury,
a hidden fury.
His crevice, *his* cavity—so close!

Maddened buzzing and flailing papery wings,
O the tiny holes are drilled with *such*
precision!

And the membrane is cut,
and the bone swung out,
and the air tickles,
and the wasp is cunning-silent.

O the instrument draws close,
very close:
a three-inch silver tweezers.

O graceless as lead you lie still,
and grateful.

The wasp is removed: a tiny fury.
It buzzes in its rage, O don't flinch!—
though the tweezers has pinched it in two.

Heavily you sleep, saved,
and too feeble to protest.
Why do we think we must live forever?
The instrument rudely wipes
the wasp on a cotton pad.
O don't flinch!—it is over.
You are grateful.

Baby

Four walls, a ceiling, and the baby grows.
Floorboards, blinded windows. Airless air.
And the baby grows.

Weeks and hours,
clambering toward you:
a plump wattled purse.

The baby grows enormous with the calendar.
Cherub-fat, quivering thighs and buttocks,
snorts of laughter escape you at the sight.
Wet wide lips, a carnivore smile, *Love me.*

Bare floor, a windowsill edged with grime.
Years have passed. *Love and feed.* The baby grows
mollusc-smug, enormous. Cannot now be stopped.
Lurid flushed cheeks, jewels for eyes.
Ah, a Cupid-toad! And yours.
Inside these walls, below this ceiling,
yours. Cannot be stopped.

Love and feed. Swollen sausages for fingers.
He grows filling the room, the space. You.
Fat knees cutely dimpled. Ears pink and delicate
as shells. O Love you are enormous, clambering
toward me, filling the room, the space.
The air glistens. There is no air.
The baby grows.

First Dark

First dark. The exuberance of the night.
Insects in their music.
Razor-ribbons of noise.

First dark, and green wet air,
close as a breath.
My feet are damp, my fingers snatch at weed-flowers
drowsy with pollen, it is long ago,
I am not yet born, I am invisible,
prowling forbidden in first dark,
far from the lighted house.

At the pond the young frogs leap with their new legs,
small yelps of green. Sheer emerald.
You can't imagine. You can't exaggerate
that green.
Or the surprise, the yelps and leaps,
the splashes in the water,
small emeralds of alarm.
The way they disappear one by one
as you approach.

I am prowling, my feet are damp.
I am snatching at things to prove my life.
Wait!—where are you going!
That child I have never seen except in snapshots,
and cannot love,
where are you going?—isn't this forbidden?

How small the soul, cupped in a child's hand.
Held over the pocked water.
Ready to leap, and sink, and disappear.

The Child-Bride

Fortunately for you I am resurrected in one piece, or nearly.
In my ancient wedding gown. With my mummy's wise grimace.
My skull partly covered with hairy moss, the lace at my wrists

grown into my wrists, my eye-sockets not quite eyeless.
Much publicity, of course, attends my resurrection.

Approximately four-feet-four-inches tall, in life.
Approximately eleven years of age.

I am resurrected gently, with caution. With gauze, tweezers,
patience. *The bridal gown used as a shroud, an old custom.*
Buried with her own infant.

I am immortal, my hide is weathered and thick,
I am brittle, I may fall apart, here is my wedding ring,
here is my gold cross, my bracelet of braided hair.
I am sorry if I have frightened you.

Resurrected from my grave after centuries of sleep,
resurrected in one remarkable piece. Or nearly.
Overhead the raw North Atlantic sky, on all sides
nibbled grave-mounds and eroded crosses and winds funnelled
to a howl, centuries, days, each day the same day,
each hour weathering my shy smile into this grimace.
Everywhere in the soil bones, bone-fragments, bone-dust.
The bones of human beings, the bones of rats, mice, sheep.

The same dwarf sheep wander the island, clumsy, grazing
calm and sure-footed amid the rocks, the broken crosses,
the moss. Starving, rheumy-eyed, unhurried, the same sheep,
approximately eleven years of age, a child-bride, buried
with her own infant, her skin mummified though not "perfectly
preserved"—

Fortunately for you I offer no resistance, I am a curiosity
under no spell of evil, I bring no curse, my husband lies
nearby but I have forgotten him, my mother, all my mothers,
my sisters, brothers, perhaps I had husbands, bone
and bone-fragments and bone-dust, relics, crosses grown
into the skeleton, the tiny bones of mice and birds ground
into the soil, we might all be resurrected with tweezers.
What do the dead know, what is their secret—

Much publicity, of course, attends my resurrection.
But it has all happened long ago.

But it is the same hour.
The bridal gown used as a shroud, an old custom.

Dreaming America

for my mother, Carolina Oates

When the two-lane highway was widened
the animals retreated.
Skunks, raccoons, rabbits,—even their small corpses
were transformed into rags
and then into designs
and then into stains
then nothing.

When the highway was linked to another
and to another
six lanes, then nine, then twelve arose
sweeping nobly to the horizon
along measured white lines.
The polled Herefords were sold.
The barbed-wire fences dismantled.
When the cornfields were bulldozed
the farmhouses turned to shanties;
the barns fell;
the silos collapsed.

When the fields were paved over
Frisch's Big Boy reared seventy feet in the air.
Sunoco and *Texaco* and *Gulf* signs gaily competed
on hundred-foot stilts.
Eyeballs on stalks:
miraculous!
And illuminated all night.

Where that useless stretch of poplars lay
an orange sphere of gigantic proportions
announces *Wonderland East*, open
for Thursday evening shopping.
Here, tonight, packs of teenagers hunt

one another.
The terrazzo footprints are known by heart.

Where did the country go?—cry the travelers, soaring
past. *Where did the country go?*—ask the strangers.
The teenagers never ask.

Where sway-backed horses once grazed in a dream that had no
     history,
tonight a thirteen-year-old girl stands dreaming
into the window of Levitz's Records & Hi-Fi Equipment.
We drive past, our speed accelerating. We disappear.
We return.

Night

> *We call Night the privation of relish*
> *in the appetite for all things.*
> St. John of the Cross

She remembers the episode taking place at night.
It is a nighttime tale, an allegory perhaps,
she is seized from behind, a forearm across her neck,
snug beneath her chin. She is a child of eleven.

It happens so quickly, it always happens so quickly,
she hasn't time to scream. And then she hasn't breath.
It is night, she has begun to choke, she is losing
consciousness, she will forget.
Forgetting is generally recommended.

Her weight, in opposition to *his,* must be slight.
She will choke, she can't scream or sob, if she faints
perhaps his anger will be placated.
Nor does she tug roughly at the arm. Nor claw at the face.
(In fact there is no face, because it is night.)

He will not harm her. She is tall for her age, so
he might have been misled.
She often lies. She can't be trusted.
When she falls to the pavement (they are in an underpass

beneath the railroad tracks) he will release her.
She is not clinically "molested."
There is no blood except from her scraped knees.
There is no scar or enduring wound
except the nighttime tale, the memory.

It is always night, she cannot not remember it as night,
though wasn't it afternoon?—she was returning home
from school, descending the steps from the street,
an old route, absolutely safe by daylight.

Still, she remembers the episode taking place at night.
In which she will be proved, twenty years later, a liar.
As for the rest of the tale—isn't it fictitious?

You've always had a queer imagination, she is told.

New Jersey White-Tailed Deer

i.
Your great sin
is "overbreeding"—
which might be defined as the modest greed
to populate the world
with your kind.

For this—
death by starvation.

ii.
Prowling the January woods
(a skeletal forest, black-on-white,
Japanese in execution)
you exhale desire
in tiny spasms
of steam.

In sympathy
our souls are drawn after you:
a fiction:
but one that offers comfort.

iii.
Morning dawns opaque
and dream-muddled.
And outside our bedroom windows
the snow is madly churned
as if by heraldic beasts—
not seven or eight starving deer.
Not an antlered figure among them.

iv.
Tonight—last night—
the years before yesterday—
these childhood apparitions
meaning no harm—
Pray for us.

Creatures of legend and perfection—
cloven-hoofed
with erect white "flags" of tails
for hunters' sights—
great-eyed
doe-eyed—
Pray for us.

That doomed fawn about whose neck
Alice slipped a graceful arm—
figures of earthen beauty—
dun-colored,
camouflaged,
finite—
Pray for us.
Our souls *are* drawn after you
in your flight.

v.
January midnight,
January moonlight,
and the riddle of all poetry
is revealed!—
as the deer disturb our sleep
eating, chewing
ivy—vines—dried leaves—the smaller evergreen branches—
browsing

starving
outside our window.

Hunger is promiscuous,
hunger is dun-colored,
hunger requires camouflage
but grows too reckless, finally
in the presence of "food."

And all this wisdom,
by January moonlight.

vi.
(When I trotted to join them
my hooves, my weight didn't break through
the snow's hard crust.
How marvelous the strength
of our dreaming muscles!—
the ease of our great moist eyes
in their sockets—

The Eucharist crackles between our teeth.
It is tough, sinewy, dry,
mainly briars.
It will not melt but must be chewed.)

GREGORY ORR

GREGORY ORR *was born in Albany, New York, in 1947, and raised in the rural Hudson River Valley.* He has degrees from Antioch College and Columbia University, where he won an Academy of American Poets Prize and the YMHA Discovery Award. *From 1972-1975 he was a Junior Fellow of the University of Michigan Society of Fellows.* He now lives near Charlottesville, Virginia, where he teaches at the University of Virginia. *The author of three volumes of poetry—*Burning the Empty Nests *(1973),* Gathering the Bones Together *(1975), and* The Red House *(1980)— he has recently completed a critical study of Stanley Kunitz.* (Photo by John Unterecker)

Some Notes:

I've spent a large part of the last three years writing a book about Stanley Kunitz's poetry and I suspect that the book contains numerous of my own opinions about poetry along with a few more objective insights and observations. What follows here is perhaps woefully schematic and abstract, but I'd rather say something than nothing. It might be of some help in terms of orientation to say that the following opinions emanate from a lyrical-mythological perspective on poetry rather than, say, its antitype—a didactic-historical perspective.

#

We usually live with the Isness of things by projecting onto them the unconscious egotism that structures our day-to-day lives. But when that blank Isness overwhelms the ego (as it does so easily), it seems to me that it calls up something deeper in the human spirit that responds with a deeper affirmation of our existence.

#

The kind of poem that interests me is one that is called into being as a response to a negation of meaning. The poet's primary task is to discover or create meaning; the poem's task is to embody meaning.

#

Certainly, personal death is one of the most intense forms of negation, and it calls out of us the meaning-making power—the pattern of magical language that will allow us to live above the abyss without denying that the abyss is there.

#

Periodically, our lives intersect with the great mysteries of eros and thanatos, or with the lesser mysteries (joy, suffering, rebirth—the list becomes long and personal). These mysteries have the power to move us to that other personal/universal level beyond the ego where something in us creates or discovers meaning.

#

The poem struggles into being against the negation of the blank page. The blankness of the page is analogous to the blank Isness of things. Such blankness is actually a great darkness. When the words appear they give off light, because each word is a lens that gathers in, intensifies, and focuses what little light there is.

#

The process of writing happens independently of these ideas. The way poems happen for me has to do with those two most non-rational and ancient forms of meaning: story and symbol, and with the incantatory magic of rhythmical language.

Silence

The way the word sinks into the deep snow of the page.

The deer lying dead in the clearing,
its head and antlers transparent.
The black seed in its brain
parachuting toward earth.

The Room

With crayons and pieces of paper, I entered the empty room.
I sat on the floor and drew pictures all day.
One day I held a picture against the bare wall:
it was a window. Climbing through,

I stood in a sloping field
at dusk. As I began walking, night settled.
Far ahead in the valley, I saw the lights
of a village, and always at my back I felt
the white room swallowing what was passed.

Love Poem

A black biplane crashes through the window
of the luncheonette. The pilot climbs down,
removing his leather hood.
He hands me my grandmother's jade ring.

No, it is two robin's eggs and
a telephone number: yours.

The Project

My plan was to generate light
with no outside source.
To accomplish this, I lived alone
in a burrow under the earth.
Previously I had observed
that in darkness my body
gave off a faint light. Suspecting
that this glow came from the bones,
I scraped the flesh from my right hand.
I'd been underground so long
the meat came off
painlessly, like wet clay.
But when the flesh was gone,
the light was gone too.

Gathering the Bones Together

for Peter Orr

When all the rooms of the house
fill with smoke, it's not enough
to say an angel is sleeping on the chimney.

1   A Night in the Barn

The deer carcass hangs from a rafter.
Wrapped in blankets, a boy keeps watch
from a pile of loose hay. Then he sleeps

and dreams about a death that is coming:
Inside him, there are small bones
scattered in a field
among burdocks and dead grass.
He will spend his life walking there,
gathering the bones together.

Pigeons rustle in the eaves.
At his feet, the German shepherd
snaps its jaws in its sleep.

2

A father and his four sons
run down a slope toward
a deer they just killed.
The father and two sons carry
rifles. They laugh, jostle,
and chatter together.
A gun goes off,
and the youngest brother
falls to the ground.
A boy with a rifle
stands beside him, screaming.

3

I crouch in the corner of my room,
staring into the glass well
of my hands; far down
I see him drowning in air.

Outside, leaves shaped like mouths
make a black pool
under a tree. Snails glide
there, little death-swans.

4   *Smoke*

Something has covered the chimney
and the whole house fills with smoke.
I go outside and look up at the roof,
but I can't see anything.
I go back inside. Everyone weeps,
walking from room to room.
Their eyes ache. This smoke
turns people into shadows.
Even after it is gone, and the tears are gone,
we will smell it in pillows
when we lie down to sleep.

5

He lives in a house of black glass.
Sometimes I visit him, and we talk.
My father says he is dead,
but what does that mean?
Last night I found a child
sleeping on a nest of bones.
He had a red, leaf-shaped
scar on his cheek. I lifted him up
and carried him with me, even though
I didn't know where I was going.

6   The Journey

Each night, I knelt on a marble slab
and scrubbed at the blood.
I scrubbed for years and still it was there.
But tonight the bones in my feet
begin to burn. I stand up
and start walking, and the slab
appears under my feet with each step,
a white road only as long as your body.

7   The Distance

The winter I was eight, a horse
slipped on the ice, breaking its leg.
Father took a rifle, a can of gasoline.
I stood by the road at dusk and watched
the carcass burning in the far pasture.

I was twelve when I killed him;
I felt my own bones wrench from my body.
Now I am twenty-seven and walk
beside this river, looking for them.
They have become a bridge
that arches toward the other shore.

After a Death

I heard the front door close
and from my window saw

my father cross the moonlit lawn
and start up the orchard road.
Then I was with him,
my mittened hand in his,
and Peter, my brother, his dead son,
holding his other hand.
The way the three of us walked
was a kind of steady weeping.

Driving Home After a Funeral

The boy watched the sun
set: gold seed squeezed
in the mountain's cleft
beak until it bled. He sat,
distant in the back
seat, unable to move.
When the moon rose
its blue light formed
patches of mold
on his father's shoulder.
In the dark, a wadded
kleenex his mother pressed
against her cheek
was a white snail
eating holes in a leaf.

Spring Floods

1
Later that week, when the reddish
silt-laden water subsided,
we found a deer
high in a tree, wedged
there by the flood; its legs
outstretched as if leaping,
its neck snapped and fallen
back along its flank.
It was my dead brother;

his body lifted, held
forever in the arms
of my twelfth year.

2

In a muddy field:
an open coffin
only I could see;
it was a boat my mother
sent to fetch me,
just as she sent the flood.
Water roiled so deeply
who could calm it
as she once did,
laying her cool hand
on my forehead in the dark
room before sleep?

The Lost Children

for Mark Strand

Years ago, as dusk seeped from the blue
spruce in the yard, they ran to hide.
It was easy to find those who crouched
in the shadow of the chicken coop
or stood still among motionless
horses by the water trough.
But I never found the willful
ones who crossed the fence and lay
down in the high grass to stare up
at the pattern of stars
and meandering summer firefly sparks.

Now I stand again by the fence
and pluck one rusted strand of wire,
harp of lost worlds. At the sound
the children rise from hiding
and move toward me:
eidolons, adrift on the night air.

On the Lawn at Ira's

for Ira and Dianne Sadoff

Six years ago in Ohio we argued free will
versus fate as we weeded your garden
and hosed out a mole tunneling toward corn.
Your father walked out when you were thirteen
and everything you'd since done you called
an act and measure of your will.
At twelve, I killed a brother by accident,
my mother died soon after: my whole life
I sensed as a lugged burden
of the invisible and unforgiving dead.

Now we're sitting on a summer lawn in Maine.
The sun's out; it's the same argument
but I see it another way: you never
let the early hurt be felt and so
it governs you; I now admit I'm mostly
happy, even feel blessed among so many friends.
Hearing a sharp "thump" we investigate
and find a least flycatcher
stunned in the grass below a window.
I hold it in my palm: its small hot heart
beats so rapidly its whole body heaves.
We sit down and continue talking; the bird
lies there with one wing awry, shits in my hand,
stares up with a glazed eye. Ten minutes later
it pulls in its wing, tries to grip
with its tiny feet my too-large finger.
While we talk, joke, and argue
it suddenly flies, unwavering, away.

A Last Address to My Ghosts

You accompanied me so far
and with such ambiguous
fidelity: my guides, my ghosts.

I've seen the candles you carried
going out, one by one,
in the darkness of deep woods.

And the path? The destination?
There never was one,
I learned that from you.
There was only the light
edging the leaves,
and now that's gone.

Branches above my head
extend their dark blessing.

ROBERT PHILLIPS

ROBERT PHILLIPS *was born in Delaware in 1938. A graduate of Syracuse University, he has for many years worked in advertising in New York City, commuting from his home in Katonah in Westchester County. His criticism includes books on Denton Welch and William Goyen, and* The Confessional Poets *(1973).* The Land of Lost Content, *a volume of short stories, was published in 1970. Among the books he has edited are* Aspects of Alice: Lewis Carroll's Dreamchild *(1971),* Last and Lost Poems of Delmore Schwartz *(1979), and* Letters of Delmore Schwartz *(1984). His books of poetry are* Inner Weather *(1966),* The Pregnant Man *(1978), and* Running on Empty: New Poems *(1981). (Photo by Layle Silbert)*

A Second Look

In graduate school I wrote a thesis, on gothic themes in Carson McCullers. Since Ms. McCullers was alive, I thought it a good idea to share my discoveries with her. After a polite exchange of letters, she agreed to read the thing. Her response was instructive: no, she had not been aware of such imagery in her fiction. But, "the writer is no critic, especially of his own work."

I believe this is true. In my own case, I'm frequently unaware of what I've actually written until someone points it out. Once I thought I had written a scathing poem about the personality of a difficult woman I knew, and everyone told me it was about courting the Muse! Certainly my most successful poems are those which wrote themselves under the pressure of a combination of emotion and idea, with emotion (or intuition) far outweighing the impulse to "say something." With luck, emotion and idea coalesce into a whole, a poem: something which is more than the sum of its paraphrasable parts.

When I try to will a poem into being, the results are less than satisfactory. This happens most when I discover that the individual poems I've written actually constitute a sequence, like the body poems from *The Pregnant Man,* and the Delaware poems from *Running on Empty.* Whenever I deliberately attempt to fill out a sequence, the new poems are inferior to those which spontaneously insisted upon being written. A poem must catch me unawares. André Gide says, "Art is a collaboration between God and the artist, and the less the artist does the better."

All of which is why I am grateful for this opportunity to take a second look at these six poems—not all among my personal favorites. So much the better. What has the editor seen in them? What, if anything, do they have in common? And what do they say about "my work"?

First, I am surprised to see these are nearly all poems about metamorphoses. Individuals suddenly become whole or unwhole, healthy or maimed, human or inhuman. There are even houses which transform into ships. These physical changes relate to the unattainable, or perhaps symbolize strong psychological yearnings toward fulfilling the unfulfilled, the what-might-have-been.

Second, I see a shared urban/suburban intensity. Two poems literally deal with suburban houses, one is largely set in a YWCA swimming pool, and another addresses a crime in the subways. The poems also share nautical imagery, probably a throwback to my childhood on the Eastern Shore of Delaware and Maryland: In "The Married Man" the narrator's nervously ticking mouth is compared to a fish flailing on a hook; "Miss Crustacean" is compared to a crab; and (I'd never noticed before) the houses in "Decks" and "Inside and Out" are similarly compared to ships. The essential difference is that in the former the houses/boats imaginatively set sail, while in the latter the house and its inhabitants are going nowhere, geographically or emotionally. The two poems were written in different decades. Both traffic with pathos and fragility.

I see that all these poems have a narrative thrust, and display a direct, wide-eyed attentiveness to objects, places, and personal experience. There are deliberate alliteration and assonance and half-rhymes, and a ceremonial tightening here and there into strict meters for calculated dramatic effect. Three are cast in the first person, and one is a dramatic monologue by a garrulous persona. Most are developed about a single extended metaphor—those houses that can or cannot sail, a man who wears his heart on his sleeve, a man with a split personality, etc.

The exception is "The Persistence of Memory, the Failure of Poetry." Its very premise is the inadequacy of language and metaphor to convey horror or to comprehend suffering. Tragedy is what happens to someone else. As La Rochefoucauld says, "All of us have enough strength to endure the misfortunes of others." The use of nursery-rhyme echoes in the third stanza not only invokes Humpty Dumpty, who (like the girl pushed before the subway car) had a great fall, but also helps me to avoid emotional overstatement. The problem here is to tell the story of a talented music student who loses her hand without dipping into gross heresies of sentimentality. The poem also balances the contrast between music and murderous intent.

In dealing with such strong emotions, I find I unconsciously resort to humor. I never set out to "be funny." This is a form of distancing myself, but not escaping. Sometimes this takes the form of puns, which I use as I use enjambments ("ports / and sherries;" "harbor / no hostilities")—to give double meanings, to project shadows. Some are blatant, as when the narrator of "Vital Message" speaks of his "Mickey Mouse days." He alludes not only to his cheap child's watch, but also to the ordinariness of his life. Sometimes I realize the wordplay may be so private that it may mean something only to me. An example is "Ingersoll" from the same poem. An Ingersoll is another brand of dime-store watch. To my ears, the word also sounds like "inner soul." On occasion the entire point of a poem is freighted in a joke; the bifurcated protagonist of "The Married Man" is lectured, "You've got to pull yourself together."

Because of these devices and effects, my work sometimes has been called light verse. I'd like readers of this anthology to see that I am damned serious. Look at the poem's subjects: nobody ever died laughing over schizophrenia, personal dissociation, human vulnerability, the collapse of family life, or the plight of housewives. ("Decks" is above all else a women's liberation poem.) Comedy can be an escape, surely—not from truth, but from despair. I'd rather laugh than cry. Comedy gives us the strength to bear existence. I'd like to think my poems constitute a narrow escape into faith.

Vital Message

The last thing I put on
    every morning is my

heart. I strap it to my
    wrist sheepishly, a man

with expensive friends
    exposing his Ingersoll.

But I strap it.
    Outside my sleeve it ticks

away the Mickey Mouse
    of my days. Some people

pretend not to notice. They look
    everywhere else but.

Some people touch it
    to see if it's warm.

It is. Warm as a hamster.
    One open-hearted friend

tried to give me
    a transplant. It wouldn't take.

I was left with my old,
    bleeding. A critic tried

to boil it in acid. It shrunk
    smaller than a chicken's.

One girl broke it. It crunched
    open, a Chinese cookie.

No fortune inside. One girl
    won it. She pats it,

a regular Raggedy Andy. And its
    worst enemy is me. I want

to eat it. Nail-chewers know
    how tempting!—a plump purple

plum just above the wrist.
    It bursts with a juicy sigh.

The skin shreds sweet. No seeds.
    So far I only nibble the edges.

There is more than half left.

The Married Man

I was cut in two.
Two halves separated
cleanly between the eyes.
Half a nose and mouth on one
side, ditto on the other.
The split opened my chest
like a chrysalis, a part
neat in the hair.
Some guillotine slammed
through skull, neck, cage,
spine, pelvis, behind,
like a butcher splits a chicken breast.

I never knew which side my heart
was on. Half of me sat happy
in a chair, stared at the other
lying sad on the floor. Half wanted
to live in clover, half to breathe
the city air. One longed to live
Onassis-like, one aspired to poverty.
The split was red and raw.

I waited for someone to unite me.
My mother couldn't do it. She claimed
the sissy side and dressed it like a doll.
My father couldn't do it. He glared
at both sides and didn't see a one.
My teachers couldn't do it. They stuck
a gold star on one forehead,
dunce-capped the other.

So the two halves lived in a funny house,
glared at one another through the seasons;
one crowed obscenities past midnight,
the other sat still, empty as a cup.
One's eye roadmapped red from tears,
the other, clear and water-bright.
Stupid halves of me! They couldn't even
decide between meat and fish on Fridays.
Then one began to die. It turned gray as old meat.

Until you entered the room
of my life. You took the hand of one
and the hand of the other
and clasped them in the hands of you.
The two of me and the one of you
joined hands and danced about the room,
and you said, "You've got to pull yourself
together!", and I did, and we are two-
stepping our lives together still.

And it is only when I study hard
the looking-glass I see that one
eye is slightly high, one corner
of my mouth twitches—a fish on a hook!—
whenever you abandon me.

Decks

In the fair fields of suburban
counties there are many decks—
  redwood hacked from hearts
  of California giants, cantilevered
  over rolling waves of green
  land, firm decks which do not
  emulate ships which lean and list,
  those wide indentured boards which
  travel far, visit exotic ports of call.
  No. Modern widow's walks,

these stable decks, stacked with fold-up
chairs, charcoal bags, rotogrills,
  are encumbered as the *Titanic*'s.
  They echo Ahab pacing the *Pequod*,
  the boy who stood on the burning,
  Hart's jump into the heart of ice,
  Noah craning for a sign, a leaf . . .
  These decks are anchored to ports
  and sherries which mortgaged house
  -wives sip, scanning horizons,

ears cocked for that thrilling sound,
the big boats roaring home—
  Riviera, Continental, Thunderbird!
  Oh, one day let these sad ladies
  loose moorings, lift anchor, cast
  away from cinderblock foundations.
  Let the houses sail down Saw Mill,
  Merritt, Interstate. You will see
  them by the hundreds, flying flags
  with family crests, boats afloat

on hope. Wives tilt forward, figureheads.
Children, motley crew, swab the decks.
  Let the fleet pass down Grand Concourse,
  make waves on Bruckner Boulevard.
  Wives acknowledge crowds, lift pets.
  The armada enters Broadway, continues
  down to Wall. Docked, the pilgrims

search for their captains of industry. When
they come, receive them well. They harbor
no hostilities Some have great gifts.

The Persistence of Memory,
the Failure of Poetry

The severed hand flutters
　　on the subway track,
like a moth. No—

it is what it is,
　　a severed hand.
It knows what it is.

And all the king's doctors
　　and all the king's surgeons
put hand and stump together

again. Fingers move,
　　somewhat. Blood circulates,
somewhat. "A miracle!" reporters

report. But it will only
　　scratch and claw, a mouse
behind the bedroom wall. We forget.

At four a.m. the hand
　　remembers: intricate musical
fingerings, the metallic

feel of the silver flute.

Miss Crustacean

for Cynthia Macdonald

Each year the city of Crisfield, "Seafood Capital of the Nation,"
sponsors an event known as the National Hard Crab Derby, certainly
one of our nation's more bizarre folk celebrations . . .
    —William W. Warner, *Beautiful Swimmers*

I should have been a pair of ragged claws . . .
    —T. S. Eliot, *The Love Song of J. Alfred Prufrock*

I
"All my life I've wanted to be
Miss Crustacean!" I said into
the microphone, into the TV
cameras just after they crowned me
beauty queen at the Crab Derby.
Afterward my brother told me
what a fool I'd made of myself—

It was the first year they'd held
a beauty pageant at the Derby:
How could I have coveted the title
"all my life"? I know, I know.
But all my eighteen years ached
for recognition some way.
All my eighteen years ached.

I always had blue limbs. In high
school I bumped into every open
locker door, my upper arms and thighs
blue with bruises, clumsiness.
In the class play I tripped
on my train, forgot my lines . . .
Not everything turned out badly:

I was a good swimmer. My best stroke,
the crawl. I struggled with one poem—
About nature being "red in tooth
and claw." I longed for
Donald Lee Scruggs to ask me

to the Junior-Senior Prom.
Donald Lee was a swimmer.

When he didn't ask me, I asked him.
Only to be told he was taking
Sue-Ellen Wheatley, captain
of the girls' basketball team.
She never bumped into anything.
Fortunately, the Crab Derby
was held on Labor Day Weekend:

I hadn't been near a locker
for three months! Not one bruise.
I possessed a certain beauty.
I was confident. And that day,
a gorgeous early September day
in Crisfield, Maryland,
I became: Miss Crustacean.

II
In the year of my reign I took
my role seriously: rode through
parades in open convertibles,
attended banquets, promoted
crab meat best I could.
The following Labor Day
I returned to Crisfield to crown
my successor (Sue-Ellen Wheatley).

When I sidled up to the throne
to place my crown upon her head,
I realized I'd walked crabwise.
That was the beginning. In the years
to follow, I caught myself scuttling
about town, nails decorated
with orange-red gloss, arms bruised
cerulean blue. Scuttle, scuttle.

(I still lived at home, an old maid.
It was my own bureau drawers bruised
me blue now.) Every day I went
to swim in the unnatural blue waters
of the YWCA. In the warm element

I waved my claws in and out.
I wanted to swim nude, my pure
white abdomen lustrous alabaster.

But the Y requires tank suits.
I tread water, I wave claws
in and out. I acquire faster open
-water speed, dive to the bottom
to bury myself. For hours
I practice my crawl. Afterward,
in direct sunlight, I blink:
my stalked eyes, nubby horns.

How I hate direct sunlight!
After swimming, famine. My life
is swimming and one constant search
for food. At the Blue Dolphin Diner
they tease about how much I eat.
Anything in a pinch. I burn
it off. My parents worry:
They say my disposition has become

. . . crabby. If only they knew!
I need a new hobby, they say.
I considered shadow boxing.
Before the mirror at night
I stand in my room, slowly jabbing
the air with my powerful right
claw. I wave it like a flag.
Jab, jab, jab.

III
The preceding pages were written
(in my crabbed hand) some years ago.
They represent a reasonable account
of my existence for twenty years.
Today my swimming has slowed,

But my love of water never ceases.
My body, shell-white from every day
inside that sunless pool. I have lost

all interest in mating. My attitude
has hardened. I am more vague:

"She believes in the oblique,
indirect method," I heard someone say.
True. My walk, slower, too. Yet
that supports my illusions—walking
legs slightly doubled, ready to spring!

But suddenly my life has changed.
First I feared cancer. That seemed
predetermined, the crab's pincers biting
my guts like hell. Now I know it is
something even more insidious. Everything

about me, even my brain, is . . . softening.
I lie in a darkened room in my bed
for days. I feel it at my points,
I feel it in my joints. Any moment now
my entire shell will crack and bust.

Inside and Out

Upstairs a young man plays
the stereo. From the ceiling
he watches himself dance like a cock.
No one understands him.

Outside the rain scribbles down
into the suburban garden
once ablaze with poppies,
peonies, salvia, impatiens,

seven varieties of loneliness.
Now the plot thickens
with weeds and poison ivy.
The picket fence wants painting.

The young man wants money,
but will not paint or weed.

Before the empty fireplace
the cat bites off a mouse's head.

In the morning kitchen a lemon
slice of sunlight spills
across a woman kneading dough.
Whole wheat, health food—

there is no health in it
for the young man. The bread
she bakes is bitter to the tongue.
It tastes of acrimony.

Downstairs in the master bath
a man sings a song
from the Fifties: *Where are you,
lucky star? Now and forever?*

He would shake down his life
like a thermometer. He dries
his body, thickened like pudding.
He leaves the mirror steamed—

he's weary of looking at himself.
The house creaks, an ancient sloop
going nowhere. The basement
carries the cargo of their lives.

Outside in the two-car garage
an aluminum rowboat is suspended
like a rocket ready to blast.
It's hung around for years.

Long ago the boy begged his father
to set the two of them adrift.
But the man fears depths,
and could not save them if they tipped.

MARGE PIERCY

MARGE PIERCY *was born in Detroit, Michigan, in 1936, and has degrees from the University of Michigan and Northwestern University.* She has *published several novels and* Parti-Colored Blocks for a Quilt *(1982), a volume of essays, reviews, and interviews from which her essay here is excerpted.* Circles on the Water *(1982) selects from seven earlier volumes of her poetry. In her introduction for this book she writes, "I imagine that I speak for a constituency, living and dead, and that I give utterance to energy, insight, words flowing from many lives. I have always desired that my poems work for others, be useful." Since the selected volume, she has published* Stone, Paper, Knife *(1983) and* Fly Away Home *(1984). She lives in Wellfleet, Massachusetts.*

(Photo by Ira Wood)

from Midgame: Making It Better, Truer, Clearer, More Gorgeous

Shame gets in creation's way. We all have notions of what we should be. A writer had better have considerable tolerance for the gap between what we would like to be and what we are in a daily way; at the same time, I think it helps to have experience of how extraordinary people can be in situations that stretch them utterly. Sometimes we are ashamed of what moves us or how much we are moved; sometimes we feel we ought to have been moved and we try to pretend. Women don't only fake orgasms; people have faked orgiastic appreciation of many things that bored them, from the Grand Canyon to Rembrandt.

Women have been trained to deny our anger, and when it emerges in a poem, often we are ashamed. Poems are never total statements. In one day you can write two equally truthful poems of complete hostility and overwhelming love for one person. Sometimes if you can express the anger, you can better express the love.

I remember seeing a poem that a young man in a poetry workshop wrote that was revised from tenderness to pornography, because he was afraid to express publicly the love he felt for a woman; having to present the poem in workshop to an audience that included several other men was, I think, a factor in the evolution of the poem toward tits and ass.

I see an awful lot of poems in quarterlies that prefer boredom to risk. Writing a well-wrought poem of careful irony and shades of alienated indifference or mild self-pity comes as easily now as rimed quatrains about meadowlarks and nightingales to an earlier generation who looked out the window and like us, saw pigeons. They thought nightingales were poetic; every age has subjects it thinks nifty which turn out to be the cliches that succeeding generations prefer to forget.

Oftentimes when I am dealing with something that makes me nervous, I have the sensation of pushing myself off a cliff. Once again I think total absorption in the process and the product inhibits shame. There is a sense I have of forcing myself open. Sometimes I am not prepared to take that risk yet and must let the poem wait till I am psyched up to march onto whatever particular quaking ground I am contemplating. I am familiar too with the sense of not being able to resist a subject I know may get me into trouble, but the idea is just too good. I can't keep my mind from playing around with it till I'm hooked. I'm working on it before I've agreed to let myself do it. Then I lull myself by thinking I'll just run it through a bit and see how it goes. I can't really proceed with it; I won't send it out anyplace. It's just a lark. But I secretly and simultaneously know better. That's a propaganda technique for turning off my fear of consequences.

I think some poets who have the habit of writing drunk or stoned may be turning off that inner censor, but I can't work other than clear. The censor says, You can't say that, it will hurt your mother/father/brother/sister/husband/wife/lover/child/friend. The censor says, Write that and you'll lose that promotion or even your job. Or you'll lose custody of your kids. The censor says, What will your comrades say about that one? Is that politically correct according to the Slogan-of-the-Month Club? The censor says, Are you going to admit that in public? Nobody will want to sleep with you. Nobody will like you any more. They'll laugh at you behind your back. The censor says, That sounds crazy.

The poem in which you are finding out what you mean as you go may lead you to an insight that you might have preferred to forego. I have in fact figured things out in poems that I then had to apply to my life, to act on. I have more than once, for instance, found out how reprehensible I thought something a friend had done when I finished a poem I realized was about them. I could refuse to be judgmental in my daily self, but underneath, acquiescence was poisonous. I have discovered the same thing about myself, that something I have done that I felt good about had turned sour in me and I regretted it or felt guilty, and had not let myself know. Partway through such a poetic process, you may find yourself suddenly blocked, suddenly weary, desirous of doing anything else whatsoever: the laundry, balancing your checkbook, taking a swim, calling your mother. That is one of the times you must flog yourself forward if you want to get the poem.

And I guess I think you have to get the hard poems. You have to pay your dues by writing the ones that cost the most. I think the others get better then, but that may be superstition. . . .

One of the most important skills a workshop can teach you and support groups can show you is the kind of questions you want to ask yourself as you are finishing a poem. Sometimes it is a matter of cutting the umbilical cord. Seeing the poem as "it" rather than as "me." Seeing what I have really got down on paper, as opposed to the vision I began with or what I imagined I was capturing: It is a matter of taking a cold look.

Once in a while I write a poem and send it off, and a little oftener I will work on it through a number of drafts in a day and then send it off. Ninety-five percent of the time, however, I put the poem aside in draft two or ten and then pick it up again to give it that cold eye when the immediate involvement has receded. Sometimes I put a poem aside for months and decide not to deal with it again until I am entirely free from the circumstances, to see what I have really wrought that stands and what is just froth that has subsided. . . .

Basically I diddle and sweat over the poem because I don't think of it as primarily self-expression. I imagine the poem has a right to exist apart from me. Once I have conceived of the poem, I feel I ought to try to make it as strong and as clear and as beautiful as I am able. I revise endlessly. I write, usually, a number of drafts, although of course there are poems that come entire and that's that. What I'm concerned with here is the vast majority of poems that are built bit by bit and rebuilt and taken down and erected again. I revise when a poem comes back rejected. I revise after my first and sometimes after my second or third public reading of that work. I revise when I choose a poem to be included in a book of poetry every couple of years. When I brought together my selected poems, I revised some of those poems again.

I suppose on my deathbed, I'll still be working on a pile of poems I don't yet consider complete—some of which I probably started when I was sixteen.

Burying blues for Janis

Your voice always whacked me right on the funny bone
of the great-hearted suffering bitch fantasy
that ruled me like a huge copper moon with its phases
until I could, partially, break free.
How could I help but cherish you for my bad dreams?
Your voice would grate right on the marrow-filled bone
that cooks up that rich stew of masochism where we swim,
that woman is born to suffer, mistreated and cheated.
We are trained to that hothouse of ripe pain.
Never do we feel so alive, so in character
as when we're walking the floor with the all-night blues.
When some man not being there who's better gone
becomes a lack that swells up to a gaseous balloon
and flattens from us all thinking and sensing and purpose.

Oh, the downtrodden juicy longdrawn female blues:
you throbbed up there with your face slightly swollen
and your barbed hair flying energized and poured it out,
the blast of a furnace of which the whole life is the fuel.
You embodied that good done-in mama who gives and gives
like a fountain of boozy chicken soup to a rat race of men.
You embodied the pain hugged to the breasts like a baby.
You embodied the beautiful blowzy gum of passivity,
woman on her back to the world endlessly hopelessly raggedly
offering a brave front to be fucked.
That willingness to hang on the meathook and call it love,
that need for loving like a screaming hollow in the soul,
that's the drug that hangs us and drags us down
deadly as the icy sleet of skag that froze your blood.

To be of use

The people I love the best
jump into work head first
without dallying in the shallows
and swim off with sure strokes almost out of sight.
They seem to become natives of that element,
the black sleek heads of seals
bouncing like half-submerged balls.

I love people who harness themselves, an ox to a heavy cart,
who pull like water buffalo, with massive patience,
who strain in the mud and the muck to move things forward,
who do what has to be done, again and again.

I want to be with people who submerge
in the task, who go into the fields to harvest
and work in a row and pass the bags along,
who are not parlor generals and field deserters
but move in a common rhythm
when the food must come in or the fire be put out.

The work of the world is common as mud.
Botched, it smears the hands, crumbles to dust.
But the thing worth doing well done
has a shape that satisfies, clean and evident.

Greek amphoras for wine or oil,
Hopi vases that held corn, are put in museums
but you know they were made to be used.
The pitcher cries for water to carry
and a person for work that is real.

The market economy

Suppose some peddler offered
you can have a color TV
but your baby will be
born with a crooked spine;
you cah have polyvinyl cups
and wash and wear
suits but it will cost
you your left lung
rotted with cancer; suppose
somebody offered you
a frozen precooked dinner
every night for ten years
but at the end
your colon dies
and then you do,
slowly and with much pain.
You get a house in the suburbs
but you work in a new plastics
factory and die at fifty-one
when your kidneys turn off.

But where else will you
work? where else can
you rent but Smog City?
The only houses for sale
are under the yellow sky.
You've been out of work for
a year and they're hiring
at the plastics factory.
Don't read the fine
print, there isn't any.

Let us gather at the river

I am the woman who sits by the river
river of tears
river of sewage
river of rainbows.
I sit by the river and count the corpses
floating by from the war upstream.
I sit by the river and watch the water
dwindle and the banks poke out like sore gums.
I watch the water change from green to shit brown.
I sit by the river and fish for your soul.
I want to lick it clean.
I want to turn it into a butterfly
that will weave drunkenly from orchid to rose.
I want to turn it into a pumpkin.
I want it to turn itself into a human being.

Oh, close your eyes tight and push hard
and evolve, all together now. We can
do it if we try. Concentrate
and hold hands and push.
You can take your world back
if you want to. It's an araucana
egg, all blue and green
swaddled in filmy clouds.
Don't let them cook and gobble it,
azure and jungle green egg laid
by the extinct phoenix of the universe.

Send me your worn hacks of tired themes,
your dying horses of liberation,
your poor bony mules of freedom now.
I am the woman sitting by the river.
I mend old rebellions and patch them new.

Now the river turns from shit brown to bubbling blood
as an arm dressed in a uniform
floats by like an idling log.
Up too high to see, bombers big as bowling alleys
streak over and the automated battlefield
lights up like a Star Wars pinball machine.

I am the old woman sitting by the river scolding corpses.
I want to stare into the river and see the bottom
glinting like clean hair.
I want to outlive my usefulness
and sing water songs, songs
in praise of the green brown river
flowing clean through the blue green world.

Hummingbird

Metallic apparition whirring
like a helicopter,
the golden nightingale of the Chinese
emperor breaking the sound
barrier, you seem almost
a weapon, too exquisite,
too expensive to be
useful, flashing
like a jeweled signal.
You could be a miniature
spacecraft from the Vegan
system.

Then I watch you at the orange-
salmon faces of the canna
and you are avid.
Your long beak darts,
pokes, stabs and stabs
deep in the flesh
of the flower as you sip
hovering, standing still
in the middle of the air.

Impatient, you waste no time
in going but materialize
before the bee balm, then
fast as a spark shot
from the heart of a fire
you at once thirty feet
distant drink at the phlox.

Keen at your pleasures
you zip through the garden.
Like seeing a falling
star from the corner
of my eye, as I question
the sight, it's gone.
But before the lilies
you dance probing
the last drop of nectar.

Baby at every breast,
your clean greed dazzles.
Passion has streamlined you,
no waste, no hesitation.
Every dawn hones
your hunger gleaming sharp
till death seizes
and drinks you down.

The watch

At this moment hundreds of women
a few miles from here are looking
for the same sign of reprieve, the red
splash of freedom. We run to check,
squirming through rituals of If I don't
look till two o'clock, if I skip lunch,
if I am good, if I am truly sorry,
probing, poking, hallucinating changes.
Flower, red lily, scarlet petunia
bloom for me. And some lesser number
of women in other bedrooms and bathrooms
see that red banner unfurl and mourn!
Another month, another chance missed.
Forty years of our lives, that flag
is shown or not and our immediate
and sometimes final fate determined,
red as tulips, red as poppies satin,
red as taillights, red as a stoplight,
red as dying, our quick bright blood.

The common living dirt

The small ears prick on the bushes,
furry buds, shoots tender and pale.
The swamp maples blow scarlet.
Color teases the corner of the eye,
delicate gold, chartreuse, crimson,
mauve speckled, just dashed on.

The soil stretches naked. All winter
hidden under the down comforter of snow,
delicious now, rich in the hand
as chocolate cake: the fragrant busy
soil the worm passes through her gut
and the beetle swims in like a lake.

As I kneel to put the seeds in
careful as stitching, I am in love.
You are the bed we all sleep on.
You are the food we eat, the food
we ate, the food we will become.
We are walking trees rooted in you.

You can live thousands of years
undressing in the spring your black
body, your red body, your brown body
penetrated by the rain. Here
is the goddess unveiled,
the earth opening her strong thighs.

Yet you grow exhausted with bearing
too much, too soon, too often, just
as a woman wears through like an old rug.
We have contempt for what we spring
from. Dirt, we say, you're dirt
as if we were not all your children.

We have lost the simplest gratitude.
We lack the knowledge we showed ten
thousand years past, that you live
a goddess but mortal, that what we take
must be returned; that the poison we drop

in you will stunt our children's growth.

Tending a plot of your flesh binds
me as nothing ever could, to the seasons,
to the will of the plants, clamorous
in their green tenderness. What
calls louder than the cry of a field
of corn ready, or trees of ripe peaches?

I worship on my knees, laying
the seeds in you, that worship rooted
in need, in hunger, in kinship,
flesh of the planet with my own flesh,
a ritual of compost, a litany of manure.
My garden's a chapel, but a meadow

gone wild in grass and flower
is a cathedral. How you seethe
with little quick ones, vole, field
mouse, shrew and mole in their thousands,
rabbit and woodchuck. In you rest
the jewels of the genes wrapped in seed.

Power warps because it involves joy
in domination; also because it means
forgetting how we too starve, break
like a corn stalk in the wind, how we
die like the spinach of drought,
how what slays the vole slays us.

Because you can die of overwork, because
you can die of the fire that melts
rock, because you can die of the poison
that kills the beetle and the slug,
we must come again to worship you
on our knees, the common living dirt.

STANLEY PLUMLY

STANLEY PLUMLY *was born in Barnesville, Ohio, in 1939, and educated at Wilmington College and Ohio University. He has taught at Columbia, the Universities of Washington and Iowa, and the University of Houston, where he is now a writer in residence. His first book,* In the Outer Dark *(1970), won the Delmore Schwartz Memorial Award, and* Out-of-the-Body Travel *(1977) was nominated for a National Book Critics' Circle Award in 1978. His other collections are* Giraffe *(1973) and* Summer Celestial *(1983). (Photo by Alvilda McWilliams)*

Poetry and Intimacy

Sometimes I've sat up all night trying to get a few lines down, trying to sort out memory from the matter in front of me. I'm never sure how helpful remembering is; it's simply built in. So why not surrender. Yet when you're sitting there with the pieces of a poem you long for the intervention of some inhering, immediate good sense, the good god who draws lines of connection. Loneliness, it seems to me, is being isolated in memory. If we love the language for anything we love its ability to focus the moment, to put us in place, to make the moment more possible, to build passage between what has happened and who we are.

The moment, though, is not just the flesh tilling the air. It is also sitting down at the end of the day or rising with the morning to try to do nothing more than write a good sentence. It is the moment within the word. Language may be the metaphor for memory—how we enter the house justified—but the moment is the language alive.

Language cannot make things up; it can only make them from. The making is of the moment, as Keats, under the plum tree at evensong, having heard the nightingale, makes of his brother's death his secret elegy. It is word-of-mouth, spoken into the silence.

Intimacy can be the difference between a word written and a word said. Poems are words said—one solitude speaking to another, to quote Rilke, one speaker to one listener, as if a poem, for all its publicity, were personal, rumor, spoken in secret. Metaphor is the language of secrets, a go-between, the messenger and the message confused. Perhaps that is why poetry and dreaming, dreaming and musing, are so closely connected. The poet passes on the information, having heard it through cupped hands in the privacy of sleep. Secrets, like dreams, are invented out of memory.

We write in rooms, a secret space. As a table is a smaller, secret space, and a bed a smaller, intimate space. Even the page is blind to what we will put there. It has its secret too. In 1928, Yeats, a sixty-year-old smiling public man, sees, as if from memory, his aging muse, Maud Gonne, as hollow of cheek, as though it drank the wind and took a mess of shadows for its meat. The metaphor of *mess* reads in the first American printing of the poem as *mass*. If it's a mistake it nevertheless teaches us the difference between description and evocation, written and spoken. *Mass* is of descriptive value alone. The discovered word, the word we now read, speaks from the intimacy of its context as a secret from its source.

"Among School Children" offers the processional skill of a man without answers, whose heart by now is an open secret. It is no accident that it takes place in a schoolroom, the most secret institutional space there is. In a country school in Ohio, on warm days, with the big windows open, the blackboard filled with names and numbers, you could almost imagine the world. I remember once a bird flew in—it was May and we were mad to be outside. We were children. We screamed and covered our heads. We were terrified, as was the bird, which had begun hitting the walls. Finally, thankfully, within moments, it flew back out. For some while after no one said anything; one or two of us cried, head on the desk. The room had changed, the out-of-doors had come in, suddenly, like a sign or signal. A little spot in time. A message.

What the signal means, what the sign says. The secret is kept by being shared, passed on. Intimacy is the act of secrets kept. Letters, like poems, are secrets passed between individuals. Yet when we put the letters of Emily Dickinson beside her poems we must wonder who her correspondent really is. There can be no question, though, that Keats, writing his great and painful and fraternal letters, means to be overheard, means to provide us with the fullest possible context for his poems. Companionable, his letters are metaphors of resources.

Whether he is providing axioms for poetry—"I think Poetry should surprise by a fine excess and not by Singularity"—or news of his brother's death—"I have scarce a doubt of immortality of some nature or other—neither had Tom"—Keats is aware that his respondent is also his reader, the one who understands, the one to whom the feeling, the voice of the information is passed, the one who knows that little of what is promised is possible. Against the imperatives of time, his letters challenge the interest of the poems in how much can be shared in secrecy, in how much the word can carry, and in how much a life can be story, memory, or lucky.

The Iron Lung

So this is the dust that passes through porcelain,
so this is the unwashed glass left over from supper,
so this is the air in the attic, in August,
and this the down on the breath of the sleeper . . .

If we could fold our arms, but we can't.
If we could cross our legs, but we can't.
If we could put the mind to rest . . .
But our fathers have set this task before us.

My face moons in the mirror, weightless,
without air, my head propped like a penny.
I'm dressed in a shoe, ready to walk out
of here. I'm wearing my father's body.

I remember my mother standing in the doorway
trying to tell me something. The day is thick
with the heat rising from the road. I am
too far away. She looks like my sister.

And I am dreaming of my mother in a doorway
telling my father to die or go away.
It is the front door, and my drunken father falls
to the porch on his knees like one of his children.

It is precisely at this moment I realize
I have polio and will never walk again.
And I am in the road on my knees, like my father,
but as if I were growing into the ground

I can neither move nor rise.
The neighborhood is gathering, and now
my father is lifting me into the ambulance
among the faces of my family. His face is

a blur or a bruise and he holds me
as if I had just been born. When I wake
I am breathing out of all proportion to myself.
My whole body is a lung; I am floating

above a doorway or a grave. And I know
I am in this breathing room as one
who understands how breath is passed
from father to son and passed back again.

At night, when my father comes to talk,
I tell him we have shared this body long enough.
He nods, like the speaker in a dream.
He knows that I know we're only talking.

Once there was a machine for breathing.
It would embrace the body and make a kind of love.
And when it was finished it would rise
like nothing at all above the earth

to drift through the daylight silence.
But at dark, in deep summer, if you thought you heard
something like your mother's voice calling you home,
you could lie down where you were and listen to the dead.

Out-of-the-Body Travel

1
And then he would lift this finest
of furniture to his big left shoulder
and tuck it in and draw the bow
so carefully as to make the music

almost visible on the air. And play
and play until a whole roomful of the sad
relatives mourned. They knew this was
drawing of blood, threading and rethreading

the needle. They saw even in my father's
face how well he understood the pain
he put them to—his raw, red cheek
pressed against the cheek of the wood . . .

2
And in one stroke he brings the hammer
down, like mercy, so that the young bull's

legs suddenly fly out from under it . . .
While in the dream he is the good angel

in Chagall, the great ghost of his body
like light over the town. The violin
sustains him. It is pain remembered.
Either way, I know if I wake up cold,

and go out into the clear spring night,
still dark and precise with stars,
I will feel the wind coming down hard
like his hand, in fever, on my forehead.

Now That My Father
Lies Down Beside Me

We lie in that other darkness, ourselves.
There is less than the width of my left hand
between us. I can barely breathe,
but the light breathes easily,
wind on water across our two still bodies.

I cannot even turn to see him.
I would not touch him. Nor would I lift
my arm into the crescent of a moon.
(There is no star in the sky of this room,
only the light fashioning fish along the walls.
They swim and swallow one another.)

I dream we lie under water,
caught in our own sure drift.
A window, white shadow, trembles over us.
Light breaks into a moving circle.
He would not speak and I would not touch him.

It is an ocean under here.
Whatever two we were, we become
one falling body, one breath. Night lies down
at the sleeping center—no fish, no shadow,

no single, turning light. And I would not touch him
who lies deeper in the drifting dark than life.

Posthumous Keats

The road is so rough Severn is walking,
and every once in a while, since the season is
beautiful and there are flowers on both sides,
as if this path had just been plowed,
he picks by the handful what he can

and still keep up. Keats is in the carriage
swallowing blood and the best of the bad food.
It is early November, like summer,
honey and wheat in the last of the
daylight, and above the mountains a clear

carnelian heartline. Rome is a week
away. And Severn has started to fill
the carriage with wildflowers—rust, magenta,
marigold, and the china white of cups.
Keats is floating, his whole face luminous.

The biographer sees no glory in this,
how the living, by increments, are dead,
how they celebrate their passing half in love.
Keats, like his young companion, is alone,
among color and a long memory.

In his head he is writing a letter
about failure and money and the ten-
thousand lines that could not save his brother.
But he might as well be back at Gravesend
with the smell of the sea and the cold sea rain,

waiting out the weather and the tide—
he might as well be lying in a room,
in Rome, staring at a ceiling stylized
with roses or watching outside right now
a cardinal with two footmen shooting birds.

He can still remember the meadows near
St. Cross, the taste in the air of apples,
the tower and alms-square, and the River
Itchen, all within the walk of a mile.
In the poem it is Sunday, the middle

of September, the light a gold conglomerate
of detail—"in the same way that some pictures
look warm." He has closed his eyes.
And he is going to let the day close down.
He is thinking he must learn Italian.

By the time they reach the Campagna the wind
will be blowing, the kind that begins at sea.
Severn will have climbed back in, finally a
passenger, with one more handful to add
to what is already overwhelming.

My Mother's Feet

        How no shoe fit them,
and how she used to prop them,
having dressed for bed,
letting the fire in the coal-stove blue

and blink out, falling asleep in her chair.
How she bathed and dried them, night after night,
and rubbed their soreness like an intimacy.
How she let the fire pull her soft body through them.

She was the girl who grew just standing,
the one the picture cut at the knees.
She was the girl who seemed to be dancing
out on the lawn, after supper, alone.

I have watched her climb the militant stairs
and down again, watched the ground go out from under her.
I have seen her on the edge of chances—
she fell, when she fell, like a girl.

Someone who loved her said she walked on water.

Where there is no path nor wake. As a child
I would rise in the half-dark of the house,
from a bad dream or a noisy window,

something, almost, like snow in the air,
and wander until I could find those feet, propped
and warm as a bricklayer's hands,
every step of the way shining out of them.

Blossom

And after a while he'd say his head was a rose,
a big beautiful rose, and he was going to blow it
all over the room, he was going to blast blood.

And after a while he'd just put his head in his one good
hand the way children do who want to go into hiding.

I still can't get the smell of smoke from a woodstove out of my head.
A woman is frying bacon and the odor is char and sour and
      somebody
running a finger over your tongue. All those dead years and the
      grease

still glue in the wall. In Winchester, Virginia, the year the war
ended, the blacks were still dark clouds. My uncle had a knife
pulled on him holding his nose.

                              When the Guard marched eleven
German prisoners of war down from Washington they marched
      them
right through town, and it was spring and a parade like apple
      blossom.
Black and white, we lined up just to watch.

I still can't get the smell of apples out of my head—
trees in orchards all over the county, like flowers in a garden.
The trees the Germans planted that spring looked like flowers,

thin as whips. Even so the branch of a full-grown apple tree

is tested every summer: when I didn't watch I picked along with
every black boy big enough to lift a bushel. Frederick County.

The National Guard in nineteen forty-five was my father and any
other son who stayed home. Next door the father of my friend
had been home two long years, one arm, one leg gone. He was

honorary. He was white sometimes, and black, depending.
He was leaf and woodsmoke and leaning always into the wind.

And everybody called him Blossom because of the piece of apple
he kept tucked at one side of his mouth. When he was drinking
he'd bring his bottle over and talk to my father about Germans.

They go down, he'd say, they all go down on their guns.

Each five-petaled flower on the tree means an apple come summer.
I still can't get the bourbon smell of Blossom out of my head.
He spits his apple out and shoots himself in the mouth with his
   finger.

American Ash

The day is late enough you could stand
within the time it takes a door to drift
back shut and watch half a tree go dark,
the other half still green with the afternoon.
I have in mind the big one down the street,
west of the house, the light so stacked and split
it bottles up, brilliant at the top.
Downing going the other way is shade.
Upstairs the light is candle-in-a-shell.
Someone is getting ready to go to bed.
The house is rich with camphor, mint, and oil
of wintergreen, and on the dining table
roses in a bowl.
                    I think it is nineteen
forty-five. Sepia will never get
quite right the year in color, my mother's
dress, for instance, red and yellow daisies
on a regimental blue to end the war,

nor my father home from work to work his garden.
He has a lantern. It is almost May,
the streetlights coming on, one to a corner.
If it is true the soul is other people,
then the antique finish of the thing
is how we love the past, how the aging
of a photograph becomes, like leaves, deciduous.
At the head of the stairs my mother's
mother's bedroom and beside hers the mahogany
and cedar of her father's . . . For a hundred years
the sun has set against the high side of the house.
I could climb those stairs, I could sleep and be
filled with the dead odors of moths and wools
and silks, with the sweet addictions of the flesh.
I could float a little lifetime above the kitchen talk,
branch, green, the sudden burden of the leaves.

Waders and Swimmers

The first morning it flew out of the fog
I thought it lived there.
It floated into shore all shoulders,
all water and air. It was cold that summer.
In the white dark the sun coming up was the moon.
And then this beautiful bird,
its wings as large as a man, drawing the line
of itself out of the light behind it.
A month or more it flew out of the fog,
fished, fed, gone in a moment.

There are no blue herons in Ohio.
But one October in a park I saw a swan
lift itself from the water in singular, vertical strokes.
It got high enough to come back down wild.
It ate bread from the hand
and swallowed in long, irregular gestures.
It seemed, to a child, almost angry.
I remember what I hated
when someone tied it wing-wide to a tree.
The note nailed to its neck said this is nothing.

The air is nothing, though it rise
and fall. Another year
a bird the size of a whooping crane
flew up the Hocking—
people had never seen a bird that close
so large and white at once.
They called it their ghost and went back to their Bibles.
It stood on houses for days, lost,
smoke from the river.
In the wing-light of the dawn it must have passed

its shadow coming and going. I wish I knew.
I still worry a swan alive
through an early Ohio winter, still worry
its stuttering, clipped wings.
It rises in snow, white on white, the way
in memory one thing is confused with another.
From here to a bird that flies
with its neck folded back to its shoulders
is nothing but air, nothing but first light and summer
and water rising in a smoke of waters.

Merriman's Cove, Maine

WILLIAM PITT ROOT

WILLIAM PITT ROOT *was born in 1941 in Austin, Minnesota, but spent his childhood near the Gulf coast of Florida. He has degrees from the University of Washington and the University of North Carolina, Greensboro. Currently a professor of English at the University of Montana, he has often served as writer-in-residence at other colleges and universities, and many Poetry-in-the-Schools programs. His awards include a Wallace Stegner Writing Fellowship at Stanford University, and grants from the Rockefeller and Guggenheim Foundations. He is a prolific poet whose books have appeared from both large and small presses.* The Storm and Other Poems *(1969) was followed by, to name just three,* Striking the Dark Air for Music *(1973),* In the World's Common Grasses *(1981), and* Reasons for Going It on Foot *(1981).*
(Photo by Pamela Uschuk)

How Would We Know There Was A Sun If We Were Blind?: Some Notes On Poetry

I write poems because I've never learned to play blues harmonica or flamenco guitar, and had to make words my instruments or be riddled with the silences of the music I could not otherwise tell.

* * *

Whether you are left-handed or right-handed makes little difference if you compose on a typewriter, which I often do; I assume working with both hands stimulates the right and left sides of the brain simultaneously, enjoining the critical-rational faculties as well as the intuitive-creative impulses. I certainly wouldn't want to be the one to research this notion, though.

* * *

This morning I interrupted this session of note-taking to instruct my daughter, Jennifer, in driving with a four-speed stick shift; the first and hardest part is learning to get the car in motion without killing the engine or any stray dogs, each gear after the first being relatively easy to engage smoothly. That process is not unlike learning to write: first the sitting down and concentrating on what's at hand to express it in literate terms, then as that becomes easier, shifting into more accelerated thinking and visualization, until finally the impulse to go forward is so automatically implemented at the mechanical level that impulse seems immediately to realize itself. And things start to move.

* * *

"Confessional" poetry: to be authentic, confession requires several elements wholly lacking from this poetry. It requires not only the admission of guilt but a sense of shame or regret and a willingness to attempt self-reformation. It also requires an audience, but that audience is not a mirror and is not the reading public; it is God, or a sense of something greater than one's own ego. To parade one's follies is not to repent them; to exploit one's self by such a light is an act not of faith but of despair. These poets did not so much confess as complain—that their follies were not fulfilling enough.

* * *

"Fleshflower" is a poem I wanted to write for some years before I could attempt it. The notion formed in part as a response to a poem by Denise Levertov, one in which she said she believed men must find the cunt ugly to look at. Other poets, of course, have approached the subject with varying degrees of directness and eloquence. Some of the ancient Sanskrit poets, for instance, and the Taoist authors of *The Yellow Book*. More recently, in her "Caritas" poems, Olga Broumas has stunning passages about female sexuality, luminously graphic and wonderfully tender. But it was not until I heard from the poet and Sinologist Sam Hamill about the Chinese character I refer to at the end of my poem, that I had that bit of hard evocative fact around which the poem began to form, rather as droplets form in the track of a cosmic ray shot through a cloud chamber. I'm aware the image of the cunt as a flower is not only a standard image, a veritable archetype, but that in feminist circles it is a laughable romanticism. If the image is evoked mechanically or superficially, it warrants amusement. Nonetheless, I take seriously Dylan Thomas' claim that one of the tasks of the poet is to reclaim words and images degraded by careless usage. It's what I've tried to do.

* * *

"Under the Umbrella of Blood" was the first poem I wrote after turning forty. My book *Reasons for Going It on Foot* had recently been reviewed by a critic who opened with a quote he attributed to Delacroix: "When a twenty-year-old writes poetry, he is twenty; when a forty-year-old writes poetry, he is a poet." He meant it as a compliment, but he had miscalculated the age at which I'd been writing the poems in that book, which came out when I was thirty-nine. So I put off writing any new poems until I could feel that the one coming on would be worthy of inaugurating this era in my life. It came as I took the shower in the first line. The vinegar-Turk association is mysterious even to me, but that I wrote the poem with poets vs. critics at the back of my mind is clear enough. I also had the conclusion from an early poem of Kenneth O. Hanson in mind, in which he describes a wandering song-writer "anxious to get the set of the lines just right," which he certainly did. The story itself, of the Turks, is one I heard— overheard, really—when I was a small child and have never been able to forget.

* * *

The method of "Sea-grape Tree and the Miraculous" was identical to that which produced "The Storm" almost twenty years earlier. I began with the expectation that I would go from A to Z, straight through, in an unbroken rush of energy; instead, I made false start after false start, each time bogging down twenty or thirty lines into the poem and despairing of ever finding the right point of entry. Only after a week or ten days of such failures did I see that the poem was indeed occurring, but in segments rather than in that undauntable charge I had imagined would carry me, without interruption, from start to finish.

A tiny newspaper article about the "miracle," and a subsequent follow-up describing the results, spurred me to start the poem, out of a rather reflexive sort of indignation; only when the poem was underway did the various recollections of my own experiences with a sea-grape tree in our backyard in Florida during my childhood begin to flood me and commandeer portions of the poem.

* * *

Which poems are good, which not so good, and which bad: How to tell.

Public applause is by no means the only or best cue to the goodness or badness of a poem. In *The Man Who Killed the Deer* by Frank Waters, there's a trial method (Navajo or Hopi?) which is instructive. After the accused has given his testimony, a silence follows during which the Indian jurors consider the quality of the silence itself for indications of truthfulness or deception, innocence or guilt. At readings, it is sometimes the case that certain kinds of silence are a stronger index of power than the applause that follows.

Publication is a sorry test. Not only are books full of weak poems, but magazines and lit mags as well, in which poems are chosen for reasons inscrutable to a discerning reader. Many of my own best poems have never appeared in lit mags—"Fleshflower," "Song of Returnings," "Under the Umbrella of Blood," "Sea-grape Tree and the Miraculous"—despite numerous times out in the mail. I've twice had entire books rejected because I refused to remove the long poems which were their strongest features.

Reviews, even favorable ones, often seem to be about books by someone else—I still find that baffling. Often it is as though the reader has approached the book with certain preoccupations so overwhelming that only the poems which trigger those associations are dealt with, though they may constitute a minor element of the whole. Good readers are rarer than we dare believe.

* * *

Watching how sea-horses navigate with those tiny delicate wings on their heads, the image of Mercury with his similarly winged feet gains a new credibility. I once took a 35 mm black and white photograph of some boys playing soccer in a Roman plaza. When I blew it up to 11 × 14, I saw the cornerstone for one of the buildings had carved into it a marvellous sea-horse I hadn't noticed before. It struck me as being a secret, revealed but mysterious, as the true secrets always are, especially in what we call the poetic realms.

* * *

Personality and character: the first we develop to get along with our fellow human beings, the second to get along with our secret gods. It isn't difficult to tell which poets have gods to deal with and which are content with social devotions.

* * *

Syntax may well be the most intimate aspect of a poet's work. It is there—rather than in image, idea, or diction—that we learn the most about the complexities of a mind and the convolutions of grace in a spirit, just as we know so much more after observing someone dancing than we could ever glean from a driver's license or lecture.

* * *

True poems fill your heart full of their moment.

* * *

Have poets always been so possessive of their art? Surely not. But today, in this country, specialization afflicts poets, and their audiences as well, to the extent that few poets would dare read to an unspecialized audience at a Grange or Union Hall. Neruda could, and did. Voznesensky, Sandburg, Woodie Guthrie. While the development of universities and critics has encouraged the practice of poetry as a literary art, the much older tradition of the troubador and harper has kept poetry alive in the hearts of living audiences on a scale American poets now only dream of.

* * *

An interesting experiment: psychologists interested in perceptual education held up a quarter before a classroom of pre-school children asked to draw exactly what they saw. Some drew the black-board as well as a stick figure, some included the classroom windows as well— with birds, clouds or trees outside—but most drew the quarter, in shapes ranging from a straight line (if they sat at the very edge of the front row) through oval shapes to the full circle (if they sat at the center). The same request after two years of formal education drew different results: all students simply drew the quarter and all the quarters were perfectly round. The young still saw with their eyes; in two years they saw with ideas. When Joyce declared "We must wipe off our glosses," he was pointing out a prerequisite to his better-known dictum that artists must "forge the uncreated conscience of our race." Consciousness precedes conscience. Poets and other artists must shed the acquired scales on their eyes since they must see clearly to speak truly.

* * *

How would we know there was a sun if we were blind? If we were all blind, always had been blind, we would know neither the sun nor our blindness. It is because we all were children once with pristine vision that we can respond so powerfully to the paradisiacal notion of Eden; and because we all learned blindness at the foot of the Tree of Knowledge that we know the places east of Eden; and because of artists and poets that we can be restored, even briefly, to the magical first knowledge got by returning to our senses, quickening.

Song of Returnings

All the bones of the horses rise in moonlight
on the flatlands, dropping
from trees, squeezing out from
under rocks, disengaging themselves
from the earth and things that live from the earth
and the scattered uniforms assemble
   to the sounds of bugling come back from the stars
and what has rotted into dust reforms with a furious sound
   of whirlwind tearing the faces from the astonished living
and gold flows molten from the mouth of Cortez
   and returns to the stones and the water and the air
and the redwoods collapse back into cones
and Christ is pried from the cross and flogged and spat upon
   and let loose among fishermen who scatter to their ships
   and enters his mother's womb and enters into the stars
and Babylon reassembles and Sodom and Gomorrah reassemble

and David sings then babbles in his mother's arms
and all living things return to their sources
and the waters return to their sources
and the sun returns to the source
and the vast darkness returns
and all things are
and are not.

Fleshflower

1.
   There is one flower,
one blossom,
exotic and common,
blooming only in the dark
despite sunlight and moonlight.

Despite starlight and streetlight
it blooms
   only in darkness
and is blooming everywhere
around us, always.

Unblinking.

2.
It is the flower of electric muscle
darkrimmed, half concealed,
   and at the hollow core
pink as sunrise, a white rabbit's eye. Closeup

it can be opened as a honeyburdened
blossom, by tongue,
by fingertip,
by the right words sung at the right pitch.

Closeup you see that it is blind, is
slowly weeping. It trusts

simply the genius
   native to those complex roots

extending outward to the stars and
in toward each cell's center
to determine,
Is this friend or foe prying
the leaves

apart, trying

some kind of entry, some
visitation?

3.
   If the ground
the plant is bedded in
entirely approves the care
afforded by your gardening hands,
if you tender it with gentleness
enough, with strength enough
and of the right kind,

and with songs vibrant as the
humming of the bee is
to the blind heart of its most random choosing
in the world that blossoms
only at its and at the wind's
wandering but insistent touch,

it will take you in
to the radiant secret chamber,
it will set beating your wild second heart
in its good time and yours.

It will accord you morning and evening glory.
It will cause you a sweet crown of joy.

4.
In a tongue not ours
but human as we are human

there is a written character
which makes three names:

Call it *Tulip* you will name it truly.

Call it *Cunt* you speak its second name.

Or let truth have its home
for a moment on your tongue,
and utter it in praise

for its last name is called *Gates of Paradise.*

Under the Umbrella of Blood

In the shower not ten minutes ago and blind from the vinegar rinse
I was thinking 40, I'm 40
when the stinging reminded me of how Turks used to bet on
just how far a headless man could run.
                                            —It was orderly, in its way,
with a band of selected prisoners, troops in attendance, distance
    markers,
the executioner with his two-handed sword and another man
    holding
a hammered copper plate glowing like the sun at the end of a pole;
as the prisoners one at a time ran past, the sword took off their
    heads
and the plate scorched the neckstumps shut to keep blood pressure
    up
so the runners ran farther, each stumbling on under the umbrella of
    blood
until the disfigured collapse, all legs and loose elbows.

Do you suppose as each head fell staring and revolving
that it could hear the tossed coins clink on the outspread blanket?
Could it see the body running off without it?
As it lay speechless, facing dirt or the sky, as chance would have it,
would it know whether it won or lost for its learned critics?

I wonder, and I rush off to the typewriter wiping my eyes clear,
knowing if I am to get it right

the images under the final downpour must be running
faster than the applauding coins of the world can ever fall.

Sea-grape Tree and the Miraculous

1.
The laboratories explain it away in retrospect as chemistry,
a compound in the pitch; their researchers
have worked with it for years, experimenting
on cataracts in caged rats and drugged monkeys.

Alfredo Verona, at 92, in Miami's Little Havana,
a free man too poor for doctors,
never had heard of
such researchers the day he reached out
to the sea-grape tree, the night he saw the moon rise
for the first time in a dozen years.

And I had not heard of that man before his quick miracle
restored for him a world polished in new tears,
nor had I thought, since childhood,
of the sea-grape tree I grew up with, never
imagining I would forget it
or that news of a miracle would restore it.

And what is the true nature of the miraculous?

Surely it is not science, arrived at by logic
and repeated demonstrations which would open
the unknown with the knock of a committee;
there's a cunning beyond such calculation
once the rationalist, vexed by paradox,
surrenders to the vision in a dream
and receives an image of the double helix.
The diamond that vanishes perfectly in water
reappears exactly when the thirsty man drinks.

2.
How young I must have been to
stand there
in the grasses

behind my parents' house
on the enormous spur of land
that is Florida,
           gazing up
into and out along
the great sinuous dance of those limbs, imagining
that they were wooden
extensions of the underground rivers
I had not believed in
before I turned the gardenhose on full force
driving it nozzle-first
into the sandy earth
until it took two neighbors, both grown-ups,
to retrieve it.
          And there stood
my mother, embarrassed, baffled
by her son again, who
stood there wide-eyed, awed
by knowledge of a new river
no eye could ever see and no toe enter
except at the risk
of descending irresistibly into the earth
from which only neighbors,
           muttering and shaking their heads,
ever could haul him back up into sunlight.

3.
Out of that conjunction of my shadow and yours
           and the trajectory of
the invisible river mercuric
underfoot,
underheart, you, tree of my youth, sprang
like an aorta of forked stone,

sprang gradually, gracefully,
           a natural history of innocence
winding through blue air like the deep impulse you are,
an empire of songbirds,

and out along your vibrant limbs
           I would climb
—away from the earth, away from its underground
riddled with those inaudible waters troubling the sands

and ominously
constant, eating ground out from under my feet,
undermining that early faith in solid earth.

4.

What place could I dream of then able to withstand
the waters under the earth
suddenly real,
suddenly filled with images of a grey population
            of turtles, white-eyed garfish,
alligators ancient and goliath with milk quartz
installed in their blind skulls,
                a constellation of stiff bodies adrift
in those grim currents, pale and swollen, countless.

For this was the river of the kingdom of death and I knew
without being told
how deeply I and all living things were involved;
that's when I turned
to you again, you
whose endless thirst rooted you in that abyss
but drawing up this darkness made it blossom into foliage and song
—the same waters
that otherwise
would be sucking caskets clean. And I dared to tell no one
the contagion of that knowledge.

5.
So I climbed up into you
                and climbed until
                        the highest breezes cleansed me,
taking refuge there among your thick queer leaves
            where I could rock, singing
                    spirit songs any ear but yours would spoil,
clinging to the power of your limbs,
and they would sway
gently, bow
slowly under the swaying sun
whose broad light lay like insubstantial hands across my skin.

6.
In those sacred hours my songs were like the light
coming from everywhere at once

—from the sun scattering your shadows
and from birds flittering
among your leaves
round like green ears all about me:
     the red-winged blackbirds
like glimpses of distant fires at night,
the crowned blue jays, raucous,
tougher than the rest; the wild canaries darting among lemons,
the cardinals demure among the mangoes,
crows wisely gleaming, kingfishers and herons,
hoot-owls hooting in the hush of long nights
     lit by the moonlike eyes of rabbits.

7.
And the magical knowledge of names!

When mourning doves mourned from the telephone lines
and mocking birds startled me
    with their perfect mockery
and whip-poor-wills cried their names over and over
from both thresholds of darkness so clearly
that I would go out to stand in the tangled fields, ecstatic,

then I began to hear meaning sing.

At night, late, when I was supposed to sleep,
I lay in bed, my chameleon
nestled along my nose,
his belly a horizon rising and falling
by one eye; sometimes
I lay there hearing you like a ghost at sea
    creaking and rustling
by the sleeping porch,
giving the winds
a body to whisper through; sometimes
when the house was still
I lay for hours, radio
held to my ear and tuned to Havana,
dim red tubes miraculously
wiring my skull with a language that sang
even without the music,
songs so quick my heart skipped beats to hear.

I learned that even my homeplace, Florida,
sang with that tongue,
> sang "flowers,"
> sang tea-roses and hibiscus,
> sang jacaranda and gay bougainvillea,
> sang day's-eye daisy and sword-of-the-gladiator gladiolus,
> sang orchid double-rooted like the testicle, and tooth-of-the lion
> > dandelion,
sang honeysuckle from which we sipped the delicate sweetness,
sang croton and poinsettia, saffron crocus and rumpled
> > elephant's-ears,
sang water-lilies afloat upon the waters,
sang sea-grape trees.

8.
So this ancient man approaches you with his blinding years, daubs
his clouded eyes
with your clear pitch
. . . soon sees his own fingers crooked
tremulous and out of focus before his face,
and, as if for the first time, sees the delicately brimming
> > tissue of your skin wrinkled as his own,
your over-arching grace before the stiff Miami skyline.

And then the quizzical faces of strangers appear,
hearing this bent man groan
as old light scalds and fills his eyes again
—rumors of miracle are plucked from the charged air.

9.
Afflicted and desperate they come,
greedy and curious.
They approach you with prayers and wounds,
> candles and demands,
hang medallions and rosaries from your branches,
smear their own gnarled limbs with your pitch,
strip your twigs and branches;
then comes night with more candles and pilgrims
impatient for another miracle.

At last the hour of the scavenger must come
in the uncandled darkness,
those drunkenly crashing and breaking your branches,

and then, with the morning star, the inevitable entrepreneur
—with the snarl of a chainsaw your trunk is gone.

At dawn
the blind remain blind, the deaf hear nothing.

10.
One day you are a tree merely,
            a mystery negligible in your ordinary loveliness,
your inauspicious appetite
drawing a self up out of the soil ignored underfoot.

The next you are a remedy
            for the blind and the lame, the endlessly wretched
who hunger for a cure
imitation can secure. They hack you to a stump.

Having healed one man
            you cure no more. Your true presence is untouched,
the luminous stigmata
of your pitch, stymied in the ascent up your ghost-trunk,

blindly rises nonetheless, a flowing crown.
            A man inspired looks through his own eyes, sees;
the rest look for proofs first,
the rest look through ideas, remaining blind

to all the eye has seen.
            They reduce you to a tourist's curiosity.
Never have I known the green stone
of your fruit, opaque as milk, to be anything but bitter,

collapsing the cheeks of the wide-eyed
            and muting the fury of curses spat out with the pulp.
What is the nature of the miraculous?
Sure not event alone, surely a process rare in the witness as well.

11.
The blind remain blind, the deaf hear nothing.

But the old man, illiterate, whose tongue is the singing tongue,
has listened to the language
as a child,
as the blind must listen, careful to detect the spell

—*the see-grape tree, the see-grape tree!*—

and all of us are walking upon the waters under the earth.

ROBERT SIEGEL

ROBERT SIEGEL *was born near Chicago, Illinois, in 1939. His degrees are from Wheaton, Johns Hopkins, and Harvard, where his Ph.D. dissertation was on Coleridge.* He has taught at Dartmouth, Princeton, and Wheaton College, and is currently a professor of English at the University of Wisconsin at Milwaukee. *His award-winning books of fiction include* Alpha Centauri *(1980),* Whalesong *(1981), and* The Kingdom of Wundle *(1982).* He has been awarded National Endowment for the Arts and Ingram-Merrill Foundation fellowships for poetry, and prizes from *Prairie Schooner and* Poetry *magazines.* His poems have been collected in *The Beasts & the Elders (1973) and* In a Pig's Eye *(1980).*
(Photo by Chris Lutes)

Participation

When asking myself what it is that moves me to write a poem, I must confess it is a desire to call things up into words. This is the alchemy that fascinates me. Whether things are common or secret (and all things are both common *and* secret), I wish to call them up by the power of words—or rather, *as* words. A sensation, impression, or image will step out from its surroundings and demand my total attention. The thing itself will appear to rise up as words. Here is the wonder of the magic, what Keats called 'natural magic': as the image reaches up toward the words, the words become the image, the thing itself. For one happy moment they are fused. Thing becomes word and word becomes thing in a process far deeper in the workings of the universe than we are aware of. Substance and meaning are fused. The terrible gap between experience and the articulation of experience is closed. The mind is one with what it perceives.

When such a moment comes, I go to my typewriter, careful to preserve the fragile image riding, as it were, on the front of my brain. Sitting down at my desk, I feel the image spring living roots through fingers and keys until the poem is rooted, however tenuously, on the page. From this point on the poem either grows or does not. A certain tact is necessary to avoid trying too hard, to avoid forcing what should not be forced—a wise passiveness. Yet the experience is not at all like automatic writing. If anything, awareness is increased at these times, as in Coleridge's description of the poet at work: "The poet . . . brings the whole soul of man into activity . . . a more than usual state of emotion, with more than usual order; judgement ever awake and steady self-possession, with enthusiasm and feeling profound or vehement." The moment of creation brings a heightened state of consciousness. In this consciousness, the critical faculty does not work slowly and laboriously, as it will during revision. Rather, it is part of a whole-souled activity. The mind follows the direction of the poem by a kind of intuition, all that one has learned by example and practice working seemingly by reflex. "Like a piece of ice on a hot stove, the poem must ride on its own melting," Frost wrote. The poet must also ride that piece of ice—an impossible feat, of course. There is always something miraculous about a poem's coming into being at all.

When a first draft arrives this way, I feel completely happy as a maker. I won't know until later whether what I've written is as good as I feel it is. (It rarely, or never, is.) The intensity of what I experience while writing is no guarantee of a poem's quality. Some of my best experiences have turned out to be failures as poems—failures often difficult to abandon. Another poem, written with less feeling and full of gaps to be filled in later, may eventually turn into something good. An idea for a poem came while I was reading a newspaper article. I then read a hopelessly dull article in an encyclopedia to gain more information. Only later, in the process of writing, did strong feeling come. All that dry information provided a kind of tinder.

Occasionally, the good poem springs forth whole. It seems, as Emerson believed, to have been "written before time was." The poet is merely the transmitter. Most often, though, the transmitter is hampered by static and the whole poem doesn't come through. The trick in revision is to restore this imperfect transcription. Sometimes the most important parts come through only during revision.

As for the experience of heightened consciousness, I would agree it is similar, though not identical, to certain states sought by the mystics. I believe it lies at the center of art. Such moments, though brief in terms of our total experience of art, form its essence. I believe they are part of a consciousness potential in all of us, artist or not, and they are a foretaste of what we might experience more regularly and not only in art. In Coleridge's famous definition, he asserts, "The primary IMAGINATION I hold to be the living Power and prime Agent of all human Perception, and as a repetition in the finite mind of the eternal act of creation in the infinite I AM." This is a complex and rich statement which, among other things, means consciousness itself is an imaginative act that mirrors—Coleridge says *repeats*—the creative act of God, the infinite I AM. Consciousness itself is an imaginative and a god-like act from which the artistic imagination differs only in degree.

This is heady stuff, but I feel it's essential to an understanding of that heightened consciousness in which word and image fuse, thought becomes thing, the perceiving mind one with what it perceives. Ordinary consciousness, what we usually mean by 'reality,' is made up of both perceived objects and the mind that perceives them. It is impossible even to think of an object without also thinking of a mind perceiving it. The two make a seamless whole. Another way to say this is that reality is not just something *out there*, as materialists and positivists say, nor is it just something *in here*, as a philosophical idealist would say, but it is *both inner and outer fused together*. Consciousness is a creative act.

What all this leads us to is that the feelings and intuitions which come along in moments of heightened consciousness are as much a part of reality as anything else we perceive. The inner is integral to the outer. As in the psalmist's "All the trees of the wood sing for joy," feeling and object are fused, inner weather and outer weather are one. Recent developments in physics tend to support this understanding of what exists. The more scientists analyze subatomic particles, the less they can say a "thing" (as we usually think of it) exists at all. What exists is a construct of mind and whatever is "out there."

The moment of intense fusion of mind and matter, when division falls away, is that heightened consciousness in which art begins and ends. It points toward a state beyond the ordinary, similar, perhaps, to that which Plotinus described where "everything is filled full of life, boiling with life. Things there flow in a way from a single source, not like one particular breath or warmth, but as if there were a single quality containing in itself and preserving all qualities, sweet taste and smell and the quality of wine with all other flavors, visions of colors and all that touch perceives, all too that hearing hears, all tunes and every rhythm."

The saints, mystics, and poets are those who move past, at least temporarily, our ordinary experience of separation, of alienation, to a state that Owen Barfield calls "final participation." This participation is what mystics elsewhere refer to as the awakening or illumination of the soul. Barfield defines it as "experiencing the presence of God in all things." Final participation assumes, of course, the basic unity of creation, but this unity is achieved only at the cost of overcoming the separation and disharmony we know all too well. At the extreme, separation and disharmony are the stuff of tragedy. The restoration of unity is ultimately divine comedy and may be accomplished only at tremendous cost. But, meanwhile, art points to it, however fleetingly.

This introduction began with mention of the source of images. The poems included here reveal my preference for images and metaphors that draw the reader into the object as something to be felt from the inside—even when that object is superficially unattractive. It is that union out of which each poem grew and may lead (I like to think) to the apprehension of something beyond itself. For I believe all that we experience to be not only real in itself, but—insofar as it is real—a means to a higher reality. The image is given transcendent significance by that which it connects us to—that which is imageless. The images have been affirmed because the imageless has joined itself to them. After all, there is no other way to express the imageless, except *through* images, as Saint Augustine reminds us: "It is not these that I love when I love my God. And yet, when I love him, it is true that I love a light of a certain kind, a voice, a perfume, an embrace; but they are of the kind that I love in my inner self when my soul is bathed in light and is not bound by space; when it listens to a sound that never dies away; when it breathes fragrance that is not borne away on the wind; when it tastes food that is never consumed by the eating; when it clings to an embrace from which it is not severed by satiety." Or, to

quote another, even more ancient authority. "Neither is this Thou,
yet this also is Thou."

A Visit to the Farm

Whoever colored the moon tonight didn't stay
within the lines—it melts across the sky.
Each leaf thrusts close its breath and frogs
white in the headlights' tunnel eye
flirt with death on quick parabolas.

At Uncle Joe's the television screen
aimed its blue dance across our faces
while a hen chuckled sleepily over an egg
deep in impenetrable darkness.
Whining, the dog dropped softly on the porch

an unweened rabbit no bigger than a mouse.
As we lingered by the car, the windmill light
burned a naked period in the dark
over a tractor comatose upon its haunches.
Cats ghosted and gleamed in the barn's murk

or wrapped their backs about our legs
pleading with small murderous motors.
Now, down miles of vanished road the light
sinks to a hardly noticeable star.
The moon lifts over fog and dashlights

show precise green teeth under a wide eye.
I stretch, glad to have escaped the city
muffled in the distance of this plain,
toward which TV towers wink with small red eyes,
each leading its oafish fellow on a chain.

Air Field

All day the great planes gingerly descend
an invisible staircase, holding up
their skirts and dignity like great ladies
in technicolor histories, or reascend,
their noses needling upward like a compass
into a wild blue vacuum,
leaving everything in confusion behind:

In some such self-deceiving light as this
we'll view the air force base when moved away
from where its sleepless eye revolves all night.
We'll smile and recollect it conversationally—
tell with what ease the silver planes dropped down
or how they, weightless, rose above
our roof. We'll pass it with the sugar and cream,

forever sheltered from this moment's sick
surprise that we have lived with terror, with pride,
the wounded god circling the globe, never resting,
that in the morning and the evening we have heard
his cry, have seen him drag his silver wings
whining with anguish like a huge
fly seeking to lay its deadly eggs.

Christmas Eve

While cattle stupidly stare
over straw damp from their breathing
and the horse lazily stirs
over his trough, and the lantern
licks at shadows in corners,

in the woods the wild ones gather,
the rabbit twitching with care,
sooty shrew, and imperial mole
with the hands of a lost politician,
to shine in the branch-broken light

of a moon which in mid-career
lights up a church of snow.
Now, one paw after another
about the bones of weeds
in a soft worrying circle

the helpless ones dance out their fear,
watching the glittering air
where he shines in the eyes of the others,
naked, with nothing to wear.
Long before he comes to the stable

to the shrew's moving smudge on the snow,
to the mole's ineffectual gesture,
to the soft hide of the hare,
he comes, warming each creature
naked in the fangs of the year.

Ego

has thrust his nose under every board,
smelt out every wild carrot and white grub,
stucco'd the dirt with his tracks from side
to side, rubbed smooth the corner
posts, left his pink, red-bristled hide
on every barb of five strands of wire;

chews the bark from the one scrub pine
that pitches a ghost of shade at noon,
bangs incessantly the metal trough-lid
at off-hours, chuffs down the white meal,
raising a cloud around his ears, and cleans
each cob with the nicety of a Pharisee,

tooth for tooth, squeezing contentedly
his small bagpipe voice as he mashes
corn with a slobbery leer and leaves
turds like cannonballs across a battlefield.
Meanwhile his little pink eye is
periscoped on the main chance—

the gate ajar, the slipped board,
the stray ducky that flusters through the wire—
saliva hanging from his mouth like a crown jewel.
His jowls shake with mirth under the smile
that made a killing on the market, won the fifth caucus,
took the city against all odds.

No wonder we shake at the thought
of his getting out, electrify the wire
(At night we hear him thump his dreams
on the corrugated tin hut and shudder,
the single naked bulb in there burning
through our sleep like his eye!),

take special dietary precautions against
his perpetual rut, except that March day
we drag the yearling sow to him
through mud up to her hocks. From that handseling
comes the fat litter—the white one for the Fair,
the spotted black to be slaughtered in November.

We don't show him to the nieghbors, though in June,
framed by clover and bees stringing out the sun, he is
quite grand, an enormous blimp supporting
intelligent waggish ears, regally lidded eyes and
a pink, glistening snout
ready to shove up the privates of the world.

Rinsed with Gold, Endless, Walking the Fields

Let this day's air praise the Lord—
Rinsed with gold, endless, walking the fields,
Blue and bearing the clouds like censers,
Holding the sun like a single note
Running through all things, a *basso profundo*
Rousing the birds to an endless chorus.

Let the river throw itself down before him,
The rapids laugh and flash with his praise,
Let the lake tremble about its edges
And gather itself in one clear thought

To mirror the heavens and the reckless gulls
That swoop and rise on its glittering shores.

Let the lawn burn continually before him
A green flame, and the tree's shadow
Sweep over it like a conductor's baton,
Let winds hug the housecorners and woodsmoke
Sweeten the world with her invisible dress,
Let the cricket wind his heartspring
And draw the night by like a child's toy.

Let the tree stand and thoughtfully consider
His presence as its leaves dip and row
The long sea of winds, as sun and moon
Unfurl and decline like contending flags.

Let blackbirds quick as knives praise the Lord,
Let the sparrow line the moon for her nest
And pick the early sun for her cherry,
Let her slide on the outgoing breath of evening,
Telling of raven and dove,
The quick flutters, homings to the green houses.

Let the worm climb a winding stair,
Let the mole offer no sad explanation
As he paddles aside the dark from his nose,
Let the dog tug on the leash of his bark,
The startled cat electrically hiss,
And the snake sign her name in the dust

In joy. For it is he who underlies
The rock from its liquid foundation,
The sharp contraries of the giddy atom,
The unimaginable curve of space,
Time pulling like a patient string,
And gravity, fiercest of natural loves.

At his laughter, splendor riddles the night,
Galaxies swarm from a secret hive,
Mountains lift their heads from the sea,
Continents split and crawl for aeons
To huddle again, and planets melt
In the last tantrum of a dying star.

At his least signal spring shifts
Its green patina over half the earth,
Deserts whisper themselves over cities,
Polar caps widen and wither like flowers.

In his stillness rock shifts, root probes,
The spider tenses her geometrical ego,
The larva dreams in the heart of the peachwood,
The child's pencil makes a shaky line,
The dog sighs and settles deeper,
And a smile takes hold like the feet of a bird.

Sit straight, let the air ride down your backbone,
Let your lungs unfold like a field of roses,
Your eyes hang the sun and moon between them,
Your hands weigh the sky in even balance,
Your tongue, swiftest of members, release a word
Spoken at conception to the sanctum of genes,
And each breath rise sinuous with praise.

Let your feet move to the rhythm of your pulse
(Your joints like pearls and rubies he has hidden),
And your hands float high on the tide of your feelings.
Now, shout from the stomach, hoarse with music,
Give gladness and joy back to the Lord,
Who, sly as a milkweed, takes root in your heart.

Mr. Brunt

Beginning with C in the dank school basement,
you taught me to hold a note on the trombone
with the dented bell. Out the window grass
grew taller in the humid air. An occasional stir
brought its green smell by the upright
piano where you patiently struck C—
your finger pointing to that simple law
while my horn bellowed and wandered.
You broke an aspirin tablet, swallowed,
struck the note again—
nodding for emphasis as sweat flashed
from your eyebrows to the keys.

My second note likewise flattened, strayed.
Far above us, a musical deity frowned
in a cloud containing the marble pallors
of Handel, Mozart, Bach—promising no manna
to me, derelict in a wilderness of sound.

   Miraculously I hung on for a season
as first trombone, slid back to second,
after another year quit the band
to mouth notes silently in the all-school chrous.
From here, feeling guilty and relieved, I watched
the back of your shirt soak through
while you wrestled music from the air
over the remnant of the faithful.

   Now, hearing of your stroke, I recall
the morning you handed out scores
you'd sat up all night over. Even then
I sensed our brazen wails and clanging cymbals
didn't deserve the sacrifice.

                 Whatever
mountain you regularly ascended,
its god was overwhelming, the music of his progress,
the single note you heard as he passed by,
struck you deaf to our tinhorn blasphemies—
even as (I guessed, while reading the biography
you loaned to me in generous despair)
it must have deafened Beethoven
to hear the divine tread fall again and again.

The Revenant

I wonder why I am living at this time,
when so many millions around me arrive dead
into the world. I came with a bruised head,
possible brain damage, and a crooked eye
(through which I see many things awry,
though the other gives me single vision and fills
my whole body with light). My mother faced the ordeal—
though why she did, I'm sure she couldn't say,

her love the sort mere logic yields to.
A syringe and suction pump might have brought me off
and so I would never have written this
poem, nor you taken the small risk
of reading it. Too late now—though you shrug it off,
someday it will return to trouble you.

CHARLES SIMIC

CHARLES SIMIC *was born in Yugoslavia in 1938, emigrated to the United States in 1949, and was educated at New York University. His most recent volumes of poetry are* Dismantling the Silence *(1971)*, Return to a Place Lit by a Glass of Milk *(1974)*, Charon's Cosmology *(1977)*, Classic Ballroom Dances *(1980)*, *and* Austerities *(1982)*. *He has also published numerous translations of French, Russian, and Yugoslav poets, and co-edited with Mark Strand* Another Republic *(1976)*, *an anthology of seventeen European and South American writers. The winner of many prizes for his poetry (from P.E.N., the Poetry Society of America, the American Academy of Arts and Letters), since 1974 Charles Simic has taught at the University of New Hampshire. He has recently been awarded a five-year grant from the John D. and Catherine MacArthur Foundation.*
(Photo by Siegfried Halus)

Composition

> *There is where listening happens, unaware*
> *Blending into attention.*
> —Jorge Guillén

In the beginning, always, a myth of origins of the poetic act. A longing to lower oneself one notch below language, to touch the bottom—that place of "original action and desire," to recover our mute existence, to recreate what is unspoken and enduring in words of the poem, and thus live twice as it were. Like our ancient ancestors who inhabited an animistic universe, the poet claims the interconnectedness and sentience of all things. This is what haunts: a world where magic is possible, where chance reigns, where metaphors have their supreme logic, where imagination is free and truthful.

The act of composition is fatefully tied to the quality of introspection. To look within and catch oneself existing—the pressure of that inwardness as a kind of cause and realization that one lives in two worlds, one of which is shared and communicable, and the other which accompanies it like a shadow. And further—the possibility of making that relationship conscious, of acknowledging the duality, of submitting to its drama.

Consciousness claims and is reciprocally claimed. The reciprocity discloses the identity of the participants. It creates a dialectic which abolishes the privacy of the act and makes it open. We say then that the poem has a "voice." However, before that voice is heard something else must be taken into account. The paradox of the original experience is that it doesn't have Time. All its elements are simultaneous. It is a totality—the whole psychic weight of a single human being. Only in telling about it does Time enter.

Form is the extension of consciousness in Time. Or, form is the breaking up of the simultaneity of content for the sake of Language.

The poem manipulates Time. Out of the simultaneity of experience, the event of Language is an emergence into linear time. The verbal nucleus of the poem (that bit of language that we are initially given) contains a kind of measure—the poem is its unwinding.

The source of that movement lies in our inability to endure simultaneity precisely because the "I" disappears in that state of consciousness. Simultaneity is what doesn't have a locus. It is spherical, all encompassing. The three dimensions of Time and the place at which they intersect are the way in which we locate ourselves and give ourselves identity.

Form is the reduction, the minimum—the area our attention circumscribes. Form is expressive, a distortion and a mirror. It is a sequence imposed on the simultaneity of experience in order to recreate it. Of course, form is also tradition, and habit. It is the familiar which frames the unfamiliar. Time, too, is both law-abiding and free. The poet makes his own time-pieces to disrupt expectations and restore the memory of the timeless.

Language and form are two manifestations of the same impulse. We speak in Time. Syntax and grammar are two of the ways in which we acknowledge that process. Meter, line-breaks, and stanza-breaks are some of the places in the poem where Time is taken into account. Geometrically, prose is a straight line which goes on to infinity. A poem is a circle: the simultaneous vision of the page where every word becomes interrelated with every other word.

What makes the act of composition so complex is this mixture of deliberate and involuntary. One is continually torn between the desire to let things be and the desire to assert oneself. The peculiar intensity and weight the words have in a good poem are probably due to this split, and the turmoil it causes in the psyche. In any case, the great wish is to make visible, to let the spirit of the occasion manifest itself. A poem which would be a threshold between worlds, where the poet is simply the ceremonial doorman.

Form, in the sense that I speak of it here, thinks. Its appetite is cosmological. It mirrors its origins and reflects on the act itself. Let's say that it thinks by provoking thought. This is its aim, intrinsically. For me, the virtue of certain poems of Gertrude Stein, Robert Creeley, and Russell Edson, three poets who share this organic idea of form, is that they are thought-machines. I like that. A poetry that makes itself the object of endless meditation.

To come full circle then, let me reiterate my sincerest wish. The poem is the place where origins are allowed to think. This is the secret strength of poetry and the source of its perpetual renewal. The "difficulty" of modern poetry from Imagism to Surrealism is that it has in-

vested all its energies to permit that ancestral and archetypal thought
to become audible in its purity.

1976-1983

Evening

The snail gives off stillness.
The weed is blessed.
At the end of a long day
The man finds joy, the water peace.

Let all be simple. Let all stand still
Without a final direction.
That which brings you into the world
To take you away at death
Is one and the same;
The shadow long and pointy
Is its church.

At night some understand what the grass says.
The grass knows a word or two.
It is not much. It repeats the same word
Again and again, but not too loudly . . .

The Animals

I have no news of the animals.
Do they still exist? Those toads
I used to know so well. And the foxes,
Are they still out there in the dark?

Impossible. Where a horse used to graze
In my dream—an emptiness, edge of a cliff
On which I balance myself
With no skill and plenty of luck.

I can see now that I'll have to construct
My bestiary in some other manner:
Without a bone or an eye,
Without even a track of blood in the snow,
And the barking
Reaching over my shoulders.

Alone, without a model—
It will be up to me
To imagine, out of the stones and debris
That are left, a new species—

A tooth,
An udder
Full of milk.

Return to a Place Lit by a Glass of Milk

Late at night our hands stop working.
They lie open with tracks of animals
Journeying across the fresh snow.
They need no one. Solitude surrounds them.

As they come closer, as they touch,
It is like two small streams
Which upon entering a wide river
Feel the pull of the distant sea.

The sea is a room far back in time
Lit by the headlights of a passing car.
A glass of milk glows on the table.
Only you can reach it for me now.

Charon's Cosmology

With only his feeble lantern
To tell him where he is

And every time a mountain
Of fresh corpses to load up

Take them to the other side
Where there are plenty more
I'd say by now he must be confused
As to which side is which

I'd say it doesn't matter
No one complains he's got
Their pockets to go through
In one a crust of bread in another a sausage

Once in a long while a mirror
Or a book which he throws
Overboard into the dark river
Swift cold and deep

Progress Report

And how are the rats doing in the maze?
The big fat one with baggy pants
Appears confused. You shout.
You tell him to keep running.

A pretty girl's got him by the tail.
Now she's going to dissect him.
The instruments glitter and the beads
Of perspiration on her forehead.

The others are still in the maze.
They study the stars, defecate,
Do the tango, make valentines,
Salute the general, wear mourning bands.

Her long fingers find no resistance,
Already she's got his heart open . . .
I don't know who this girl is?
Neither does he, the spellbound one.

Prodigy

I grew up bent over
a chessboard.

I loved the word *endgame*.

All my cousins looked worried.

It was a small house
near a Roman graveyard.
Planes and tanks
shook its windowpanes.

A retired professor of astronomy
taught me how to play.

That must have been in 1944.

In the set we were using,
the paint had almost chipped off
the black pieces.

The white King was missing
and had to be substituted for.

I'm told but do not believe
that that summer I witnessed
men hung from telephone poles.

I remember my mother
blindfolding me a lot.

She had a way of tucking my head
suddenly under her overcoat.

In chess, too, the professor told me,
the masters play blindfolded,
the great ones on several boards
at the same time.

Baby Pictures of Famous Dictators

The epoch of a streetcar drawn by horses;
The organ-grinder and his monkey.
Women with parasols. Little kids in rowboats
Photographed against a cardboard backdrop depicting an idyllic
    sunset
At the fairgrounds where they all went to see
The two-headed calf, the bearded
Fat lady who dances the dance of seven veils.

And the great famine raging through India . . .
Fortune-telling white rats pulling a card out of a shoebox
While Edison worries over the lightbulb,
And the first model of the sewing machine
Is delivered in a pushcart
To a modest white-fenced home in the suburbs,

Where there are always a couple of infants
Posing for the camera in their sailors' suits,
Out there in the garden overgrown with shrubs.
Lovable little mugs smiling faintly toward
The new century. Innocent. Why not?
All of them like ragdolls of the period
With those chubby porcelain heads
That shut their long eyelashes as you lay them down.

In a kind of perpetual summer twilight . . .
One can even make out the shadow of the tripod and the black hood
That must have been quivering in the breeze.
One assumes that they all stayed up late squinting at the stars,
And were carried off to bed by their mothers and big sisters,
While the dogs remained behind:
Pedigreed bitches pregnant with bloodhounds.

Classic Ballroom Dances

Grandmothers who wring the necks
Of chickens; old nuns

With names like Theresa, Marianne,
Who pull schoolboys by the ear;

The intricate steps of pickpockets
Working the crowd of the curious
At the scene of an accident; the slow shuffle
Of the evangelist with a sandwich-board;

The hesitation of the early morning customer
Peeking through the window-grille
Of a pawnshop; the weave of a little kid
Who is walking to school with eyes closed;

And the ancient lovers, cheek to cheek,
On the dancefloor of the Union Hall,
Where they also hold charity raffles
On rainy Monday nights of an eternal November.

Crows

Just so that each stark,
Spiked twig,
May be even more fierce
With significance,

There are these birds
As further harbingers
Of the coming wintry reduction
To sign and enigma:

The absolutely necessary
Way in which they shook snow
Out of their wings,
And then remained, inexplicably

Thus, wings half-open,
Making two large algebraic x's
As if for emphasis,
Or in the mockery of . . .

Midpoint

No sooner had I left A.
Than I started doubting its existence:
Its streets and noisy crowds;
Its famous all-night cafes and prisons.

It was dinnertime. The bakeries were closing:
Their shelves empty and white with flour.
The grocers were lowering their iron-grilles.
A lovely young woman was buying the last casaba melon.

Even the back alley where I was born
Blurs, dims . . . O rooftops!
Armadas of bedsheets and shirts
In the blustery, crimson dusk . . .

*

B. at which I am destined
To arrive by and by
Doesn't exist now. Hurriedly
They're building it for my arrival,

And on that day it will be ready:
Its streets and noisy crowds . . .
Even the schoolhouse where I first
Forged my father's signature . . .

Knowing that on the day
Of my departure
It will vanish forever
Just as A. did.

DAVE SMITH

DAVE SMITH *was born in Portsmouth, Virginia, in 1942. His undergraduate degree is from the University of Virginia, Charlottesville, his M.A. and Ph.D. degrees from Southern Illinois University and Ohio University.* He is the author of the novel Onliness *(1981), and editor of* The Pure Clear Word: Essays on the Poetry of James Wright *(1982). He has taught widely, has won several awards for his poetry, is currently professor of English at Virginia Commonwealth University. His most recent books of poetry are* Goshawk, Antelope *(1979),* Dream Flights *(1981),* Homage to Edgar Allan Poe *(1981), and* In the House of the Judge *(1983).*
(Photo by Maurice Duke)

Beagling

My neighbor has a handsome adolescent beagle which, as anyone knows, is a universe of energy and assertion. Sunrise and sunset, he yips, yelps, and yodels. I have stood by the tall wooden fence that cages him and watched, impressed by the signalling range of his voice. Sometimes he is lyrical and brief, sometimes he is cumulative as a fugue. Occasionally he sits abjectly and cocks his head as charmingly as RCA's dog. He can't see beyond the fence but often appears perfectly receptive of all that is distantly, unknowably, continuingly there. When he has latched onto something which affects him, he sounds off.

To speak of a poet as a dog is reductive and comic. A beagle is not even one of God's hugely admirable creatures, scarcely wolf or dane. But a beagle is an actor and an action, fulfilled only in collaboration with the man who sets him loose and controls, loosely, what he does. The poet is both beagle and beagler. The poem is a passage from ignorance, or stasis, through particular thickets, meazes, mudholes, road-ruts, cabin debris, and—increasingly of late—suburban landscapes, to mystery. I do not say from innocence to experience, from arrogance to humility, from restlessness to contentment, from ignorance to wisdom, though the true poem is surely characterized by these patterns. The true poem is not deliberately functional but experiential. It must have its ghostly spoor, as the beagle has its rabbit, and it must proceed in successful circles but its greatest pleasure is not in arrival and cessation but in its contested, testing, revealing movement.

Beagles, like all hunting animals, are images of witness and faith and, especially, obligation. Dog hunters say it is a matter of genetics, of blood. Dogs are obliged to hunt because the world is there, because the summons is in their blood. Like poets, a beagle cannot choose *not* to hunt. Unlike poets, a beagle cannot choose what to hunt or what will be the shape of his voiced response. The other half of a hunting beagle is his owner. Some of these hunt for meat but others, the true hunters in my mind, hunt only for the mysterious pleasure derived from the sounding of their dog's circling announcements of the world's shape. These usually hunt at night and their hunting consists of sitting at a campfire, as at a desk, alone or with others where they listen intensely. Among the looping, singing voices of dogs, these hunters shape and reshape both the quality and content of what their dogs say. This is ordinarily done in a constant awareness and even reverential, sometimes debunking, evocation of history's dogs, hunts, and sounds. One has only to see the otherworldly glory in these faces to know such men have come into a direct engagement with all that is real and durable in their lives, though the hunt is partial and temporary.

Why do dogs hunt? Why do men sit in the night to hear dogs hunt? What is the nature of such hunting? The answers are never simple or complete. It suffices to say dogs hunt because of a blood-gift. Men hunt them because it gives them pleasure. Such hunting is circular, ritualistic, and ordered by manners. The poet does not choose to become a poet, I think, so much as he becomes one by default or destiny. He could choose otherwise but does not because writing poems pleases him and fulfills the demands of his nature. The poem is always circular, ritualistic, and informed by manners. Its particular form is the result of self-negotiations between what feels *right* and the continual assertions of all those voices which have been lifted before him and of which he cannot declare ignorance. For the poet, each poem must be a re-entry into the night-barking mystery, each entry having its local and inevitable logic of circumstance, personality, formal character, and meaning. Yet if the poem does not or cannot establish cohabitation with the past as with the unanswerable mysteries, it is—as hunters say—a dog that won't hunt.

I imagine my neighbors listening, as I do, to the young beagle next door. Their speculation is almost audible to me: pain? immaturity? loneliness? fear of intruders? Is it hunger for food, his mother, a young bitch? Why don't they take him in, make him feel better for Christ's sake? No questions affect the dog's noise; no answers account for it. There are no resolving answers to explain why a God's delight comes to the hunter listening confidently through the mysterious darkness nor why a similar delight comes to the poet. We do try to account for why we write what we write and how we write because that is our nature and one of our obligations. We feel obliged to know and to say, to bear witness in image and narrative and rapture and dirge, to make a discrimination of values and defects and causes and effects, just as one beagler speaking with passion to another. And like them, we slip reflections of the world into our remembering and conjecturing: the absence of the heroic dead, the meanness and infertility of our kind, the loss of good fields, the war against change and for change. While we speak critically, the right dogs keep hunting for us and with us, and we are glad to be alive then. We are glad to praise life, even in our annoyance and speculation.

I am suspicious of making prideful statements of accountability or prognostication. What may be said of poems seems to me often partial, wrong, inconsistent; or it is self-defensive, posturing, inflationary; or it is illogical, sentimental, hysterical. I mistrust the poet who would legislate my emotions, induce ameliorative behavior, or stump for a patriotism of aesthetics. I mistrust those who would huddle us forward as if to a doggy obedience school and distrust those who would value us according to our pedigree charts or our field-trial certificates. Even in poets the critical effort is proprietary and oppressive. The true poem will have none of this. It has all it can do to answer the opposing calls of the poet and the world.

Milton thought of the poet as God's translator. Others have regarded him as physician, legislator, policeman, psychologist, etc.—all distinct and distinguished functions, social functions. Conrad describes him as a kind of therapist of the senses, Eliot as a catalyst, and Adrienne Rich as a self-appointed Equal Opportunity Officer. Auden reflects the world's opinion: the poet makes nothing happen. All of these figures are true. And false. They reveal only that the poet values what he signifies and suggest the particular subjects to which he is most susceptible. I might have chosen the figure of the poet as spy (John Hollander and others have done so) since in the jittery instability of contemporary existence the spy has moral authority, privileged perspective, formal control, and all the world to roam in. Even television's archetypal gumshoe, Columbo, constantly journeys from ignorance to revelation. But, no. For me there is something appealing in the homely, divided figure of the beagle and his hunter that rings true. One is useless without the other. I write because it is a blood-gift I can't ignore. I write about what I know and have known and would know better: evocative places, significant human actions, ethical and moral and consequential mysteries, the indifferent and holy urge to live, which is freedom. I write to go beyond fences I did not erect but must acknowledge.

Of all a man might say about his poems, the least reliable observations concern form, or sound. All poetry exists on the spectrum from image-pictograph to abstract rhetoric. There is too little heartbeat in the image and there is no body in the rhetoric. Neither organic nor mechanical metaphors unequivocally explain what balance we choose—and the poet does choose—for the individual poem. I find my poems occupy various positions on that spectrum and I regard that as healthy. But the poems I take the greatest pleasure in are those whose principal organizing feature is neither a dominant picture nor a faithful metric, but is a circling, a slowly circling forward motion that is the movement of planets. Or the mind. Or of beagles on a night hunt. It is a motion whose cadences are strong, repetitive, idiosyncratic; whose pleasure is to seek, to apprehend, to announce; whose source is in the blood-beat of my ear; whose end is in its beginning. It is a kind of beagling that swings away and back to the self that waits before the looming fence of the night, the self who must find within the lovely orchestra and chorus his own rising, falling, entirely alive voice. To find the poem one must lose the poem, letting it go and drawing it back, letting it become as Frost says "a wild tune"—though not so wild that it escape intelligible, necessary, and revealing witness. The poem, then, that sings as it hunts, simultaneously and significantly. Not the poem that merely sounds off.

Mending Crab Pots

The boy had run all the way home
from school to tell the old man
about a book he'd found which put
the whole thing in a new light:
'The beautiful sea, grandfather,
in a poem you might have written,
out there always to be touched
or swum in, or worked, or just
looked at, the way you told me.'

The old man gave the wire trap
one extra twist, like a chicken's
neck, relit his dead cigar, said
he heard the slovenly bitch still
ranted around, couldn't be got
rid of, or lived with. He slit
the head from a blowfish, stuffed
it in the mouth of the pot, grinned.
'Them poets, goddam 'em, always
in school with their white hands.'

On a Field at Fredericksburg

The big steel tourist shield says maybe
fifteen thousand got it here. No word
of either Whitman or one uncle
I barely remember in the smoke

that filled his tiny mountain house.

If each finger were a thousand of them
I could clap my hands and be dead
up to my wrists. It was quick
though not so fast as we can do it
now, one bomb, atomic or worse,
the tiny pod slung on wing-tip,
high up, an egg cradled
by steel mockingbirds.

Hiroshima canned nine times their number
in a flash. Few had the time
to moan or feel the feeling
ooze back in the groin.

In a ditch I stand
above Marye's Heights, the book-
pale faces of Brady's fifteen-year-old
drummers, before battle, rigid
as August's dandelions
all the way to the Potomac
rolling in my skull.

If Audubon came here, the names
of birds would gush, the marvel
single feathers make
evoke a cloud, a nation,
a gray blur preserved
on a blue horizon, but

there is only a wandering child,
one dark stalk snapped off
in her hand. Hopeless teacher,
I take it, try to help her
hold its obscure syllables
one instant in her mouth,
like a drift of wind
at the forehead, the front door,
the black, numb fingernails.

Night Fishing for Blues

Fortress Monroe, Virginia

Tonight, not far from where Jefferson Davis

hunched in a harrowing cell, gray eyes quick
as crabs' nubs, I come back over planks
deep drummed under boots, tufts of hair

floating at my ears, everything finally right
to pitch through tideturn and mudslur
for fish with teeth like snapped sabers.

In blue crescents of base lights, I cast hooks

baited with Smithfield ham: they reel, zing,
plummet, coil in corrosive swirls, bump on
scum-skinned rocks. No skin divers prowl here,

visibility an arm's length, my visions

hand-to-hand in the line's warp. A meat-
sugared lure limps through limbs nippling the muck,
floats free, shoots forward, catches a cruising Blue

sentry's eye, snags and sets

cold steel barbs. Suddenly, I am not alone:
three Negroes plump down in lawn chairs, shudder-
casting into the black pod plodding under us. One
ripples with age, a grandmotherly obelisk,

her breath puffing like a coal stove. She swivels
heavily, chewing a dark nut, spits thick juice
like a careful chum, and sings.

When I yank the first Blue,
she mumbles, her eyes roll far out on the black
and blue sea-billowing. I hear her canting

to Africa, a cluck in her throat, a chain

song from the fisherman's house. As if they
understand, Bluefish are pouring at me in squads.
I haul two, three at a time, torpedoes, moon-shiners,
jamming my feet into the splintered floor, battling
whatever comes. I know I've walked this way
a whole life for this minute. Hypnotic as dreams

graven on cold cell walls, Blues fly over

our heads, ground on fin-wings, and audibly groan.
They cluster, rings of blue and silver, tiaras
of lost battalions. I can smell the salt of ocean
runners as she hollers *I ain't doing so bad*
for an old queen. No time to answer. Two

car-hoods down her descendents swing bare-armed

in Superfly shirts, exotic butterflies: I hear them
pop beer cans, the whoosh released like stale breath
through a noose no one remembers. We hang

fast flat casts, artless, no teasing fishermen,

hungry for the biggest haul we can imagine, crudely
speeded up, centrifugal, at war with the weight
of our bodies' limitations, sweating, momentum

hinging us to the past, winging our lines out

like howitzers. Incredibly it happens: I feel
the hook hammer and shake and throw my entire self
to dragging, as if I have caught the goddamndest

Blue in the Atlantic. She screams: *Oh my God!*

Four of us fumbling in beamed headlight and blue
arclight cut the hook from her face. Gnats butterfly
and nag us: I put it in deep and must gouge it out
like shrapnel. When it's free, I hear Blues not yet

dead flopping softly. *It's a lucky thing*

she can see, I say. She mops blood in the blue
glitter of her teeth, opens her arms so her dress

fins wide as a caftan. *Let's just fish*

all night, she says. I hand her her pole, then cast
as far as I can. She pumps, wings a sinker and naked
hooks into flashing slop, then reels. As if by design,

our lines leap crisp as daguerreotypes; we have

caught each other out in the mindless deep and thrash
our lines in midair too high for any Blue to know.
Like ghosts cruising the brain's black room
we seem to pull at nothing, but feel a way
to sit on the shaky pier like prisoners. Coil
by coil we trace a fester of knots backward,

unlooping, feeling for holes, giving, taking,

our skins crawling with gnats. Harried, unbound,
we fling ourselves apart and leap at last
to be fishers again. But now a gray glow
shreds with morning clouds, an old belly-fire

guts the night. Already the tide humps

itself around. Lights flicker like campfires, duty windows
at Ft. Monroe. She hooks up, saying *Sons, they done*
let us go. I cast again, but nothing bites. Everywhere

ranks of Blues bleach, stiffen

in scales of blood. We kneel, stuff styrofoam
boxes with blankets of ice, break their backs
to keep them fresh and sweet, the woman gravely
showing us what to do. By dawn the stink has passed

out of our noses. We drink beer like family.

All the way home thousands of Blues fall from my head,

falling with the gray Atlantic, and a pale veiny lignt
fills the road with sea-shadows that drift in figure

eights, their knotted, snarling march all

that draws me forward.

Under the Scub Oak, a Red Shoe

Wrapped in a twisted brown stocking, strangled in the rolled
nylon of our grandmothers, it was wedged at the heart
of what little cool shade ever accumulated there.
You would have to walk out of your way, back
along an arroyo twisting and empty as memory, back
from the road out of town so far the sky itself
signals another world. To find it you do that,

though, in any case, you are simply walking and it appears,
something red shining through the gray-green glaze
of stunted limbs. If you were looking for a lost child,
your steps deliberate and slow, you might see it.
Otherwise you will go on. That is what we do.
But it waits to reveal itself, like an eye
in the darkness, and you may innocently look into that

moment, and may imagine why it lacks the slender heel which
must, once, have nailed many boys against a wall
where she walked. I kneel and pick it up
as you would, hearing though it is noon
the moony insects cry around her, hearing also
the nylon flake like pieces of skin against my skin,

feeling the sound of its passage from her shaven calf, a screech
like the hawk's when he is distant and not hungry.
In this arroyo no one could have seen her stop,
not as drunk as she pretended, sitting long
and, in time, methodically undressing, beyond
thinking now, placing her bundled shoe with care.
She must have been small and would have borne the usual

bruises, so we would have had no fear of any we might add,

when we stood smoking by the wall, cat-calling lightly.
It would have been one of those nights the breath
aches it is so pleased with itself, then she
appeared in that red like the first cactus buds,
something clearly wrong with her but that, by God,
no concern of any red-blooded buck she might want.
In the junk car someone squealed, some rose
and fell. There were no names. I did not mean

whatever I said, but said it because she was so small, she
could not hide her fear and shivered on her back.
Such moments we tell ourselves to walk away from,
and we do, as now I have walked in my hoping
for absence, but there is no absence, only
what waits, like this shoe, to reach, to say please
as best it can for whoever comes along, as if forgiveness
were what it meant, and love, as if any weather
that red shining endured was the bruise
you might have kissed and might not yet refuse.

The Roundhouse Voices

In full glare of sunlight I came here, man-tall but thin
as a pinstripe, and stood outside the rusted fence
with its crown of iron thorns while
the soot cut into our lungs with tiny diamonds.
I walked through houses with my grain-lovely slugger
from Louisville that my uncle bought and stood
in the sun that made its glove soft on my hand
until I saw my chance to crawl under and get past
anyone who would demand a badge and a name.

The guard hollered that I could get the hell from there quick
when I popped in his face like a thief. All I ever wanted
to steal was life and you can't get that easy
in the grind of a railyard. *You can't catch me
lardass, I can go left or right good as the Mick,*
I hummed to him, holding my slugger by the neck
for a bunt laid smooth where the coal cars
jerked and let me pass between tracks

until, in a slide on ash, I fell safe and heard
the wheeze of his words: *Who the hell are you, kid?*

I hear them again tonight Uncle, hard as big brakeshoes,
when I lean over your face in the box of silk. The years
you spent hobbling from room to room alone crawl
up my legs and turn this house to another
house, round and black as defeat, where slugging
comes easy when you whip the gray softball over
the glass diesel globe. Footsteps thump on the stairs
like that fat ball against bricks and when I miss
I hear you warn me to watch the timing, to keep
my eyes on your hand and forget the fence,

hearing also that other voice that keeps me out and away
from you on a day worth playing good ball. Hearing
Who the hell . . . I see myself, like a burning speck
of cinder come down the hill and through a tunnel
of porches like stands, running on deep ash,
and I give him the finger, whose face still gleams
clear as a B & O headlight, just to make him get up
and chase me into a dream of scoring at your feet.
At Christmas that guard staggered home sobbing,
the thing in his chest tight as a torque wrench.
In the summer I did not have to run and now

who is the one who dreams of a drink as he leans over
tools you kept bright as a first-girl's promise? I
have no one to run from or to, nobody to give
my finger to as I steal his peace. Uncle, the light
bleeds on your gray face like the high barbed wire
shadows I had to get through and maybe you don't remember
you said to come back, to wait and you'd show me
the right way to take a hard pitch
in the sun that shudders on the ready man. I'm here

though this is a day I did not want to see. In the roundhouse
the rasp and heel-click of compressors is still,
soot lies deep in every greasy fingerprint.
I called you from the pits and you did not come up
and I felt the fear when I stood on the tracks
that are like stars which never lead us
into any kind of light and I don't know who'll

tell me now when the guard sticks his blind snoot
between us: take off and beat the bastard out.
Can you hear him over the yard, grabbing his chest,
cry out *Who the goddamn hell are you, kid?*

I gave him every name in the book, Uncle, but he caught us
and what good did all those hours of coaching do?
You lie on your back, eyeless forever, and I think
how once I climbed to the top of a diesel and stared
into that gray roundhouse glass where, in anger,
you threw up the ball and made a star
to swear at greater than the Mick ever dreamed.
It has been years but now I know what followed there
every morning the sun came up, not light
but the puffing bad-bellied light of words.

All day I have held your hand, trying to say back that life,
to get under that fence with words I lined
and linked up and steamed into a cold room
where the illusion of hope means skin torn in boxes
of tools. The footsteps come pounding into words
and even the finger I give death is words
that won't let us be what we wanted, each one
chasing and being chased by dreams in a dark place.
Words are all we ever were and they did us
no damn good. Do you hear that?

Do you hear the words that, in oiled gravel, you gave me
when you set my feet in the right stance to swing?
They are coal-hard and they come in wings
and loops like despair not even the Mick
could knock out of this room, words softer
than the centers of hearts in guards or uncles,
words skinned and numbed by too many bricks.
I have had enough of them and bring them back here
where the tick and creak of everything dies
in your tiny starlight and I stand down
on my knees to cry, *Who the hell are you, kid?*

Elk Ghosts: A Birth Memory

Tirelessly the stream licks the world until
from snow they do not come, but are

hoof-deep and standing, silhouettes
stark on the stones under stars.

Gathered, they seek a way to reenter
paths graven on the bone-walls.
Their white breath is alive. It is
possible to walk into and out

of monstrous, gentle eyes, knowing no link
exists except your face anchored
in the herd's dream. They are beyond
stillness and memory, their

revelation the lapping fire-fleck of water
and the starbright lintel of stones.
They come here to wait for change,
to be dreamed among pine and spruce.

There is no hawk who could hook them
out of the blue they breathe
effortlessly. Each moon-swollen
needle leads them more into vision.

Time conspires with you at night's window
and cannot help but hope for this
birth of joy. No longer do they
wait, no more nuzzle the future.

They glide through desire on earth.
Their thin song has entered each reed,
it has risen in your sleep and wails
forth these white shadows

you have summoned. They become electric
in your blood. One after another
they bear the stars, walking on water,
beasts with backs of pure light.

There is no world they cannot carry.
They are love's magi. Hooves flare
with a way through the darkness.
Composed, they suffer your coming.

The Purpose of the Chesapeake & Ohio Canal

Thick now with sludge from the years of suburbs, with toys,
fenders, wine bottles, tampons, skeletons of possums, and
edged by blankets of leaves, jellied wrappers unshakably
stuck to the scrub pines that somehow lift themselves
from the mossed wall of blockstone headlined a hundred
years back, this water is bruised as a shoe at Goodwill.
Its brown goes nowhere, neither does it remain, and elms
bend over its heavy back like patient fans, dreamlessly.
This is the death of hope's commerce, the death of cities
blank as winter light, the death of people who are gone
erratic and hopeless as summer's glittering water-skimmers.
Yet the two climbing that path like a single draft horse
saw the heart of the water break open only minutes ago,
and the rainbow trout walked its tail as if the evening
arranged an offering in an unimaginable room where plans
inched ahead for the people, as if the trout always meant
to hang from that chain, to be borne through the last shades
like a lure sent carefully, deviously in the blue ache of
air thickening in still streets and between brown walls.

MARK STRAND

MARK STRAND *was born of American parents in Summerside, Prince Edward Island, Canada, in 1934. His degrees are from Antioch College and Yale University. He has taught at many colleges and universities, has won Rockefeller, National Institute of Arts and Letters, and Guggenheim awards, among others. He has edited (w. Charles Simic)* Another Republic *(1976) and* Art of the Real: Nine American Figurative Painters *(1983), and translated Raphael Alberti's* The Owl's Insomnia *(1973). A book of prose,* The Monument, *appeared in 1978. His* Selected Poems *(1980) includes work from five earlier books. He is a member of the American Academy of Arts and Letters, and is currently a professor of English at the University of Utah.*
(Photo by Lilo Raymond)

A Statement About Writing

The degree to which a poem is resolved before I set it on paper is the degree to which its chances of ever getting on paper are diminished. I am lured to writing by suggestions, vague promptings, a desire for order. I always wish to write something that will not declare itself too soon as one of my poems—in fact, writing is often the act of postponing such a declaration. Writing as a sort of unwriting.

I must entertain the illusion that I am saying something new—new for me, that is. But as the poem is worked on, ignorance of my enterprise becomes more difficult to sustain, and I begin to lose interest in my work as it becomes familiar. I am more attached to those poems that persist in their strangeness, that resist my tactics of conversion. My attachment, however, is almost never rewarded, for the poems, if they are to remain strange, can never be mine. I sometimes wish I were someone else, someone to whom such poems could belong.

I would have an easier time, I imagine, if I were less self-aware. But then, any reduction of self-awareness would mean no poems at all. Ideally, it would be best to just write, to suppress the critical side of my nature and indulge the expressive. Perhaps. But I tend to think of the expressive part of me as rather tedious—never curious or responsive, but blind and self-serving. And because it has no power, let alone appetite, for self-scrutiny, it fits the reductive, dominating needs of the critical side of me. The more I think about this, the more I think that not writing is the best way to write.

Whether I admit it or not, I write to participate in the delusion of my own immortality which is born every minute. And yet, I write to resist myself. I find resistance irresistible.

The Babies

Let us save the babies.
Let us run downtown.
The babies are screaming.

You shall wear mink
and your hair shall be done.
I shall wear tails.

Let us save the babies
even if we run in rags
to the heart of town.

Let us not wait for tomorrow.
Let us drive into town
and save the babies.

Let us hurry.
They lie in a warehouse
with iron windows and iron doors.

The sunset pink of their skin
is beginning to glow.
Their teeth

poke through their gums
like tombstones.
Let us hurry.

They have fallen asleep.
Their dreams
are infecting them.

Let us hurry.
Their screams rise
from the warehouse chimney.

We must move faster.
The babies have grown into their suits.
They march all day in the sun without blinking.

Their leader sits in a bullet-proof car and applauds.
Smoke issues from his helmet.
We cannot see his face:

we are still running.
More babies than ever are locked in the warehouse.
Their screams are like sirens.

We are still running to the heart of town.
Our clothes are getting ragged.
We shall not wait for tomorrow.

The future is always beginning now.
The babies are growing into their suits.
Let us run to the heart of town.

Let us hurry.
Let us save the babies.
Let us try to save the babies.

The Dress

Lie down on the bright hill
with the moon's hand on your cheek,
your flesh deep in the white folds of your dress,
and you will not hear the passionate mole
extending the length of his darkness,
or the owl arranging all of the night,
which is his wisdom, or the poem
filling your pillow with its blue feathers.
But if you step out of your dress and move into the shade,
the mole will find you, so will the owl, and so will the poem,
and you will fall into another darkness, one you will find
yourself making and remaking until it is perfect.

The Dance

The ghost of another comes to visit and we hold
communion while the light shines.
While the light shines, what else can we do?
And who doesn't have one foot in the grave?

I notice how the trees seem shaggy with leaves
and the steam of insects engulfs them.
The light falls like an anchor through the branches.
And which one of us is not being pulled down constantly?

My mind floats in the purple air of my skull.
I see myself dancing. I smile at everybody.
Slowly I dance out of the burning house of my head.
And who isn't borne again and again into heaven?

Elegy for My Father

(Robert Strand 1908–68)

1 THE EMPTY BODY

The hands were yours, the arms were yours,
But you were not there.
The eyes were yours, but they were closed and would not open.
The distant sun was there.
The moon poised on the hill's white shoulder was there.
The wind on Bedford Basin was there.
The pale green light of winter was there.
Your mouth was there,
But you were not there.
When somebody spoke, there was no answer.
Clouds came down
And buried the buildings along the water,
And the water was silent.
The gulls stared.
The years, the hours, that would not find you
Turned in the wrists of others.
There was no pain. It had gone.
There were no secrets. There was nothing to say.
The shade scattered its ashes.
The body was yours, but you were not there.
The air shivered against its skin.
The dark leaned into its eyes.
But you were not there.

2 ANSWERS

Why did you travel?
Because the house was cold.
Why did you travel?
Because it is what I have always done between sunset and sunrise.
What did you wear?
I wore a blue suit, a white shirt, yellow tie, and yellow socks.
What did you wear?
I wore nothing. A scarf of pain kept me warm.
Who did you sleep with?
I slept with a different woman each night.
Who did you sleep with?

I slept alone. I have always slept alone.
Why did you lie to me?
I always thought I told the truth.
Why did you lie to me?
Because the truth lies like nothing else and I love the truth.
Why are you going?
Because nothing means much to me anymore.
Why are you going?
I don't know. I have never known.
How long shall I wait for you?
Do not wait for me. I am tired and I want to lie down.
Are you tired and do you want to lie down?
Yes, I am tired and I want to lie down.

3 YOUR DYING

Nothing could stop you.
Not the best day. Not the quiet. Not the ocean rocking.
You went on with your dying.
Not the trees
Under which you walked, not the trees that shaded you.
Not the doctor
Who warned you, the white-haired young doctor who saved you
    once.
You went on with your dying.
Nothing could stop you. Not your son. Not your daughter
Who fed you and made you into a child again.
Not your son who thought you would live forever.
Not the wind that shook your lapels.
Not the stillness that offered itself to your motion.
Not your shoes that grew heavier.
Not your eyes that refused to look ahead.
Nothing could stop you.
You sat in your room and stared at the city
And went on with your dying.
You went to work and let the cold enter your clothes.
You let blood seep into your socks.
Your face turned white.
Your voice cracked in two.
You leaned on your cane.
But nothing could stop you.
Not your friends who gave you advice.
Not your son. Not your daughter who watched you grow small.

Not fatigue that lived in your sighs.
Not your lungs that would fill with water.
Not your sleeves that carried the pain of your arms.
Nothing could stop you.
You went on with your dying.
When you played with children you went on with your dying.
When you sat down to eat,
When you woke up at night, wet with tears, your body sobbing,
You went on with your dying.
Nothing could stop you.
Not the past.
Not the future with its good weather.
Not the view from your window, the view of the graveyard.
Not the city. Not the terrible city with its wooden buildings.
Not defeat. Not success.
You did nothing but go on with your dying.
You put your watch to your ear.
You felt yourself slipping.
You lay on the bed.
You folded your arms over your chest and you dreamed of the world
    without you,
Of the space under the trees,
Of the space in your room,
Of the spaces that would now be empty of you,
And you went on with your dying.
Nothing could stop you.
Not your breathing. Not your life.
Not the life you wanted.
Not the life you had.
Nothing could stop you.

4 YOUR SHADOW

You have your shadow.
The places where you were have given it back.
The hallways and bare lawns of the orphanage have given it back.
The Newsboys Home has given it back.
The streets of New York have given it back and so have the streets of
    Montreal.
The rooms in Belém where lizards would snap at mosquitos have
    given it back.
The dark streets of Manaus and the damp streets of Rio have given it
    back.

Mexico City where you wanted to leave it has given it back.

And Halifax where the harbor would wash its hands of you has given it back.

You have your shadow.

When you traveled the white wake of your going sent your shadow below, but when you arrived it was there to greet you. You had your shadow.

The doorways you entered lifted your shadow from you and when you went out, gave it back. You had your shadow.

Even when you forgot your shadow, you found it again; it had been with you.

Once in the country the shade of a tree covered your shadow and you were not known.

Once in the country you thought your shadow had been cast by somebody else. Your shadow said nothing.

Your clothes carried your shadow inside; when you took them off, it spread like the dark of your past.

And your words that float like leaves in an air that is lost, in a place no one knows, gave you back your shadow.

Your friends gave you back your shadow.

Your enemies gave you back your shadow. They said it was heavy and would cover your grave.

When you died your shadow slept at the mouth of the furnace and ate ashes for bread.

It rejoiced among ruins.

It watched while others slept.

It shone like crystal among the tombs.

It composed itself like air.

It wanted to be like snow on water.

It wanted to be nothing, but that was not possible.

It came to my house.

It sat on my shoulders.

Your shadow is yours. I told it so. I said it was yours.

I have carried it with me too long. I give it back.

5 MOURNING

They mourn for you.

When you rise at midnight,

And the dew glitters on the stone of your cheeks,

They mourn for you.

They lead you back into the empty house.

They carry the chairs and tables inside.

They sit you down and teach you to breathe.
And your breath burns,
It burns the pine box and the ashes fall like sunlight.
They give you a book and tell you to read.
They listen and their eyes fill with tears.
The women stroke your fingers.
They comb the yellow back into your hair.
They shave the frost from your beard.
They knead your thighs.
They dress you in fine clothes.
They rub your hands to keep them warm.
They feed you. They offer you money.
They get on their knees and beg you not to die.
When you rise at midnight they mourn for you.
They close their eyes and whisper your name over and over.
But they cannot drag the buried light from your veins.
They cannot reach your dreams.
Old man, there is no way.
Rise and keep rising, it does no good.
They mourn for you the way they can.

6 THE NEW YEAR

It is winter and the new year.
Nobody knows you.
Away from the stars, from the rain of light,
You lie under the weather of stones.
There is no thread to lead you back.
Your friends doze in the dark
Of pleasure and cannot remember.
Nobody knows you. You are the neighbor of nothing.
You do not see the rain falling and the man walking away,
The soiled wind blowing its ashes across the city.
You do not see the sun dragging the moon like an echo.
You do not see the bruised heart go up in flames,
The skulls of the innocent turn into smoke.
You do not see the scars of plenty, the eyes without light.
It is over. It is winter and the new year.
The meek are hauling their skins into heaven.
The hopeless are suffering the cold with those who have nothing to
    hide.
It is over and nobody knows you.
There is starlight drifting on the black water.

There are stones in the sea no one has seen.
There is a shore and people are waiting.
And nothing comes back.
Because it is over.
Because there is silence instead of a name.
Because it is winter and the new year.

The Garden

for Robert Penn Warren

It shines in the garden,
in the white foliage of the chestnut tree,
in the brim of my father's hat
as he walks on the gravel.

In the garden suspended in time
my mother sits in a redwood chair;
light fills the sky,
the folds of her dress,
the roses tangled beside her.

And when my father bends
to whisper in her ear,
when they rise to leave
and the swallows dart
and the moon and stars
have drifted off together, it shines.

Even as you lean over this page,
late and alone, it shines; even now
in the moment before it disappears.

Nights in Hackett's Cove

Those nights lit by the moon and the moon's nimbus,
the bones of the wrecked pier rose crooked in air
and the sea wore a tarnished coat of silver.
The black pines waited. The cold air smelled

of fishheads rotting under the pier at low tide.
The moon kept shedding its silver clothes
over the bogs and pockets of bracken.
Those nights I would gaze at the bay road,
at the cottages clustered under the moon's immaculate stare,
nothing hinted that I would suffer so late
this turning away, this longing to be there.

A Morning

I have carried it with me each day: that morning I took
my uncle's boat from the brown water cove
and headed for Mosher Island.
Small waves splashed against the hull
and the hollow creak of oarlock and oar
rose into the woods of black pine crusted with lichen.
I moved like a dark star, drifting over the drowned
other half of the world until, by a distant prompting,
I looked over the gunwale and saw beneath the surface
a luminous room, a light-filled grave, saw for the first time
the one clear place given to us when we are alone.

My Mother on an Evening in Late Summer

1
When the moon appears
and a few wind-stricken barns stand out
in the low-domed hills
and shine with a light
that is veiled and dust-filled
and that floats upon the fields,
my mother, with her hair in a bun,
her face in shadow, and the smoke
from her cigarette coiling close
to the faint yellow sheen of her dress,
stands near the house
and watches the seepage of late light
down through the sedges,
the last gray islands of cloud

taken from view, and the wind
ruffling the moon's ash-colored coat
on the black bay.

2
Soon the house, with its shades drawn closed, will send
small carpets of lampglow
into the haze and the bay
will begin its loud heaving
and the pines, frayed finials
climbing the hill, will seem to graze
the dim cinders of heaven.
And my mother will stare into the starlanes,
the endless tunnels of nothing,
and as she gazes,
under the hour's spell,
she will think how we yield each night
to the soundless storms of decay
that tear at the folding flesh,
and she will not know
why she is here
or what she is prisoner of
if not the conditions of love that brought her to this.

3
My mother will go indoors
and the fields, the bare stones
will drift in peace, small creatures—
the mouse and the swift—will sleep
at opposite ends of the house.
Only the cricket will be up,
repeating its one shrill note
to the rotten boards of the porch,
to the rusted screens, to the air, to the rimless dark,
to the sea that keeps to itself.
Why should my mother awake?
The earth is not yet a garden
about to be turned. The stars
are not yet bells that ring
at night for the lost.
It is much too late.

MICHAEL WATERS

MICHAEL WATERS *was born in New York City in 1949. He has degrees from SUNY at Brockport, the University of Iowa, and Ohio University. Currently an English professor at Salisbury State College on the Eastern Shore of Maryland, he has read his poems widely and has worked in the Poetry-in-the-Schools programs in New York, Ohio, and South Carolina. In addition to several limited editions, he has published* Fish Light *(1975) and* Not Just Any Death *(1979).*
(Photo by Teresa Folks)

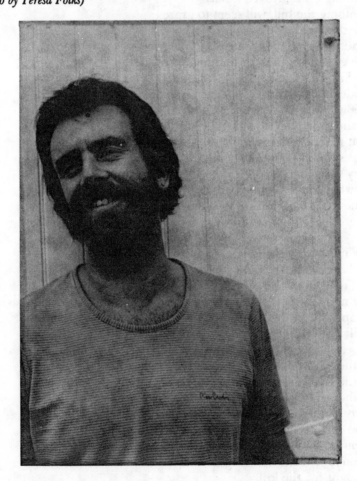

The Stories in the Light

On April 15, 1887, Walt Whitman posed for photographs in the studio of George C. Cox on Broadway and 12th, where the Strand Bookstore now flourishes. I think Whitman must have walked north from the ferry slip that morning, along the Bowery where a few men still slept in doorways, past Grace Church where General Tom Thumb, the famous midget brought to New York by P.T. Barnum, married Lavinia Warren. It must have been a lovely morning, the advent of another spring touching all the senses, so I imagine Whitman a little late, but taking his time, nodding to the passersby, sniffing the air like any dog, eyeing everything: the trash baskets stuffed with newspaper, the signs in windows—NO MYSTERY ABOUT OUR HASH—framed with new electric lights, the horse-drawn trolleys along Broadway crowded with men with a purpose, rushing to work. And Walt must have shaken his head with wonder—such changes! How could a body keep track? And then the surprise awaiting him at Cox's studio—two children, "soul extensions," to coax onto his lap, to distract with stories, to contrive to have stare into the huge camera without fear.

Here in the Twentieth Century we continue to shake our heads with wonder. So often the seemingly insignificant—a word, a gesture, the scent of oranges, the changing of a traffic light—will touch me in such a way as to demand fleshing out. What compelled my attention in the first instance? What requires language to burgeon in air? As a finger on the metal of a mailbox on a winter's morning will convey a chill to the whole body, as a splash of ink on a blotter will slowly blossom even as I write this, so too something as simple as, say, an apple decomposing on a lawn will suddenly whisper its particular and momentary significance in this world.

Poetry is story-telling, pure and simple. Sometimes we employ the narrative mode, sometimes the lyrical, more often a balance of both. Of course there is more, but the basis of poetry, the line, means to convey information. Poetry is a form of speech, an attempt to articulate something as indefinite as that gesture, one moment, to define a feeling that passes with the twitch of an eye-muscle. "Who knows the curious mystery of the eyesight?" wrote Whitman. Years later, James Wright, musing on Whitman's contribution, would write: "He also understands how the past continues to exist: it exists in the present, and comes into living form only when some individual man is willing to challenge it." Poetry attempts to transcribe the stories in the light.

The Stories in the Light

stopping on the green
uniform of the schoolgirl
crossing Fifth Avenue—

her fingers smoothing the skirt
against gusts, against thighs,
while holding her hat to her hair—

begin to come true those evenings
after the skirt has been folded,
the legs bathed and forgotten:

now your lover inherits a past
fashioned from such pure moments,
lovely before you knew her,

before the light began traveling
and gathered you together,
because such stories at best

are false, cut-out silhouettes,
because the past changes
each time traffic stalls,

because the light one particular
autumn afternoon struck me
and I have never seen it again,

but I have this task:
to consider the source of stories,
to allow that skinny schoolgirl

to blossom into someone's lover,
maybe yours, maybe mine,
though even now she is sleeping.

I haven't had much to say about my poems. "The truth is that poets
are human beings, and that what a poet has to say about his work is
often far from being the most illuminating word on the subject,"
wrote Jung. Theodore Roethke was more blunt: "Frankly, I don't

think what the instrument says about his tune (or sperm) is v. important."

Recently, though, I've been staring at the New York etchings of John Sloan, "an incorrigible window watcher," admiring his humanistic realism, noting his influence on Edward Hopper. Sloan would spend hours at the back window of his 23rd Street studio, staring into the tenement flats, the railroad apartments facing his alley. He recorded the lives glimpsed there—women pinning workshirts to clotheslines, the weariness of their husbands after work, their brief pleasures between supper and sleep, the desires suggested by a man lighting his pipe on the roof, a woman brushing her hair with one hundred strokes, or reading the fashion page of the weekly. Having grown up in New York City, I can't help walking through ghosts: these people, their buildings, the reservoir on 42nd Street where the Public Library now stands, the trout stream that once angled through what's now Minetta Lane in the Village. I try to squint enough to see the various layers, the overlapping lives, the rich stories, the past flowing into the present. "Nothing will happen until we pause to flame what we know," William Stafford has written. I'm tired of rushing into the future, of keeping pace with progress. I'm tired of what passes for originality now, especially in literature. "It isn't so hard to be original—," says Louis Simpson, "it's a sight harder to say something true and useful."

With my poems, I mean to slow the passage of light, to attempt to say something true and useful, to offer stories that the reader—*you*— might trust as the world drags us along. I keep in mind what William Dean Howells said to Stephen Crane in an interview published in *The New York Times* on October 28, 1894: "A man should mean something when he writes. Ah, this writing merely to amuse people—why, it seems to me altogether vulgar. A man may as well blacken his face and go out and dance on the street for pennies."

A century later, Whitman still presses his hand upon my shoulder. Where does the poet go for inspiration? Whitman wrote: "He shall go directly to the Creation." Each new morning the various lights stress something familiar, yet unique, in our surroundings, this American landscape. I want to stare at the world long enough and hard enough to make it come true. I want to grasp what's offered to me. Randall Jarrell once wrote about Picasso: ". . . he loves the world so much he wants to steal it and eat it." So the apple that is the world tempts us again and again, and because we remain only human . . .

June 1983, Yaddo

The Mystery of the Caves

I don't remember the name of the story,
but the hero, a boy, was lost,
wandering a labyrinth of caverns
filling stratum by stratum with water.

I was wondering what might happen:
would he float upward toward light?
Or would he somersault forever
in an underground black river?

I couldn't stop reading the book
because I had to know the answer,
because my mother was leaving again—
the lid of the trunk thrown open,

blouses torn from their hangers,
the crazy shouting among rooms.
The boy found it impossible to see
which passage led to safety.

One yellow finger of flame
wavered on his last match.
There was a blur of perfume—
mother breaking miniature bottles,

then my father gripping her,
but too tightly, by both arms.
The boy wasn't able to breathe.
I think he wanted me to help,

but I was small, and it was late.
And my mother was sobbing now,
no longer cursing her life,
repeating my father's name

among bright islands of skirts
circling the rim of the bed.
I can't recall the whole story,
what happened at the end . . .

Sometimes I worry that the boy
is still searching below the earth
for a thin pencil of light,
that I can almost hear him

through great volumes of water,
through centuries of stone,
crying my name among blind fish,
wanting so much to come home.

Apples

                    for my father

I was the clumsy child
who stole apples
from your favorite tree
to toss them into the lake.

I have no excuse, but
those apples were never lost.
Each night, while you slept,
as apples bobbed in moonlight,

I waited in shallow water
until the apples washed ashore.
Each night I gave you an apple.
Sometimes I remember that desire

to take whatever belongs to you
so I can return it.
Now, on windless nights,
when the lake lies still,

I have another dream:
I gather you in my arms,
after death, and ease you
like a basketful of apples

into the moonlit water,
and we float home,

with an awkward grace,
to a continent dark with apples.

Among Blackberries

Her lips blue from tasting, her eyes so blue,
she stares at the boy on the bicycle
who stares at her breasts
through the thin, cotton blouse.

I was fourteen and didn't know
our lives come down to moments,
to small things forgotten
until so many miles later, perhaps

stuck in the slow bloom of traffic,
the sun pressing its memory
into thighs, the horns
blare us back from another country

where I have been bicycling again
among hills, among blackberries.
Noon strikes its dumb chord
through the part in my pale hair.

I stop pedaling now to stare—
her lips blue from tasting, eyes so blue,
the struck moment of her breasts,
the blackberries sweating in their bucket.

Preserves

I found the preserves in the cellar,
canned decades ago
by the woman who brought this house
on wheels from Missouri.

The black raspberries were still
delicious, each cluster

burning like years in the brain.
I could almost hear the song

used to press those raspberries
into jars thinner, now, than dust,
almost imitate each gesture
as the stain rose on my fingers.

The stuffed owls are crumbling now
like rags left too long in bins,
the black rafters warp,
but the slow spirals of dust

still resist sweeping,
having been written in the journal
of the lost, to keep track
of what passes, what preserves.

Frank Sinatra

I love to listen to men in bars,
the lonely drinkers

who finger their last ice-cubes
until frost surrounds the skin
like a wedding ring,

who hum softly to themselves
tunes popular decades ago,

whose wives sweat through sleep
in rooms only streetlights away.

*

Every drunk thinks he's Frank Sinatra

and each bored husband has a story
that has nothing to do
with the worn face mooning
above the bottles into the mirror,

but the story touches you
like the man who hopes to bum a drink.

*

One night some guy showed me his hands—
swollen, humped with scar-tissue,
navy-blue at the knuckles.

Those hands had done everything—
fought in the Golden Gloves,
hauled barrels of nails,
patted the ass, once, of Lana Turner.

He told me his bare right hand
had driven nails into bar-tops.

*

And he took a nail from his pocket
and, for whiskey,
raised his palm above my eyebrows
and brought it down, *hard*,
onto the flecked & ragged head . . .

*

I won't tell you what happened,
but after several beers,
after the ballgame flickered off,
that man began to sing,
loud enough for everyone to hear . . .

Hello, young lovers, whoever you are
I hope your troubles are few . . .

and soon other men stopped drumming
their tables with finger-tips,
stopped lifting their glasses,
their miserable swizzle
sticks . . .

*

His voice swept onto the street
and maybe his wife slept on . . .

dreaming of that night, years ago,
when she & her handsome young sailor
held hands in the balcony
of the Paramount

where Frank Sinatra sang only for them.

Singles

I don't know anyone more lonely
than the woman listening
to the late news, memorizing
baseball scores for coffee break.

She must undress so carefully,
folding her beige blouse
as if for the last time,
not wanting to be found unkempt

by detectives in the morning.
Sometimes I hear her talking
as she roams from room to room
watering her plumeria,

the only splash of color.
She sets two places at the table
though no one ever comes,
then turns to the boredom of bed

thinking *Indians 7 - Yankees 3,
Cardinals 11 - Mets 2*
until she rises before dawn
and drives crosstown to work.

Could anyone be more lonely?
She doesn't acknowledge, again,

the man in the tollbooth
who's spent the whole night there,

not even a magazine before him,
grateful now to be making change
and touching fingers, briefly,
with such a beautiful stranger.

C. K. WILLIAMS

C. K. WILLIAMS *was born in Newark, New Jersey, in 1936. He attended*
Bucknell University, and after a period of travel in Europe, graduated from
the University of Pennsylvania in 1959. Currently a professor at George
Mason University in Virginia, he also teaches in the Writing Division of the
School of the Arts at Columbia University. He has translated (w. Gregory
Dickerson), Sophocles' Women of Trachis *(1978), and rendered poems*
from Issa, The Lark. The Thrush. The Starling. *(1983). His books of*
poetry are Lies *(1969),* I Am the Bitter Name *(1972),* With Ignorance
(1977), and Tar *(1983).*
(Photo by Layle Silbert)

Contexts

I think that the primary business of poetry in our time—or at least poetry as I conceive it—is to offer evidence. We have to know what is there before us, we have to have the facts, and to get them straight, because without a clear and at least relatively detailed knowledge of our condition and the condition of our world, how can we expect to accomplish what are our obvious tasks: to confront, to cure or comfort, solace or succor, to change, correct, resolve, take into account, come to terms with, redeem, surmount, transfigure or transform? . . . How will we save ourselves and save this vulnerable world which so desperately needs to be protected from its protectors?

Because our capacity for blindness, for forgetfulness and for distortion is so limitless, we have to be reminded again and again of what is really in the world, or what is there before our eyes and what is within us—those double theaters offering us their tragedies and comedies, their grand guignol and slapstick—and we have to be recalled again and again to the difficult knowledge that not only are there two theaters, but that each of us is at once the tormented and exalted and valiant hero, the rapacious and licentious villain, and the spear-bearer in the dumb-show chorus, and that each of us is in some undeniable sense responsible for all the identities of all our fellows.

We have to know again and again what our tasks are and what our capacities are, because despite our best intentions, and despite the fact that we all think we nobly and incessantly attempt all we can, we still manage to leave out so much, to omit so unconscionably much of what implores us or hints subtly to us of the necessity of our intervention. Our shortcomings, our unfulfilled potentials, our desires, acknowledged or agonizingly private, our ability to think like angels and to gibber like hyenas, the splendors of our ideals and the paucity of the means we have developed to implement these ideals, our overcomings and our capitulations, our willingness to confront our false fantasies and our weary wishes, and our submission to our incessant and erratic and wistful and impotent longings for something we are not and are not even able to specify very clearly—it is perhaps all of this that poetry must take into account now, and what is most astonishing, as always, is that poetry is not merely to offer evidence for all of this, but to *sing* that evidence.

It is within this apparent contradiction, this clearly unresolvable but ever-vibrant paradox that poetry exists. The poem, every poem, is to confront our two theaters, or our many theaters, or the endless bits of seemingly random information which flutter before us, and still do these two things at once: mean, and sing.

The language of poetry is narcissism itself. It calls attention to itself at every possible opportunity. It is as vain and self-conscious and as tensioned and competitive as an adolescent. It wishes all eyes to be on it: we are to hear its voice only, to love only it and to spurn its competition, although this competition is life, is everything else in reality, everything which has not yet been transfigured not only into language but into the particular language and the particular music of this poem. The language of the poem desires to be opaque: nothing is to pass through it. The subject is utterly incidental to it. We are to be conscious only of it, of its inexhaustible capacity for energy and play, of the delight it can offer even in the most dire recitation, of harmony and counterpoint, elegant association and brutal, lovely disjunction. And, further, in our age, in the epoch of the democratic, the language of poetry also wants us to know how it loves *us*: we are to be aware of how deeply poetry can delve into the language of our every speaking, thinking moment and still recover and display the poetry that is there, muffled in guises of function or of commerce or of chat. We are to know that we are musicians in our speech: our poems convince us that we are geniuses of music even in the most abashed recitations of ourselves.

The paradox of course is that at the same time the subject of the poem, whatever it is, flower or star, love or war or scrap of lost ambition, also makes clear and absolute demands. The subject is jealous of us: it, too, requires all of our attention, we are to bring upon it all that we possess: our language, our emotions, our most acute mental discrimination, even our passions, even our most banal experience: all is to be committed to doing justice to what is under consideration. The poem makes enormous demands: we are to be confronted with all our disattentions, with how small mind we pay to what is offered us. We are to become aware of how little we have allowed experience to actually touch us, and at the same time we are to face the responsibilities implied in our awareness of that experience.

Consciousness by definition desires freedom for itself before all else, because consciousness by definition *is* freedom. But we also sadly know that consciousness has the uncanny and unpredictable gift of weaving veils before us, veils of habit, of inertia, of indolence and fear—there is even a veil of love which is the most touching of all. The poem is song and play and evidence and the process of our interaction with it is also a stripping away of what is between ourselves and the realities which sorrow so for our engagement with them, and in this sense the language of the poem and even the poem itself seem to want not to exist at all. The poem is in the deepest sense to be a medium through which our attention flows, uncolored by any necessity whatsoever.

The essential mystery of poetry is that these two disparate elements, so contradictory, somehow intensify each other, when by any logical reasoning they should be distracting and subtracting from each other. Perhaps it is this paradox which makes poetry so forbidding, so "difficult" for many of the otherwise fine minds of our time. Or perhaps it is because poetry has assumed for itself—and all of us don't know this yet, don't understand what's at stake—many of the passions and concerns and quandaries which have traditionally been the realm of religion or moral or social philosophy, but which the withdrawal of god from our active affairs, or our exorcism of him, or our dedication to the realization of human promise, have redistributed through the continents of consciousness and of art. Or perhaps it is because at the same time that all of this has occurred, the means of poetry, and the nature of poetry, have not changed and probably cannot and should not change very radically. Poetry is always being seduced to become what it is not: to be philosophy or fiction, theosophy or myth, but all of these quickly become mere means for the essential activity of poetry; they are means and moments, of no more urgency than anything else. There is that in the human which apparently always wishes to be what it is not: we are all in our souls young gods, dedicated only to what is most pure and profound in the universes of our existence, but if it is one thing that life actually and truly and undeceivedly teaches us it is that it is always the day to day, the lover's smile, the friend's death, the evident suffering of the stranger, or the scent of morning air, which determines who we really are in relation to everything else: to god, to our consciousness and our community, to the very notion of our essence. If poems are written which are not overtly committed to the quotidian, there is no poem which can afford not to take it into account, and if those to whom poetry is a foreign language find that often it chooses apparently inconsequential strips of reality to brood or to reflect upon, poetry knows that this apparent inconsequence is not the question, but that it is rather our so-called deeper, or higher, or broader visions which are most susceptible to processes of selection, of abstraction, of generalization, of false raptures of transcendence.

In our moment, our terribly difficult historical moment, it seems as though our particular struggle is against how much of our public experience seems to consist of attempts to deceive us, to make what is evidence, what is there before us, have the consistency and contingency and mutability of dream. War is peace, terror is security, poverty is moral affront. Our politicians wish us to sleep and dream, the educational systems we submit to wish us to be functional, and what poetry offers us is a more acute awareness not only of this, but of everything, and it is an awareness that by its nature must be *felt*, with all the force of our being, not with mind or partial consciousness nor with easy compassion or a reprehensibly abstract pity.

Our poetry will paint the stripes on the tulip, this is its limitation and its glory, but as we paint the stripe we will also know and tell who owns the garden in which the tulip grows, and where the bulb came from and under what condition it was brought to us and who shovelled the manure upon its root and who picked and vased it on their shelf . . . and even perhaps what that room looks like and where the person who lives there is going out tonight, and how much they might know of all of this.

And we also probably have to know, we of the poem, how conscious that poem has been of *itself*, how much it has been forced to omit or elide, to avoid or evade or skip or skim because of the exigencies of structure or of form, or of that glorious song. For the form of the poem, and the quality and intensity of its song, is a part, and not a small part, of the evidence.

Downwards

This is the last day of the world. On the river docks
I watch for the last time the tide get higher
and chop in under the stinking pilings. How the small creatures
who drift dreaming of hands and lungs must sting,
rotting alive in the waste spill, coming up dead
with puffy stomachs paler than the sky or faces.
There is deep fire fuming ash to the surface.
It is the last tide and the last evening and from now
things will strive back downwards.
A fish thrown up will gasp in the flare
and flop back hopelessly through the mud flats to the water.
The last man, an empty bottle with no message, is here, is me,
and I am rolling, fragile as a bubble in the upstream spin,

battered by carcasses, drawn down by the lips of weeds
to the terrible womb of torn tires and children's plastic shoes
and pennies and urine. I am no more, and what is left,
softly baled with wire, floating
like a dark pillow in the hold of the brown ship, it is nothing.
It dreams. Touching fangs delicately with cranes
and forklifts, it rests silently in its heavy ripening.
It stands still on the water, rocking, blinking.

A Day for Anne Frank

> *God hates you!*
> —St. John Chrysostom

1.
I look onto an alley here
where, though tough weeds and flowers thrust up
through cracks and strain
toward the dulled sunlight,
there is the usual filth spilling from cans,
the heavy soot shifting in the gutters.
People come by mostly
to walk their dogs or take the shortcut
between the roaring main streets,
or just to walk
and stare up at the smoky windows,
but this morning when I looked out
children were there running back and forth
between the houses toward me.
They were playing with turtles—
skimming them down the street
like pennies or flat stones,
and bolting, shouting, after the broken corpses.
One had a harmonica, and as he ran,
his cheeks bloating and collapsing like a heart,
I could hear its bleat, and then the girls' screams
suspended behind them with their hair,
and all of them: their hard, young breath,
their feet pounding wildly on the pavement to the corner.

2.
I thought of you at that age.
Little Sister, I thought of you,
thin as a door,
and of how your thighs would have swelled
and softened like cake,
your breasts have bleached
and the new hair growing on you like song
would have stiffened and gone dark.
There was rain for a while, and then not.
Because no one came, I slept again,
and dreamed that you were here with me,
snarled on me like wire,
tangled so closely to me that we were vines
of underbrush together,
or hands clenched.

3.
They are cutting babies in half on bets.
The beautiful sergeant has enough money to drink
for a week.
The beautiful lieutenant can't stop betting.
The little boy whimpers
he'll be good.
The beautiful cook is gathering up meat
for the dogs.
The beautiful dogs
love it all.
Their flanks glisten.
They curl up in their warm kennels
and breathe.
They breathe.

4.
Little Sister,
you are a clot
in the snow,
blackened,
a chunk of phlegm
or puke

and there are men with faces
leaning over you with watercans

watering you!
in the snow, as though flowers would sprout
from your armpits
and genitals.

Little Sister,
I am afraid of the flowers sprouting from you

I am afraid of the silver petals
that crackle
of the stems darting
in the wind
of the roots

5.
The twilight rots.
Over the greasy bridges and factories,
it dissolves
and the clouds swamp in its rose
to nothing.
I think sometimes the slag heaps by the river
should be bodies
and that the pods of moral terror
men make of their flesh should split
and foam their cold, sterile seeds into the tides
like snow
or ash.

6.
Stacks of hair were there
little mountains
the gestapo children must have played in
and made love in and loved
the way children love haystacks or mountains

O God the stink
of hair oil and dandruff

their mothers must have thrown them into their tubs
like puppies and sent them to bed

coming home so filthy stinking

of jew's hair

of gold fillings, of eyelids

7.
Under me on a roof
a sparrow little by little
is being blown away.
A cage of bone is left,
parts of its wings,
a stain.

8.
And in Germany the streetcar conductors go to work
in their stiff hats,
depositing workers and housewives
where they belong,
pulling the bell chains,
moving drive levers forward or back.

9.
I am saying good-bye to you before our death. Dear
Father: I am saying good-bye to you before my death.
We are so anxious to live, but all is lost—we are not
allowed! I am so afraid of this death, because little
children are thrown into graves alive. Good-bye
forever.
                    I kiss you.

10.
Come with me Anne.
Come,
it is rotten not to be anywhere at all,
to have no one
like an old whore,
a general.

Come sit with me here

kiss me; my heart too is wounded
with forgiveness.

There is an end now.
Stay.
Your foot hooked through mine
your hand against my hand
your hip touching me lightly

it will end now
it will not begin again

Stay
they will pass
and not know us

the cold brute earth
is asleep

there is no danger

there is nothing

Anne

there is nothing

The Rampage

a baby got here once who before
he was all the way out and could already feel the hindu
pain inside him and the hebrew and the iliad
decided he was never going to stop crying no matter what
until they did something he wasn't going
to turn the horror
off in their fat sentences
and in the light bulb how much murder to get light
and in the walls agony agony for the bricks for the glaze
he was going to keep screaming
until they made death little like he was
and loved him too and sent

him back to undo all this
and it happened
he kept screaming he scared them he saw them
filling with womblight again like stadiums
he saw the tears sucked back into the story the smiles
opening like sandwiches
so he stopped
and looked up and said all right
it's better now
I'm hungry now I want just to sleep
and they let him

Blades

When I was about eight, I once stabbed somebody, another kid, a little
    girl.
I'd been hanging around in front of the supermarket near our house
and when she walked by, I let her have it, right in the gap between her
    shirt and her shorts
with a piece of broken-off car antenna I used to carry around in my
    pocket.
It happened so fast I still don't know how I did it: I was as shocked as
    she was
except she squealed and started yelling as though I'd plunged a knife
    in her
and everybody in the neighborhood gathered around us, then they
    called the cops,
then the girl's mother came running out of the store saying "What
    happened? What happened?"
and the girl screamed, "He stabbed me!" and I screamed back, "I did
    not!" and she you did too
and me I didn't and we were both crying hysterically by that time.
Somebody pulled her shirt up and it was just a scratch but we went on
    and on
and the mother, standing between us, seemed to be absolutely ter-
    rified.
I still remember how she watched first one of us and then the other
    with a look of complete horror—
You did too! I did not!—as though we were both strangers, as though
    it was some natural disaster

she was beholding that was beyond any mode of comprehension so all
  she could do
was stare speechlessly at us, and then another expression came over
  her face,
one that I'd never seen before, that made me think she was going to
  cry herself
and sweep both of us, the girl and me, into her arms to hold us against
  her.
The police came just then, though, quieted everyone down, put the
  girl and the mother
into a squad-car to take to the hospital and me in another to take to
  jail
except they really only took me around the corner and let me go be-
  cause the mother and daughter were black
and in those days you had to do something pretty terrible to get into
  trouble that way.

I don't understand how we twist these things or how we get them
  straight again but I relived that day I don't know how many times
  before I realized I had it all wrong.
The boy wasn't me at all, he was another kid: I was just there.
And it wasn't the girl who was black, but him. The mother was real,
  though.
I really had thought she was going to embrace them both
and I had dreams about her for years afterwards: that I'd be being
  born again
and she'd be lifting me with that same wounded sorrow or she would
  suddenly appear out of nowhere,
blotting out everything but a single, blazing wing of holiness.
Who knows the rest? I can still remember how it felt the old way.
How I make my little thrust, how she crushes us against her, how I
  turn and snarl
at the cold circle of faces around us because something's torn in me,
some ancient cloak of terror we keep on ourselves because we'll do
  anything,
anything, not to know how silently we knell in the mouth of death
and not to obliterate the forgiveness and the lies we offer one another
  and call innocence.
This is innocence. I touch her, we kiss.
And this. I'm here or not here. I can't tell. I stab her. I stab her again.
  I still can't.

Floor

A dirty picture, a photograph, possibly a tintype, from the turn of the
century, even before:
the woman is obese, gigantic; a broad, black corset cuts from under
her breasts to the top of her hips,
her hair is crimped, wiry, fastened demurely back with a bow one
incongruous wing of which shows.
Her eyebrows are straight and heavy, emphasizing her frank, unin-
trospective plainness
and she looks directly, easily into the camera, her expression some-
where between play and scorn,
as though the activities of the photographer were ridiculous or be-
neath her contempt, or,
rather, as though the unfamiliar camera were actually the much more
interesting presence here
and how absurd it is that the lens be turned toward her and her part-
ner and not back on itself.
One sees the same look—pride, for some reason, is in it, and a sur-
prisingly sophisicated self-distancing—
in the snaps anthropologists took in backwaters during those first,
politically pre-conscious,
golden days of culture-hopping, and, as Goffman notes, in certain
advertisements, now.

The man is younger than the woman. Standing, he wears what looks
like a bathing costume,
black and white tank top, heavy trousers bunched in an ungainly heap
over his shoes, which are still on.
He has an immigrant's mustache he's a year or two too callow for, but,
thick and dark, it will fit him.
He doesn't, like the woman, watch the camera, but stares ahead, not at
the woman but slightly over and past,
and there's a kind of withdrawn, almost vulnerable thoughtfulness or
preoccupation about him
despite the gross thighs cast on his waist and the awkward, surely
bothersome twist
his body has been forced to assume to more clearly exhibit the genital
penetration.
He seems, in fact, abstracted—oblivious wouldn't be too strong a
word—as though, possibly,

as unlikely as it would seem, he had been a virgin until now and was
    trying amid all this unholy confusion—
the hooded figure, the black box with its eye—trying, and from the
    looks of it even succeeding
in obliterating everything from his consciousness but the thing itself,
    the act itself,
so as, one would hope, to redeem the doubtlessly endless nights of the
    long Victorian adolescence.

The background is a painted screen: ivy, columns, clouds; some muse
    or grace or other,
heavy-buttocked, whory, flaunts her gauze and clodhops with a half-
    demented leer.
The whole thing's oddly poignant somehow, almost, like an antique
    wedding picture, comforting—
the past is sending out a tendril to us: poses, attitudes of stillness we've
    lost or given back.
Also, there's no shame in watching them, in being in the tacit com-
    merce of having, like it or not,
received the business in one's hand, no titillation either, not a tangle,
    not a throb,
probably because the woman offers none of the normal symptoms,
    even if minimal, even if contrived—
the tongue, say, wandering from the corner of the mouth, a glint of
    extra brilliance at the lash—
we associate to even the most innocuous, undramatic, parental sorts
    of passion, and the boy,
well, dragged in out of history, off Broome or South Street, all he is is
    grandpa:
he'll go back into whatever hole he's found to camp in, those higher-
    contrast tenements
with their rows of rank, forbidding beds, or not even beds, rags on a
    floor, or floor.
On the way there, there'll be policemen breaking strikers' heads, or
    micks', or sheenies',
there'll be war somewhere, in the sweatshops girls will turn to stone
    over their Singers.
Here, at least peace. Here, one might imagine, after he withdraws, a
    kind of manly focus taking him—
the glance he shoots to her is hard and sure—and, to her, a tender-
    ness might come,
she might reach a hand—Sweet Prince—to touch his cheek, or
    might—who can understand these things?—

avert her face and pull him to her for a time before she squats to flush him out.

Tar

The first morning of Three Mile Island: those first disquieting, uncertain, mystifying hours.

All morning a crew of workmen have been tearing the old decrepit roof off our building,

and all morning, trying to distract myself, I've been wandering out to watch them

as they hack away the leaden layers of asbestos paper and disassemble the disintegrating drains.

After half a night of listening to the news, wondering how to know a hundred miles downwind

if and when to make a run for it and where, then a coming bolt awake at seven

when the roofers we've been waiting for since winter sent their ladders shrieking up our wall,

we still know less than nothing: the utility company continues making little of the accident,

the slick federal spokesmen still have their evasions in some semblance of order.

Surely we suspect now we're being lied to, but in the meantime, there are the roofers,

setting winch-frames, sledging rounds of tar apart, and there I am, on the curb across, gawking.

I never realized what brutal work it is, how matter-of-factly and harrowingly dangerous.

The ladders flex and quiver, things skid from the edge, the materials are bulky and recalcitrant.

When the rusty, antique nails are levered out, their heads pull off; the under-roofing crumbles.

Even the battered little furnace, roaring along as patient as a donkey, chokes and clogs,

a dense, malignant smoke shoots up, and someone has to fiddle with a cock, then hammer it,

before the gush and stench will deintensify, the dark, Dantean broth wearily subside.

In its crucible, the stuff looks bland, like licorice, spill it, though, on your boots or coveralls,

it sears, and everything is permeated with it, the furnace gunked with burst and half-burst bubbles,

the men themselves so completely slashed and mucked they seem almost from another realm, like trolls.

When they take their break, they leave their brooms standing at attention in the asphalt pails,

work gloves clinging like Brer Rabbit to the bitten shafts, and they slouch along the precipitous lip,

the enormous sky behind them, the heavy noontime air alive with shimmers and mirages.

Sometime in the afternoon I had to go inside: the advent of our vigil was upon us.

However much we didn't want to, however little we would do about it, we'd understood:

we were going to perish of all this, if not now, then soon, if not soon, then someday.

Someday, some final generation, hysterically aswarm beneath an atmosphere as unrelenting as rock,

would rue us all, anathematize our earthly comforts, curse our surfeits and submissions.

I think I know, though I might rather not, why my roofers stay so clear to me and why the rest,

the terror of that time, the reflexive disbelief and distancing, all we should hold on to, dims so.

I remember the president in his absurd protective booties, looking absolutely unafraid, the fool.

I remember a woman on the front page glaring across the misty Susquehanna at those looming stacks.

But, more vividly, the men, silvered with glitter from the shingles, clinging like starlings beneath the eaves.

Even the leftover carats of tar in the gutter, so black they seemed to suck the light out of the air.

By nightfall kids had come across them: every sidewalk on the block was scribbled with obscenities and hearts.

CHARLES WRIGHT

CHARLES WRIGHT *was born in Pickwick Dam, Tennessee, in 1935, and has degrees from Davidson College and the University of Iowa.* Country Music *(1982), which selects poems from four of his earlier books, shared the 1983 American Book Awards prize for poetry. A sixth book of poems,* The Southern Cross, *was published in 1981. Other of his awards include the PEN Translation Prize for Eugenio Montale's* The Storm and Other Things, *and the Academy of American Poets' Edgar Allan Poe Award. He currently teaches at the University of Virginia at Charlottesville. His most recent book of poetry is* The Other Side of the River *(1984).*
(Photo by Holly Wright)

10 Questions, 9 Answers and 1 Retort

(Questions by Elizabeth McBride)

- But eventually you concentrate on what you are trying to say. I'm asking what you can tell me about what you are saying, and to whom you are saying it?

- I'm saying it to the better part of myself, the part of myself who understands everything I say, all the nuances, who really knows what I mean to say. Now that person doesn't really exist in the temporal world, but one hopes that he exists somewhere so one can write to him. What I'm trying to say is—I don't know what I'm trying to say. I think if I knew what I was trying to say, I'd say it and stop.

- So you think of it as more of a search?

- Oh sure, constantly. A search for the small, still center of everything. It's what one looks for. I don't know whether that exists. Zen people say it really exists here; maybe it does. I don't know. Anytime you start getting into that kind of questioning, I feel terribly embarrassed because I'm very unsure of what I'm trying to do and that's why I keep writing the poems, trying to figure out what I'm trying to say. A lot of what I want to say changes, but the place I want to get to never changes. There are different ways of approaching it through language, metamorphosis, other changings, but I do want to get to that still, small pinpoint of light at the center of the Universe, where all things come together and all things intersect. And that sort of answer stops conversation, because what can one say but Good Luck. So that's what I say to myself. Good Luck.

- What about the dead? You've said you write for the dead?

- I facetiously have said that I write for my mother and in fact I do write for her because she always wanted me to be a writer. There are very few mothers who want their children to be writers and she desperately wanted me to. I think. And so I do write for her. To write for the dead. I know I made that statement and I still believe it. I write for the ghosts of Thomas Hardy and Hart Crane, for Emily Dickinson and Arthur Rimbaud. When you say you write for the angels, for the dead, for that which is beyond you, you write for that part of yourself better than you are, for all of those things that are in this imaginary, mythical, still, brightly lit center of attention at the heart of the Universe. Of course, we suspect it's all talk. But it's the kind of talk that interests me and it's the kind of speculation and belief in a constructed reality which keeps me trying to work in language, because ultimately what we are doing is playing with words. Some people play with words in one way and some in another. I think there's a serious way and a non-serious way of playing with words. I think poetry is the most serious way in the world of playing with words; it certainly is for me. And it is the one way (to mix the image(s)), the one boat I will ever catch, if I'm going to catch one, that's going to get me across the river. Other people will get there differently, perhaps, but that's the only way I'm going to get there and therefore I try to pay as serious and lasting and constant attention to that as I can. Otherwise I'm slough-ing off. Contrary to what a lot of people believe, you get only one chance to do it. If you slough off, you're a damn fool.

- I see your work as a constant reach toward the ultimate, and perhaps that is what all serious writers are doing. But in a Western sense, that kind of effort seems almost like an imitation of Christ. Do you ever feel that burden?

- Never.

- But poetry is a search for perfection.

- Sure. Poetry is, as I said, my way across the river, but I don't pre-sume any of those other changes. What a presumption! Lightning bolts will come down from heaven. But it is true that poetry, for many people, is a substitute for religion, and I don't mean just the worship of words or style or of worldly success. It does substitute for me in many ways. So I play with words and try to use them as little prayer wheels, as little wafers. Poems are sacred texts. Perhaps it's presump-tuous to say we write sacred texts; perhaps we write notes toward sacred texts, notations on what we think of as the real sacred texts. Notations are as close as I ever get. Otherwise we would be like Saul on the road to Damascus. If we ever saw the book of light, we would be blinded.

- So, in a sense, the poems are prayers?

- Oh yes, all my poems are prayers and songs. Little sacraments. Hymns.

- I understand well that Dante is very important to you. I wanted to ask you to talk about that. What effect did Dante have on your work?

- Reading Dante has an effect on anyone's *life*. On my work, tech-nically, none. What can you take from Dante other than a great awe and a great admiration? I suppose if you were a practicing Catholic and a believer in Aquinas and a believer in the medieval theological systems which went into *The Divine Comedy,* there would be some spillover and influence, but I'm not and I don't. Or if you're looking for a tripartite structural paradigm or palimpsest. Seriousness. Seriousness from Dante. It is the most serious thing there is. That's how *he* tried to get there, through language, through the structuring of that incredible story, but it's through language that he got there. I think maybe he actually did go up and come back down. Not really, but he might have, the poem is that good. But with the three different Dantes, the writer, the pilgrim, the character, one sees the possibilities that one can try to explore, but nobody . . . What I'm trying to say is that it is presumptuous of me even to try to talk about Dante. He changed my life in the way that Pound changed my life. Reading Pound changed my life by the fact that I saw that one could write poems without having to write like Robert Frost. I admire Frost, but I can't write like that. I can write synaptically, in 'gists and piths.'

- So Pound gave you permission to do what you *could* do?

- What I could do, exactly. And Dante gave me the opportunity to think that I could do more than I can. I think it's important to think that you might be able to do more than you can, because then you *will* try to do more than you can and you will, of course, stub your toe and you'll sometimes look like a fool, but then if you try hard enough you *will* do more than you can. If you're lucky. You see, it's such a terrible phrase, but it is truly a religious experience to read Dante if you read him seriously. No matter what religion you are. I'm not Catholic, but reading Dante and Gerard Manley Hopkins were two of the great experiences of my life. And there's something about the medieval writing that appeals to me. Medieval thought is very basic and uncluttered and sure of itself and I like that.

- One of the things that interests me most about your poetry is that you write in forms. Not traditional forms—you don't write sonnets, you don't write sestinas, you create your own forms.

- Architecture, structure. I don't care what you call it, there is a great overall form. And so you've got to have structures. And so I'm extremely interested in the way my poems are put together and the way the lines are put together. I'm a fanatic about lineation.

- Why don't you talk about the line?

- I think about 10% of the people writing poems now know anything at all about the way to write a line. There are so few, particularly among the young people coming up, *so* talented, but they write mostly an ordered prose. These blocky poems. Pound said a lot of things as we all know, and a lot of them were wrong, but a lot of them were true. One of the truest things he ever said is that "rhythm is a form *cut* into time . . . ," and the word is *cut.* Lines have reason for being. They are entities and one line after the other builds the form. So you're always working in a formal condition. I write free verse, as there's no repetition of a particular line length or pattern of repetition, but it is all formal.

The New Poem

It will not resemble the sea.
It will not have dirt on its thick hands.
It will not be part of the weather.

It will not reveal its name.
It will not have dreams you can count on.
It will not be photogenic.

It will not attend our sorrow.
It will not console our children.
It will not be able to help us.

Blackwater Mountain

That time of evening, weightless and disparate,
When the loon cries, when the small bass
Jostle the lake's reflections, when
The green of the oak begins
To open its robes to the dark, the green
Of water to offer itself to the flames,
When lily and lily pad
Husband the last light
Which flares like a white disease, then disappears:
This is what I remember. And this:

The slap of the jacklight on the cove;
The freeze-frame of ducks

Below us; your shots; the wounded flop
And skid of one bird to the thick brush;
The moon of your face in the fire's glow;
The cold; the darkness. Young,
Wanting approval, what else could I do?
And did, for two hours, waist-deep in the lake,
The thicket as black as death,
Without success or reprieve, try.

The stars over Blackwater Mountain
Still dangle and flash like hooks, and ducks
Coast on the evening water;
The foliage is like applause.
I stand where we stood before and aim
My flashlight down to the lake. A black duck
Explodes to my right, hangs, and is gone.
He shows me the way to you;
He shows me the way to a different fire
Where you, black moon, warm your hands.

Cloud River

The unborn children are rowing out to the far edge of the sky,
Looking for warm beds to appear in. How lucky they are, dressed
In their lake-colored gowns, the oars in their oily locks
Taking them stroke by stroke to circumference and artery . . .

I'd like to be with them still, pulling my weight,
Blisters like small white hearts in the waxed palms of my hands.
I'd like to remember my old name, and keep the watch,
Waiting for something immense and unspeakable to uncover its face.

Spider Crystal Ascension

The spider, juiced crystal and Milky Way, drifts on his web through
    the night sky
And looks down, waiting for us to ascend . . .

At dawn he is still there, invisible, short of breath, mending his net.

All morning we look for the white face to rise from the lake like a
 tiny star.
And when it does, we lie back in our watery hair and rock.

Clear Night

Clear night, thumb-top of a moon, a back-lit sky.
Moon-fingers lay down their same routine
On the side deck and the threshold, the white keys and the black
 keys.
Bird hush and bird song. A cassia flower falls.

I want to be bruised by God.
I want to be strung up in a strong light and singled out.
I want to be stretched, like music wrung from a dropped seed.
I want to be entered and picked clean.

And the wind says "What?" to me.
And the castor beans, with their little earrings of death, say "What?"
 to me.
And the stars start out on their cold slide through the dark.
And the gears notch and the engines wheel.

Holy Thursday

Begins with the *ooo ooo* of a mourning dove
In the pepper tree, crack
Of blue and a flayed light on the hills,
Myself past the pumpkin blooms and out in the disked field,
Blake's children still hunched in sleep, dollops
Of bad dreams and an afterlife.
Canticles rise in spate from the bleeding heart.
Cathedrals assemble and disappear in the water beads.
I scuff at the slick adobe, one eye
On the stalk and one on the aftermath.

There's always a time for rust,
For looking down at the earth and its lateral chains.
There's always a time for the grass, teeming

Its little four-cornered purple flowers,
                             tricked out in an oozy shine.
There's always a time for the dirt.
Reprieve, reprieve, the flies drone, their wings
Increasingly incandescent above the corn silk.
No answer from anything, four crows
On a eucalyptus limb, speaking in tongues.
No answer for them, either.

It's noon in the medlar tree, the sun
Sifting its glitter across the powdery stems.
It doesn't believe in God
And still is absolved.
It doesn't believe in God
And seems to get by, going from here to there.
Butterflies blow like pieces of half-burned construction paper over
    the sweet weeds,
And take what is given them.
Some hummer is luckier
Downwind, and smells blood, and seeks me out.

The afternoon hangs by a leaf.
The vines are a green complaint
From the slaking adobe dust. I settle and stand back.
The hawk realigns herself.
Spatter of mockingbird notes, a brief trill from the jay.
The fog starts in, breaking its various tufts loose.
Everything smudges and glows,
Cactus, the mustard plants and the corn,
Through the white reaches of 4 o'clock . . .
There's always a time for words.

Surf sounds in the palm tree,
Susurrations, the wind
                   making a big move from the west,
The children asleep again, their second selves
Beginning to stir, the moon
Lop-sided, sliding their ladder down.
From under the billowing dead, from their wet hands and a saving
    grace,
The children begin to move, an angle of phosphorescence
Along the ridge line.
                Angels

Are counting cadence, their skeletal songs
What the hymns say, the first page and the last.

Laguna Blues

It's Saturday afternoon at the edge of the world.
White pages lift in the wind and fall.
Dust threads, cut loose from the heart, float up and fall.
Something's off-key in my mind.
Whatever it is, it bothers me all the time.

It's hot, and the wind blows on what I have had to say.
I'm dancing a little dance.
The crows pick up a thermal that angles away from the sea.
I'm singing a little song.
Whatever it is, it bothers me all the time.

It's Saturday afternoon and the crows glide down,
Black pages that lift and fall.
The castor beans and the pepper plant trundle their weary heads.
Something's off-key and unkind.
Whatever it is, it bothers me all the time.

Portrait of the Artist with Hart Crane

It's Venice, late August, outside after lunch, and Hart
Is stubbing his cigarette butt in a wine glass,
The look on his face pre-moistened and antiseptic,
A little like death or a smooth cloud.
The watery light of his future still clings in the pergola.

The subject of all poems is the clock,
I think, those tiny, untouchable hands that fold across our chests
Each night and unfold each morning, finger by finger
Under the new weight of the sun.
One day more is one day less.

I've been writing this poem for weeks now
With a pencil made of rain, smudging my face
And my friend's face, making a language where nothing stays.
The sunlight has no such desire.
In the small pools of our words, its business is radiance.